Economic Criminal Law

Luciano Anderson de Souza

Economic Criminal Law

An Analysis from a Brazilian Perspective

Springer

Luciano Anderson de Souza
Department of Criminal Law, Forensic Medicine and Criminology
University of São Paulo
São Paulo, São Paulo, Brazil

ISBN 978-3-031-87235-8 ISBN 978-3-031-87236-5 (eBook)
https://doi.org/10.1007/978-3-031-87236-5

Translation from the Portuguese language edition: "Direito Penal Econômico" by Luciano Anderson de Souza, © Author 2022. Published by Thomson Reuters Brasil Conteúdo e Tencnologia Ltda. All Rights Reserved.

The original submitted manuscript has been translated into English. The translation was done using artificial intelligence. A subsequent revision was performed by the author(s) to further refine the work and to ensure that the translation is appropriate concerning content and scientific correctness. It may, however, read stylistically different from a conventional translation.

This Springer imprint is published by the registered company Springer Nature Switzerland AG
The registered company address is: Gewerbestrasse 11, 6330 Cham, Switzerland

Those who desire to give up freedom in order to gain security will not have, nor do they deserve, either one.

Thomas Jefferson

Contents

Chapter 1
Economic Criminal Law: Between Protection and Delegitimization

The focus of the present investigation is questioning the legitimacy of the legal-criminal branch in an attempt to control the economic order. This analysis will be delimited by the confrontation of the legal finding of economic criminal protection, identified as revealing the phenomenon of the administrativization of Criminal Law, in tension with its harmful character and, also, the theory of cumulative delinquency.

Concepts of Economic Law and Administrative Law will, therefore, be tools to be used in the course of the research, in the face of criminal science, to which the focus will be mainly on the expansion of Economic Criminal Law in contradiction with the fundamental characteristics of the penal dogmatics of the European-continental matrix, developed since the Enlightenment.

Contemporary Criminal Law clearly exhibits a hypertrophied, expanded character, wrapped in an unprecedented existential limit situation. Beyond the global levels of transformation into a blank slate of the principle of *ultima ratio*, elevating to the category of crimes the most diverse novel social interests, especially those still little sedimented by society, emanate typifying formulations of dubious consistency. In other words, there has been a trivialization of Criminal Law.

Thus, the Law has been taking care of supra-individual interests, and, in this way, ethereal, by the legal-criminal branch, as well as yielding to social pressures for preventive protection of certain themes by the criminalizing formulation, enhancing the symbolic aspect of Criminal Law. And more: in a true vicious circle delegitimizing the most serious means of formal social control of conduct, once the incapacity of such a legal branch for the protection of specific goods, or even as the promoter of human behaviors considered positive, the solution is the repressive aggravation, tearing the punitive posture.

Not to mention the difficulties of assimilating unprecedented and little tangible interests in a complex, globalized, multifaceted society, permeated by conflicting groups, beyond being highly technological (bringing new challenges such as artificial intelligence), criminal protection still abuses inconsistent formulations. This is what happens, for example, with the constant use of categories of abstract danger,

L. A. d. Souza, *Economic Criminal Law*,
https://doi.org/10.1007/978-3-031-87236-5_1

blank criminal norms, and negligent and open types, compromising, even more, the intended effectiveness of the drastic option for criminal protection.

It is in this context of deconstruction of the liberal paradigm of Criminal Law, mitigating the principle of legality in the orders of European-continental tradition, flaunting a rampant typification and curtailing guarantees of the accused, that the legal-criminal branch has been trying to intervene in the economic order, which justifies the intended study. And this happens not only because of questioning the real necessity of this legislative posture, but also because of its serious social consequences.

Globalization, in turn, further strains the situation in the sense of expanding the borders of Economic Criminal Law. If globalization is, above all, an economic phenomenon of reaffirmation of the capitalist mode of production, consisting in the narrowing of wealth production agents, ignoring national borders, with the promotion of economic interconnection, division of labor and production stages, distribution of products and facilitation of consumption and assumption of capital, the current economic system reveals unique characteristics of reflexive modernization, that is, of exacerbation, or radicalization, of its traditional characteristics.

In this influx, economic agents seek the intensification of social control formulas for revalidation of their own values. The Criminal Law, then, is used by the contemporary globalized capitalist system as a supposedly efficient and guaranteeing option for the correct functioning of productive forces. There is strong international pressure in this regard, including with respect to the imposition of *compliance* mechanisms.

The legal representation of the socioeconomic model in focus consecrates the elevation to the category of criminal offenses of the most varied and complex behaviors supposedly offensive to the current economic model. Thus, crimes said against economic and financial order, against the environment, against consumer relations, against tax order, money laundering, etc., are within this context, generally understood as economic delinquency.

Criminal Law sees itself, in this way, as a supposed guarantor of economic systemic normality, leaving all actors of criminal repression astonished. In practice, what seems to emerge is the delegitimization of the legal-criminal branch in the face of its weakness in controlling such situations.

In light of these findings, it is imperative to study criminal legitimacy in relation to the economic order. This branch of Law has been showing the characteristic of anticipatory protection to situations often within the scope of Administrative Law, hence the talk of its "administrativization," which is questioned in the face of the necessary criminal harmfulness justifying the typification of behaviors, but, on the other hand, perhaps supported by the theoretical foundation of the construction of cumulative crimes, a topic with which it is intended to confront. This last theoretical construction, once confronted by the absence of harmfulness to a legal good by individual behavior, is understood to justify the typification because the set of behaviors—by the realization of conducts by the community—would culminate in injury to the mentioned good.

Thus, the complex dogmatic-criminal reality today is paradigmatically faced with the search for economic regulation by this grievous means of social control, which will be analyzed through this study, aiming to ascertain its legitimacy for this, offering the legal community a novel scientific guiding contribution.

In this sense, the topic proposed for scientific investigation goes through specific fundamental questions which will subsidize the intended conclusions—and which will permeate the chapters of this work—namely:

In Chap. 2, after a historical overview of the intersection between Criminal Law and Economics, what is doctrinally understood by Economic Criminal Law will be investigated, as well as its relationship with the theory of the legal good. Next, an approach will be made to the concept of economic order, considered fundamental to allow the identification of legal-criminal protection aimed at it. In this vein, as well as in the face of the necessary realization of the linguistic communication of criminal actors for the disvalue conclusion of behavior, trust must be analyzed as an important element for the reproduction and circulation of wealth.

Noting the penal experience of guaranteeing the economic system in contemporary legislation, it will allow the construction of criticisms and questions to Economic Criminal Law, fueled, as mentioned, by the use of porous and anticipatory formulations of repressive protection, such as those of open types, of types of administrative accessory, highlighting the blank criminal norms, of abstract danger crimes, of omissive types and of negligent crimes. In this context, the contradictions of the legitimizing discourse of the purposes of the penalty for this specific penal focus will be noted.

Next, in Chap. 3, the research will confront the attempt at criminal protection of the economic order in the face of the concept of criminal harmfulness. Thus, passing through the classic view of the concept of harmfulness as a necessary element to the finding of offense or serious threat of offense to a legal good of dear social interest, until its apprehension as revealing a transgression to the order, or injury of duty, its occurrence or not in economic criminal typification will be verified. This proves to be an essential element for the reflection of the need or not for criminal intervention in a specific branch of human activity.

The next step of the scientific-legal investigation, to be developed in Chap. 4, is the confrontation of the criminal protection of the economic order with the theoretical construction of cumulative crimes, or accumulation. In this way, the notions of cumulative criminality, the emergence of the concept of cumulativity, the apprehension of such crimes as of danger or result, as well as their assimilation in the face of criminal harm, will allow us to conclude by the capacity or incapacity justifying the criminal economic protection according to this specific thought.

The criminal protection of the economic order, as mentioned, represents a paradigmatic example of the characteristic of the administrativization of Criminal Law, which is why it is imposed on the interpreter of this science a careful reflection on this, which shows something typical of the unprecedented legislative-penal expansionism that we experience. This is what will guide the research in Chap. 5. On the occasion, the so-called "Frankfurt School" and the discourse of resistance to the expansion of Criminal Law; the proposal of an "Intervention Law"; the proposal of the so-called "two-speed" Criminal Law, and the administrative-sanctioning reading will be the objects of analysis concerned.

Finally, in Chap. 6, entitled "Criminal Law and Economic Infractions," a conclusive reflection is intended on what has been previously investigated, allowing to ascertain, from the discourse of diffuse criminalization, the purpose and legal-criminal efficiency in economic protection, confronting this with the principle of *ultima ratio*, the structural and conjunctural contradictions of Economic Criminal Law and the search for alternative solutions. For this, it will be necessary to study the most appropriate legal formulations for economic crime, proposing legal options as *lege ferenda*.

Since it is intended to verify the characteristics of contemporary economic criminalization in the face of the outlines of criminal science, aiming to conclude by the legitimacy or not of the legal-criminal branch for the protection of the economic order, the present work is aimed at the conclusion of the relevance or not of such grievous legal intervention in this branch of human activity.

Chapter 2
Economic Order: Conceptualization and Attempts at Criminal Protection

2.1 Historical Overview

The relationship between Criminal Law and economics is not recent, nor is it exclusive to the capitalist system, as can be verified through a historical reference. Initially remote and sparse, the cases of such intertwining will assume a greater sense of economic protection only from liberalism and, in a third moment, characteristic of the Welfare State, display an ordering foundation with the simultaneous intention of protecting the current state economic model and ensuring the public policies of this model. Finally, there is a last phase, which moves away from the Welfare State, of retraction of the state's role in relation to the economy.

Given the peculiarities of the Brazilian reality, this will receive a separate mention at the end of the topic.

2.1.1 First Phase: Legislative Casuistry

Initially, the scarce examples collated by the doctrine do not reveal in the legal-criminal history any trace of continuity or greater ordering, materializing in sporadic prohibitions and wrapped in peculiarities of specific social contexts.

Thus it is that already in ancient Greece, whose economic system was slave-based, coins, known to the Greeks before the Romans,[1] had their counterfeiting punished with the death penalty. Establishing the same sanction, at the end of the third century BC, the legislation in force in the city of Atia forbade the abuse in the marketing of grains, regulating stocks and limiting profits.

Still in Antiquity, in 18 BC, during the High Empire, Rome had promulgated by Octavius Augustus, of the Julian dynasty, the *Lex Julia de Annona*, which

[1] The minted currency, guaranteed by the State, dates back to the seventh century BC.

L. A. d. Souza, *Economic Criminal Law*,
https://doi.org/10.1007/978-3-031-87236-5_2

established the death penalty for price increases and the violation of rules on import and trade of foodstuffs. It was a period of governmental authoritarianism that experienced wide commercial expansionism, fostered by the economic policy of Augustus, tending to fix trade as a unifying trait of the Empire. Hence the characterization of tight trade regulation.

In the medieval period, e.g., with a punitive bias, Canon Law condemned to ex-communication those who practiced usury,[2] considering that money could never generate money, being time something sacred over which man could not create a tax. However, the economic development of humanity was, little by little, tempering this ecclesiastical understanding.

Still, about the medieval period, Tiedemann writes:

> (...) The Middle Ages brings with it a global concept of general application of the *falsum* that gathered, until the entrance of the Modern Age and in a principle without a development of a specific type of fraud (with the requirement of intentional property damage), aspects of institutional protection that are currently found in accessory criminal law and in special types of fraud (counterfeiting of food, coins and weights).[3]

Already in the eighteenth century, at the end of the Modern Age, continuing with the illustrative list of this first phase, during the reign of Maria Theresa, queen of Hungary and Bohemia, the export of cereals and fruits and the violation of norms on beer production could be punished even with death.

Until this historical moment, as the illustrative content itself shows, due to its casuistry, there is in the use of criminal control of matters of economic interest a mere sense of seeking correction of specific situations, without systematization or an evolutionary logic, whether legislative or dogmatic.

2.1.2 *Second Phase: Protection of Liberalism*

The strengthening of the liberal economic model of the nation-state, on the other hand, will for the first time in history bring about a systemic reason in economic regulation, in general, which has legal-criminal consequences (at least in legislative terms in this phase).

The legal matrix of the liberal state presupposes, notably, the narrow separation between public and private law and the predominance of private will autonomy in the economic sphere.[4] As the raison d'être of a bourgeois model that sought to overcome the limitations to economic activity typical of trade corporations, there are no major difficulties in assimilating such characteristics.

---

[2] Although usury has been prohibited since the Code of Hammurabi, there is fluctuation in history regarding his penal treatment.

[3] Tiedemann (2009), p. 78 (free translation).

[4] de Mondaca (2007), p. 18 and ss.

In this influx, economic freedom in the context of industrialization presupposes the power to conquer new consumers and markets. It happens that, at this point, it was empirically verified that the free action of economic agents ended up generating acts of capital concentration and monopoly,[5] which are factors contrary to the characteristics of the system, and should therefore be rejected with a view to its own maintenance. In this way, it is seen that the model of the absence of regulation, consistent with a liberal legal conception, proved to be inadequate.[6]

Thus, in this conjuncture of full economic liberalism and political power of the nation-state consecrated by the codifying movement, e.g., the Penal Codes of France (1810), Belgium (1867), and Italy (1889) criminally punished the speculation of goods and securities.

Also during this period was promulgated in the United States of America the *Sherman Act*, the first antitrust legislation of that country. Dated 1890, the law was named in honor of its author, Republican Senator John Sherman, dealing with legislation that criminally punished both the individual and the legal entity due to acts of monopoly. Within the evolutionary line of competition discipline, the *Sherman Act* is the crowning of the second identified period, as it consecrates competition as essential for the economic system, at the same time that it demands a state action to eliminate the distortions it can cause to the system.[7]

Despite being the consecrator of this second evolutionary phase of the criminal treatment of the economy, due to the lack of precision regarding the behaviors prohibited, however, the *Sherman Act* was replaced in 1914 by the *Clayton Antitrust Act*, followed by successive modifications.

2.1.3 Third Phase: Welfare State

It is only with the emergence of the interventionism of the Welfare State—*Welfare State*— resulting from the world wars of the twentieth century and, in the interregnum of these, the crisis of 1929, that a systematic centralization of economic regulation begins, to protect weakened national economies, widely using Criminal Law for this. From then on, dogmatic concerns begin about the relationship between this legal branch and economics.

The beginning of this third phase of economic regulation, namely, economic interventionism, in relation to which the use of Criminal Law is exacerbated, begins with the First Great War.[8] The social conflicts related to it, the need for direction and economic mobilization for the war efforts, fundamentally due to the scarcity of

[5] Berstein (2007), p. 19.

[6] Silva Sánchez (2022), p. 35.

[7] Forgioni (2008), pp. 71–72. In a similar sense, Rodrigues (2019), p. 23.

[8] Moment that marks the beginning of the history of Economic Criminal Law, according to Dias and Andrade. Cf. Dias and Andrade (1998), p. 323.

products and urgency of price control, forged a radicalization of state control of economic life in the sense of direction, conformation, and defense.[9] There is then a true "outbreak of state regulation of economic activity."[10]

> The shortages caused by the war led (in 1914) to laws that authorized the Bundesrat [German Federal Council] to take measures considered necessary in economic matters and, in particular, in the domain of prices (maximums). This was followed by an almost uncontrollable proliferation of administrative norms directing economic life that resorted (abusively, at times) to criminal sanctions as a guarantee of effectiveness and prevention. Only in the fight against speculative forms (*Kriegswuchergesetze*) were more than forty thousand criminal provisions published, which would later see their validity extended beyond the end of the war in the form of price regulation laws.[11]

The emblematic German crisis thus led to the enactment of the Weimar Constitution (1919), a milestone of state interventionism in economic life to build a state of a social nature and which influenced those elaborated later in other countries,[12] such as the Brazilian Constitution of 1934. The German decree against the abuse of economic power, from 1923, is, "(...) a typical case of legislation (penal) economic of the Weimar Republic that historically arose as an *economic state* (*Wirtschaftsstaat*) – Tiedemann."[13] The liberalism of *laissez-faire* thus transmuted into a tendency of a State concerned with social welfare.[14]

The state interventionist movement was intensified even more due to the so-called Great Depression, or crisis of 1929, triggered in the United States of America. The increase in North American productivity, a result of intense industrialization, coupled with protectionist measures, on the one hand, was not accompanied by an increase in purchasing power of the growing population, due to low wages, and on the other, faced an economic crisis in Europe, resulting from the economic fragility product of the First Great War, factors that drastically reduced the consumer market of the country's industrial park, generating a strong recession.

The fall in the shares of American companies was the subsequent consequence that led to unemployment and large-scale bankruptcies. The president elected in 1932, Franklin Delano Roosevelt, influenced by the ideas of economist John Maynard Keynes, to face the crisis, proposed a policy of great state interventionism in the economy, which became known as the *New Deal*.

This policy was implemented in three stages: (a) initially, in the years 1933 and 1934, with the adoption of a series of measures, such as the devaluation of the American currency (*Gold Reserve Act*), the stricter control of the banking system

---

[9]Dias (2009), p. 323.

[10]Forgioni (2008), p. 83.

[11]Dias and Andrade (1998), pp. 324–325.

[12]Cf., e.g., Bonavides (2009), p. 231; Fabri (2009), p. 55; Bercovici (2005), pp. 14–15. This last author properly observes that the Mexican Constitution of 1917 was the first to emerge in a sense of "social constitutionalism" or to figure as "Economic Constitution", but the most famous Political Charter representative of this model was that of Weimar. Bercovici (2005), pp. 11–12.

[13]Dias and Andrade (1998), p. 325 (original highlights).

[14]Tiedemann (1985), p. 71.

(*Banking Act*), the amortization of the agrarian debt and the destruction of agricultural stocks (*Agricultural Adjustment Act*) and the establishment of a new paradigm in the relationship between the State and companies (*National Industrial Recovery Act*); (b) then, in view of the invalidation by the Supreme Court of most of the measures adopted, a reorientation carried out in 1935, with greater combat against unemployment, strengthening of unions and greater welfare, and (c) the final moment, in 1938, of increased public spending, increased wages and stricter control over companies.

The imminence of a new war then brought in rearmament a final factor in solving the crisis, but the fact is that a posture of state dirigisme of economic life was consecrated, that is, "the State begins to direct the system, with the aim of avoiding crises."[15]

It is exactly the North American political-economic situation post-1929 crisis the analytical substrate of crime in the business world of Edwin H. Sutherland.[16] According to his theory, of differential association, crime is not the result of a dysfunction or maladjustment of less favored classes, but rather the result of learning a deviant behavior and association related to it, within the communicational context of a social group. To demonstrate his theory, Sutherland focuses on a group of people of respectability and high social status, from whom one would not expect them to commit crimes: the "white collar criminals." Thus begins the doctrinal concerns with economic delinquency, as will be analyzed below.

In legislative terms, shortly before, during, and shortly after the Second World War, state dirigisme of the economy intensified, both in the German national-socialist regime and in capitalist countries and the Soviet bloc. In this sense:

> The dirigiste character of the economy of the national-socialist regime and its subsequent commitment to war gave rise to a hypertrophied Economic Criminal Law, characterized by the administrative nature of its processing and the rigor of the sanctions. Many of the norms of this law remained in force, others perished due to lack of application, others replaced by new scattered and separate legislation to which the *economic penal law* of 1949 tried to give some arrangement. It is in this law that, for the first time, the contraposition between a *criminal law* (economic) and a *right of mere social ordering*, leading to the appearance of the *Ordnungswidrigkeitengesetz* [Law of Administrative Offenses] of 1952. The criminal law of the economy has undergone several important reforms, the last of which in 1975.[17]

State regulation of the economy has only increased since then and concerns about economic crime took on an important configuration in the second half of the twentieth century, revealing the radicalization of the incriminating formula. However, the foundations and the regulatory outlines resulting from them began to display different characteristics from the beginning of the 80s of that century.

[15] Forgioni (2008), p. 84. In the same sense, e.g., Shecaira (2023), p. 185.

[16] Sutherland (2009), *passim*.

[17] Dias and Andrade (1998), p. 325 (original highlights). On the topic, from this last author, cf. also: da Andrade (1998), p. 96 and ss.

2.1.4 Fourth Phase: Retraction of the Role of the State

After a period of economic prosperity experienced with the end of the Second World War, the United States of America began, in the 70s of the twentieth century, to suffer from a series of economic and political difficulties triggered by various factors, such as the Vietnam War, the oil shocks and the resulting global economic downturn, and the Watergate scandal. The welfare and state action models with the aim of economic recovery, implemented by Presidents Richard Nixon, Gerald Ford, and Jimmy Carter, did not contain inflation, the increase in the *deficit* budget, and unemployment, reasons that triggered a significant economic crisis in the United States of America and, consequently, in the world economy.

It is in this context that Ronald Reagan assumed the American presidency, who, aligned with British Prime Minister Margaret Thatcher, adopts a policy of reducing state intervention in the economy. This implied a decrease in taxes and public spending, going through privatizations, reduction of numbers of public employees and cutting welfare measures.

This policy of overcoming the Welfare State by a model of minimal state intervention, synthesized by the expression "Washington Consensus," consecrated in Economic Law a posture of establishment of regulatory frameworks, that is, the State only seeks to manage economic actors with a view to ensuring the current model, without interfering more significantly in the market, which should function freely.

This did not mean, however, a decrease in Criminal Law in the economic field. On the contrary, in this scenario, of transition from industrial society to post-industrial, in which new social risks were revealed, Criminal Law reaffirmed itself as a guaranteeing instrument of the current state economic policy and as a risk management instrument of a highly complex society.

The great power of transnational companies in a globalized economy made possible, for example, frauds with enormous repercussions, as happened with the Enron and WorldCom cases.[18] These American companies, as was disclosed in the years 2001 and 2002, starred in two notorious financial scandals, involving billions of dollars in losses, due to accounting frauds perpetrated by their executives.

Thus, because of these two cases, with the aim of more efficiently protecting the financial market, the *Sarbanes-Oxley Act*,[19] was enacted in July 2002 in the United States of America, legislation that changed the *United States Code* in order to intensify the criminal treatment of the subject. In essence, consecrating the value

[18] A similar financial scandal involved the Italian company Parmalat. As this only erupted in the year 2003, after the emblematic American legislative reform cited below, it was not mentioned in the text.

[19] The legislative nickname comes from the composition of the patronymic of the subscribing parliamentarians of the legal diploma: Senator Democrat Paul Sarbanes and Republican Representative Michael Oxley.

of reliability in business relations,[20] this law imposes the obligation, on the part of administrators and financial directors of companies, to include in their periodic, semi-annual and annual statements to shareholders, a commitment to the accuracy of the information provided, under penalty of committing a crime of falsehood punishable by up to 20 years of imprisonment, regardless of proof of any harm.

There are doubts about the maintenance of this state managerial model after the 2008 crisis, triggered by a strong contraction of credit in the United States of America (called the "credit bubble") due to the collapse of the mortgage system, which led to significant state intervention in the economy.[21] This took place in the form of credit release by governments around the world, increase in normative and operational regulation, as well as the occasional purchase of shares of large transnational companies by the American government.

Nevertheless, it can be said that the state financial rescue and the increase in regulation, in the form they took, did not distort the managerial policy to the point of demonstrating a return to the model of the Welfare State.[22] In any case, the expansionist trend in criminal law in economic matters remains.

2.1.5 *Economic Delinquency in Brazil*

The Brazilian case has peculiarities in the face of the outline of the western northern hemisphere. Until the first decades of the twentieth century, the relationship between Criminal Law and economy in Brazil is insignificant. Although there may be greater historical interest for Economic Law in the analysis of the colonial period, which presented the phase of simple economic exploitation and, later, the beginning of economic orientation, this with the arrival of the Portuguese Court in Brazil, in 1808, in legal-criminal terms at the time, in the Philippine Ordinances,[23] e.g., in Title XII of Book V, counterfeiting of coins was punished, and, in Title LVI of the same Book, frauds committed by goldsmiths[24] were punished.

In independent Brazil, it is observed that the Criminal Code of the Empire (1830) and the Republican Penal Code (1890) punished, for example, the counterfeiting of

[20] And, in this way, consecrating the managerial state stance.

[21] On the penal relevance of the highlighted crisis, cf. Rodrigues (2019), p. 11 and ss.

[22] Also understanding that the economic interventionism of the first half of the twentieth century gave way to a managerial stance in the second half, cf. de Sousa (2023), p. 19.

[23] First legislation effectively in force and applicable for more than two centuries in Brazilian lands. Cf., e.g., Pierangeli (2001), p. 55 and pp. 60–61; Garcia (2008), p. 175 and ss.

[24] In the same unsystematic way, casuistic, scarce decrees of the regent prince, such as that of August 14, 1809, which sought to reinforce the repression of smuggling, or that of February 12, 1810, which dealt with gold misplacement, had some legal-penal interest.

coins[25] and bankruptcy[26] (called "bankruptcy" in that). However, possibly due to the late national industrialization,[27] there are no revealing traces of identification with the corresponding phase in Anglo-Saxon or continental European law of the same time, namely, the emergence of norms tending to protect the liberal economic model.

In fact, in this influx, the country seems to have jumped from a merely casuistic phase to, from the end of the 1930s, following the trend of expanding the criminal protection of the economy,[28] but initially in a faltering way and always in a peculiar, unsystematic way, and in a way to protect the most diverse interests.[29]

To corroborate such understanding, it is observed that, although the 1934 Constitution was effectively influenced by the foundation of the interventionist State,[30] it had a short duration and, in terms of criminal law, it was not accompanied by a phenomenon of broad typification of an economic nature. In fact, for most of the 1930s, a time of effervescence of the Welfare State elsewhere, with broad economic criminalization, Brazil[31] held some interest in economic criminal law only for crimes against the freedom of work[32] and counterfeiting of coins,[33] provided for in the Consolidation of Penal Laws, and the repression of the crime of usury, by Decree No. 22,626, of 1933.

It is only from Decree-Law 869/38 that the relationship between Criminal Law and the economy begins to gain some importance in the country. Resulting from a regulation of Article 141 of the 1937 Constitution,[34] which adopted among its principles the protection of the popular economy, the Vargas legislation sought to curb specific abuses of economic power, considering the interests of the consumer.[35]

---

[25] Articles 173 to 176 of the Criminal Code of the Empire of Brazil and 239 to 244 of the Penal Code of 1890.

[26] Article 263 of the Criminal Code of 1830 and Articles 336 and 337 of the Penal Code of 1890.

[27] Pointing out the reasons for the delay, cf. Prado Júnior (1970), p. 257 and ss.

[28] "Whoever fixes the set of legislative evolution in Brazil will recognize, from 1930 onwards, the growing primacy of collective interest, in the mechanism of the State." Lyra (1940), p. 91.

[29] In the same sense regarding antitrust norms, cf. Forgioni (2008), p. 125.

[30] Its Article 115 established: "The economic order must be organized according to the principles of justice and the needs of national life, in a way that enables everyone to have a dignified existence. Within these limits, economic freedom is guaranteed."

[31] Although FORGIONI identifies that in the 1930s the Brazilian state intensified its action on and in the economic domain, the fact is that this did not occur through Criminal Law. Forgioni (2008), p. 109.

[32] Article 204 of the Consolidation of Penal Laws.

[33] Articles 239 to 244 of the Consolidation of Penal Laws.

[34] Whose content was as follows: "The law will promote the economy popular, ensuring special guarantees. Crimes against the popular economy are equated to crimes against the State, and the law must impose severe penalties and prescribe processes and trials adequate for their prompt and secure punishment."

[35] Lyra (1940), p. 93; Forgioni (2008), p.114. Although this is the same meaning, at the time the word "consumer" was not commonly used, but rather "people" or the phrase "people's economy," as was done, for example, by Hungria (1939), p. 14 and *passim*. On the subject, FORGIONI also

With the 1940 Code, whose edition did not repeal Decree-Law 869/38, there is again only sporadic intertwining between Criminal Law and the economy, as with the examples of crimes of counterfeit money and smuggling.

Next, revealing a lack of systematization regarding the theme of repression of the abuse of economic power,[36] Decree-Law 7,666/45, of an exclusively administrative nature, sought to curb acts contrary to national economic interests, defined by the diploma, and created the Administrative Commission for Economic Defense. This norm, however, had a few months of validity, having been revoked with the fall of President Getúlio Vargas, at the end of October 1945.

Later, seeking to regulate Article 148 of the 1946 Constitution,[37] which expressly provided for the repression of the abuse of economic power,[38] Law 1,521/51, enshrined the use of Criminal Law in the economic field, revealing an antitrust scope[39] and consumer protection. This is the dual aspect that emerges from the analysis of legislative discussions when drafting the law, an opportunity when it even refers to the consumer.[40]

After that, only from the 1960s, fundamentally in the period of political authoritarianism following the Constitution of 1967, laws of economic criminal nature were enacted, under questionable arguments of the need to combat inflation and monetary appreciation, without order and with little practical applicability.[41] The expansive trend, still without systematization and in a technically poor manner, radicalized in the 90s of the last century.

Despite the enactment of the Penal Code of 1940,[42] reformed in its General Part in 1984, regarding economic criminalization, the path chosen by the national legislator was predominantly the treatment of the theme in extraordinary legislation, relatively to which mention is made, in generic terms, among others, to the following significant diplomas of interest: Law 1.521/51 (crimes against the popular economy), Law 4.729/65 (tax evasion crimes), Law 7.492/86 (crimes against the national

---

notes that the State sought with said diploma not the function of conducting the system, but only the correction of any dysfunctions. Cf. Forgioni (2008), p. 116.

[36] Forgioni (2008), p. 120.

[37] Which stated: "The law will repress any and all forms of abuse of economic power, including unions or groupings of individual or social companies, whatever their nature, that aim to dominate national markets, eliminate competition and arbitrarily increase profits."

[38] About the constitutional text, Reale Júnior writes: "Thanks to the insistence of Deputy Agamenon Magalhães, the Constitution of 1946 stipulated, in art. 148, that it would be, as one of the objectives to achieving a fair economic order, repressing the abuse of economic power (…)." Reale Júnior (1999), p. 116.

[39] Forgioni (2008), p. 125.

[40] Cf. Sousa Neto (1952), *passim*. Summarizing the constitutional and historical reasons for this law, this author wrote: "(…) The State intervenes to regulate the use of property, conditioning it to social well-being; to distribute, with equal opportunity for all; and, finally, to punish abuse and exploitation, prohibiting market dominance, the elimination of competition and the arbitrary increase in profits." Sousa Neto (1952), p. 9.

[41] In this sense, cf. Ferrari (2004), p. 257.

[42] With little economic criminal interest, as asserted.

financial system), Law 8.078/90 (Consumer Protection Code), Law 8.137/90 (crimes against the tax, economic order and against consumer relations), Law 8.176/91 (types of crimes against the economic order), Law 14.133/2021 (bidding and administrative contracts law), Law 9.605/98 (environmental crimes), Law 9.613/98 (money laundering crimes), Complementary Law 105/2001 (crimes against the secrecy of operations of financial institutions), Law 10.303/2001 (crimes against the capital market), Law 12.683/2012 (new money laundering legislation) and Laws 13.254/2016 and 13.428/2017 (repatriation of assets).

It should be noted that the significant majority of legal diplomas referring to the theme were enacted after the validity of the Constitution of the Federative Republic of Brazil of 1988, thus, there should be a particular reference to it.

Of an analytical nature, or in other words, extremely detailed,[43] including in the numerous provisions that do not appear as essentially constitutional,[44] the Political Charter currently in force in Brazil—a result of the redemocratization after the end of the military period— despite adopting the free enterprise regime,[45] through which the exercise of any economic activity is free, regardless of state authorization, except in exceptional cases expressed by law, shows itself to be directive in economic terms,[46] because "it is certain that free initiative gives way to state intervention at some points."[47]

In this influx, the State, as a normative and regulatory agent of the economy, is given the supervision, the incentive, and the planning of the economic activity in Brazil (Article 174 of the Constitution of 1988), in addition to, in certain cases, directly exploring this activity (Article 173).

The fundamental pillars of the national economic activity are listed in the *caput* of Article 170 of the 1988 Charter: I – national sovereignty; II – private property; III – social function of property; IV – free initiative; V – consumer protection; VI – environmental protection, including through differentiated treatment according to the environmental impact of products and services and their processes of elaboration and provision; VII – reduction of regional and social inequalities; VIII – pursuit of

---

[43] Identifying one of the main reasons for this as the lack of adoption of a preliminary project at the time of the Constituent Assembly, which had its work scattered in multiple subcommittees, cf. Bastos (2010), p. 213. Specifically about the text edited pertaining to the economic and financial order, Gastão Alves Toledo adds: "The constitutional economic order reflects the uncertainties and perplexities reigning during the works of the constituent assembly of 1987/88. Gathered in a period marked by the climate of political resurgence, after the end of the military regime, it had as a backdrop, in the economic sphere, a chronic inflationary process, fiscal chaos, the moratorium on external debt that only brought harm and the failure of an economic plan (cross plan) that did nothing to lead the economy back to normality. On the contrary, it exacerbated the already excited spirits by the opportunity to modify the legal structure of the country, endowing it with institutions that would make it less vulnerable to economic uncertainties and able to self-determine in the field of foreign policy." de Toledo (2010), V. II, p. 307.

[44] Bonavides calls such Constitutions as verbose, cf. Bonavides (2009), p. 91.

[45] Bastos (2010), p. 632.

[46] Canotilho (2001), pp. 12, 14, 18–24, *passim*; Bercovici (1999), pp. 35–51; Ferrari (2004), p. 257.

[47] Bastos (2010), p. 632.

full employment and IX – favored treatment for small businesses established under Brazilian laws and that have their headquarters and administration in the country. In the name of these general principles,[48] which would be a plan for the transformation of Brazilian society,[49] it is established, among other details, the repression of the abuse of economic power that aims at the domination of markets, the elimination of competition, and the arbitrary increase in profits.[50]

This last aspect, of repression of the abuse of economic power, in consonance with the fundamental pillars of economic activity engraved by the constituent of 1988, thus represents the necessary interpretative sense of infraconstitutional norms with economic aspects. Discussing the hermeneutic challenges imposed by the discipline of the economic and financial order of the 1988 Charter, it is observed that:

> (…) the constitutional economic order, in a broad sense, harbors principles and guidelines capable of supporting all legislative or administrative measures necessary to confront circumstances that put the performance of the economy at risk (…).[51]

Thus, beyond a series of norms of Economic Law properly said, or Administrative, Commercial and Civil, these in cases where they present economic aspects, the hermeneutic understanding to be employed in the interpretation of economic criminal legislation produced after the Charter now in force is also similar.[52]

It should be noted, at this point, that part of the doctrine,[53] supposes there is even the need for criminalization of conduct as a result of the constitutional text,[54] in the name of interests there protected.[55] In this sense, extravagant legislation of an economic criminal nature could be understood, even if indirectly based on §§

---

[48] Eros Grau adds other constitutional directives within the economic order, such as human dignity and the construction of a free, fair and solidary society. Grau (2007), p. 216.

[49] Bercovici (2003), pp. 312–315.

[50] Article 170, § 4, of the 1988 Constitution. The following paragraph of this same provision would be the one that, according to part of the doctrine, would establish the criminal liability of the legal entity in crimes against the economic and financial order and against the popular economy.

[51] de Toledo (2010), p. 314.

[52] The theme will be developed below, Sect. 2.3, starting from the notion of the legal good economic order. But it is already observed that the *ratio essendi* of the legitimate economic penal norm can only be the one that aims, together with the other legal norms pertaining to the matter, the protection of the fundamental pillars of the national economic activity, in all its entirety. Hence why, for example, the meaning cannot be solely the defense of property (case, e.g., of crimes against property), but, beyond this, the defense of the consumer and free initiative, among other aspects.

[53] Paschoal (2003), p. 69 and following, *passim*.

[54] An example of this position can be found in Brazilian literature, with Antonio Carlos da Ponte, who states: "The mandates of criminalization indicate matters on which the ordinary legislator does not have the power to legislate, but the obligation to deal with, protecting certain goods or interests in an adequate and, as far as possible, integral way." da Ponte (2008), p. 152.

[55] According to the author, such understanding arises from the perspective that one has of Criminal Law in the face of the Constitution: "Indeed, when it ceases to be a limit, becoming a foundation, the Constitution begins to be taken as a propeller of Criminal Law, allowing that any situation of 'emergency', or apparent 'emergency', may raise questions related to the non-compliance of an indication, or constitutional determination of criminalization. This change of perspective makes it

4 and 5 of Article 173 of the Major Law, as in compliance with the aforementioned postulate.[56]

However, in line with what has already been expressed elsewhere,[57] and according to the thought of part of the doctrine,[58] such a position is not adopted. The supposed obligatory constitutional criminalization of conduct is entirely incompatible with the configuration of the Democratic State of Law, which has, by its very essence, the freedom of citizens as a rule and the most severe means of its curtailment, which is the penal regulation, as an exception, to be used only to curb the most serious attacks on the most cherished community values and only when other means of protection prove ineffective for this purpose.[59] In other words, Criminal Law is the *ultima ratio* of social control.

Therefore, the constituent could not establish a determination of criminalization of conduct, when the ordinary legislator can, in the face of the changing color of social relations, find, for example, that another form of legal regulation, less drastic, has the possibility of performing the same, or more effective, role. And in regard to the topic at hand, this discussion is crucial, since it is possible that administrative law, e.g., adequately delimits certain issues currently addressed by the criminal law branch.

Consequently, it is not understood as constitutionally justified penal expansionism in any aspect, let alone in the economic field.[60] In other words, it is not conceivable to have a legitimizing support *a priori*, of a constitutional nature, for the production of *lege lata* of types of economic content incriminators.

However, a certain practical influence of the interests signaled as worthy of protection by the constituent on the ordinary legislator is noted, which, in recent decades, has been consecrating in Brazil, as elsewhere, a global movement of expansion of Criminal Law typical of risk society, which includes the criminal-legal protection of economic interests. The relevance or not of this posture, with regard to specifically the economic order, is one of the essential aspects of this scientific investigation.

---

so that, before the Constitution, the criminalization of a certain conduct ceases to be seen only as possible, becoming constitutionally obligatory." Paschoal (2003), pp. 71–72.

[56] As some interpreters do, in the national doctrine, e.g., regarding the Environmental Crimes Law (Law No. 9.605/1998) or the Heinous Crimes Law (Law No. 8.072/1990). In this sense, cf. Paschoal (2003), p. 81 and following, *passim*.

[57] de Souza (2007), pp. 87–92.

[58] Paschoal (2003), *passim* ; Cunha (1995), *passim*; Reale Júnior (2009), p. 21 and following.

[59] "Not every good, interest or value established in the Constitution can be considered a legal good with criminal dignity. However, not every legal good needs criminal protection, often, protection by other branches of law is enough. Thus, it is evident the flaw of intending to derive from the recognition of values and interests in the Constitution the obligation of the legislator to promote their criminal protection. Therefore, in a Democratic State of Law, the normative force of the constitution in relation to criminal law, is necessarily directed towards its limitation (in order to confer legitimacy on it), and not towards its foundation, in a positive sense of determination." Bechara (2010), p. 56.

[60] Furthermore, state dirigisme of the economy is not incompatible with a minimum Criminal Law. In the same sense, Bechara (2003), p. 3; Bechara (2010), p. 40.

2.1.6 Conclusion

In terms of general historical evolution, the relationship between Criminal Law and economy presented four phases: (a) mere casuistry of treatment, which lasted from Antiquity to the Modern Age; (b) protection of the liberal economic model, which has in the *Sherman Act* its consecration; (c) assurance of the policy of the Welfare State and d) decrease of the role of the State in the economy, to mere regulatory agent, which has in the *Sarbanes-Oxley Act* its peak.

From the period of seeking protection for the liberal model to the present day, only the penal repression of actions of economic interest has been increasing, although for various reasons.

As for the Brazilian legal system, an exact correspondence with the international phases is not observed, at least until recently. This is because, from the second half of the twentieth century, economic criminalization begins to emerge in Brazil, which is consecrated, or radicalized, in the 90s, without systematization.

Therefore, given the exasperation—increasingly intense—and on a global level, of this novel criminality from the middle of the last century to the present day, it is essential to delimit the meaning, the scope, and the functionality of this link between Criminal Law and economy, with a view to reflection on its legitimacy in a Democratic State of Law. For this, it is necessary to preliminarily focus on what is understood by Economic Criminal Law and what the role of the theory of legal good is in this understanding.

2.2 Fundamental Assumptions

A fundamental preliminary question for addressing the proposed theme is exactly that of the delimitation of what Economic Criminal Law would be. Without a precise understanding of its content, one cannot advance on the inquiry into its legitimacy.

2.2.1 Understanding Economic Criminal Law

There is in the doctrine the recognition of the absence of uniformity in the conceptualization of Economic Criminal Law,[61] which beforehand brings serious difficulties for the analysis and systematization of the subject,[62] as there is not even convergence on the exact object protected by the criminal norm.

[61] Cf., among others: Tiedemann (1985), p. 9; Gracia Martín (2003), p. 66; Pimentel (1973), p. 12; Dias and Andrade (1998), p. 332; Ferrari (2004), p. 263.

[62] Tiedemann (1985), p. 9.

The initial studies of the theme, from the mid-twentieth century, due to Sutherland[63] and Clinard,[64] linked the idea of economic crime to its author, seen as a "businessman" (a "white-collar" man), in contrast to the so-called traditional delinquent, belonging to the popular classes (a "blue-collar" man). As stated, the ideology focused its analysis of the differential association on the delinquency committed by the economically better-off individuals in society.

The descriptive view, of a criminological nature,[65] of such authors cannot, however, be adopted as a normative reference for criminalization,[66] being in fact unacceptable in the face of a liberal Criminal Law, aimed at the illicit act, regardless of the personal characteristics of its author. Moreover, this view would not hold up against the simple observation that economic crime often has as its material author a simple employee or an interposed person of a "businessman" or, still, an economically deprived individual, but who aspires to a superior position with the illegality.

On the other hand, despite the undeniable importance of business contexts in economic delinquency, as the studies of Sutherland and Clinard point out, it is also not appropriate to think that relates economic criminal offense to that of a company (*corporate crime*),[67] an economic actor of major business typical of our era. This is because this understanding—abstracting at this point from the precise discussion of the possibility or not of criminal responsibility of the legal person, that is, of its consideration as an active subject of criminal offenses—presents the same reductionist flaw of the previous understanding, which ignores that the criminal norm prohibits conducts and that, in the case of economic delinquency, one can use or not a moral entity to carry out the prohibited actions.

The understanding of Corporate Criminal Law as a branch of Economic Criminal Law[68] may even prove useful in terms of study methodology, especially for criminological investigations, but it is not adequate to characterize in essence what Economic Criminal Law is. That is, despite the relevance of the business environment in the perpetration of socially undesirable economic behaviors, Criminal Law Economics is not exclusively a Corporate Criminal Law. In other words, economic

---

[63] Sutherland (2009), *passim*.

[64] Clinard (1969), *passim*; Later, cf.: Clinard and Yager (2005), *passim*.

[65] Gracia Martín (2003), p. 67. For Faria Costa, "We are facing a case of particular relevance to have a correct perception of the relations between criminal law and criminology. As is known, that happy qualification was coined by Edwin Sutherland and meant a 'small Copernican revolution' not only in the ways of criminology research but also a huge enrichment in what refers to criminal law itself (…)." Costa (2003), p. 81.

[66] Silveira (2006), p. 65, note 4.

[67] Trend of the French and Swedish doctrine, cf. Tiedemann (1985), p. 10. Cf. also, e.g., except for some nuances pointed out, Terradillos Basoco (2001), pp. 34–35; Schünemann (2002), p. 192. See also the outstanding work specifically on the subject by Alexander (2004).

[68] Terradillos Basoco (1995), p. 10; de Sousa (2023), p. 25.

crime is not exclusively business crime. The broad sense intended by certain authors[69] to Corporate Criminal Law encompasses such distinct behaviors as bankruptcy crimes, against free competition, and environmental and tax crimes, which, despite not actually having an identity of protected interest, can be perpetrated outside of a specific business reality.

Still in this context, part of the specialized German and American literature, moving away from the simple consideration of authorship or exclusive use of a collective entity for the practice of the illicit, but in a certain sense using such ideas-force, employs the concept of "occupational crime" (*occupational crime* or *occupational deviant*).[70] Thus, for a conception of this kind, economic crime would be perpetrated professionally within an economic activity.

Although it seems more appropriate than previous understandings, since there is a focus on the fact and not exclusively on its author or on the means of criminal execution, the thought of *occupational crime* truly still reveals great imprecision, since it can generically encompass the same understanding facts so distinct practiced professionally with the intention of illicit profit such as, e.g., drug trafficking, bankruptcy crime, tax evasion, extortion by kidnapping and aggression to free competition.

It has also been sought to doctrinally define economic delinquency according to a criminological perspective:[71]

> From the circumstance that economic crimes, due to their normal complexity, can only be investigated and judged through special processes, by police and magistrates endowed with knowledge of modern economic life and through the expenditure of large sums, it has gone to the point of denying any other identifying note of the crime against the economy.[72]

Thus, in the face of the specificities of their investigation, economic crimes would be qualified, which is inappropriate because it distances itself from the dogmatic foundations of the issue, clinging to something simply tied to investigative praxis.[73]

Finally, the distinction proposed by Tiedemann, adopted in Spanish doctrine by authors such as Bajo Fernández, between Economic Criminal Law in the strict sense and Economic Criminal Law in the broad sense stands out in economic criminal literature.[74]

---

[69] Terradillos Basoco (1995), *passim*.

[70] Tiedemann (1985), pp. 10–11; Pimentel (1973), p. 28.

[71] Tiedemann (1985), p. 12; Tiedemann (2009), pp. 70–71.

[72] Dias and Andrade (1998), p. 333.

[73] In the words of Dias and Andrade: "(...) It would be a matter of property crimes qualified only by the complexity of their practice and, consequently, of their investigation. It is an equally inadequate perspective. It elevates to the category of essential note of a phenomenon a characteristic (only) normal and that, therefore, does not satisfy the requirements of dogmatics and criminal policy." Dias and Andrade (1998), p. 333.

[74] García Cavero (2007), pp. 21–22.

According to the strict understanding, this branch would only cover infractions aimed at protecting state intervention in market regulation.[75] Thus, usury crimes, currency evasion, and tax evasion would be included in this spectrum, since the normative intention would be to "protect the objectives of state planning" of the economy.[76]

In a broader sense, which gains the adherence of the referred German author, Economic Criminal Law would comprehend:

> (…) firstly, the violations within the scope of Economic Administrative Law, that is, against the state's intervening and regulatory activity in the economy. It also covers infractions against other collective or supra-individual legal goods of economic life, which, by conceptual necessity, transcend individual legal goods. And finally, it includes classic property crimes (fraud, extortion, forgery, corruption, etc.), when these are directed against supra-individual assets (as in cases of fraudulent obtaining of subsidies or state credits) or when they constitute abuse of measures and instruments of economic life (as in the cases of a bounced check or a false balance sheet).[77]

Subsequently, also in the same sense, but, as we understand, broadening its understanding even more, Tiedemann specifies that it includes within the scope of the aforementioned Economic Administrative Law the topics related to taxes, subsidies, credit system, capital market, consumer protection, bills of exchange, etc., arguing that Economic Criminal Law is an integral part of Economic Law.[78]

However, this excessively broad political-criminal vision of Tiedemann does not coincide, either due to the absence of a unit of meaning to justify incriminating types of such disparate substrates as those mentioned, or due to the autonomy of Criminal Law in relation to Economic Law, as well as, finally, due to the lack of a clear and secure criterion capable of limiting the state's criminal repression. The strict view, rejected by the doctrinaire, curiously, also seems vague to us, lacking the greater concreteness necessary in a legal-criminal construction, and, specifically, unclear when trying to distinguish Economic Criminal Law from Economic Law, since the latter certainly seeks to regulate the state's direction of the economy.

In this vein, as developed below, the need to identify the economic criminal legal good is verified. This is because only the protection of legal goods with criminal dignity represents the material interpretative reference of this branch of Law.

---

[75] "Economic Criminal Law, in a strict sense, is conceived as 'law of direction of the economy by the State' (…)." Tiedemann (1985), p. 19 (free translation).

[76] Tiedemann (1985), p. 19 (free translation).

[77] Tiedemann (1985), p. 12 (free translation).

[78] Tiedemann (2009), p. 77.

2.2.1.1 The Protection of Legal Goods as a Material Interpretative Reference of Criminal Law

The methodological solution that emerges consistent with our legal-criminal evolution, which dates back to the ideals of the Enlightenment, is the preliminary inquiry about the protected legal good: "The purpose of providing security by protecting legal goods is what sets a rational limit to the ethical aspiration of criminal law (...)."[79]

The State can only curtail in the most drastic way—with criminal sanction—a human behavior that significantly offends a legal good fundamental to social coexistence, which cannot be protected in any less burdensome way.[80] This is an essential criterion for the analysis of the material reference of a criminalization that has consolidated in the tradition of legal-criminal dogmatics.[81] Only in this way is it possible, concurrently, to justify an incriminating type and provide a secure delimiter against the arbitrariness of the State.

The notion of legal good[82] dates back to the opposition made by Birnbaum in 1834 to Feuerbach's ideas of injury to subjective rights as the material core of the crime, developed by the latter years before to deny any theocratic foundations in Criminal Law. Although there are authors who glimpse in Feuerbach the origin of the concept of legal good, the majority doctrinal understanding is adopted that the closest notion will arise from Birnbaum's criticism of that author's thought, since "good" is more properly linked to the idea of object than to the right.[83]

Without using the exact expression legal good, Birnbaum expands the spectrum of consideration of the material content of the crime, developing his thought in the sense that an incrimination should always be based not on a right, but on an object, of a liberal nature, valued by the State, representative of essential interests of the individual in social life.[84] Such understanding arises from the fact that Law is based on human reason and the social contract, not justified either by a divine or natural idea.

[79] Cf. Zaffaroni and Pierangeli (2008), p. 90.

[80] Hassemer (2007), p. 95 and ss.

[81] Cf., among others: Mir Puig (2005), p. 129; da Costa (2010), pp. 1–2.; Bechara (2007), p. 171; Bechara (2010), p. 88 e ss., passim.

[82] A brief historical mention of the evolution of the concept of legal good will be made only to highlight its benchmark in a specific incrimination, as in the case of economic nature. With depth, among others, cf.: Prado (1997), p. 25 and ss.; Tavares (2002), p. 181 and following; Silveira (2003), p. 36 and following; Paschoal (2003), p. 26 and following; Coelho (2003), p. 31 and following; Bechara (2010), p. 88 and following; Polaino Navarrete (1974), *passim*; Hormazabal Malarée (1992), p. 14 and following; Bustos Ramírez (1994), p. 24 and following; da Andrade (1991), p. 42 and following; Cunha (1995), p. 29 and following.

[83] Regarding the topic, cf., e.g., Cunha (1995), p. 30.

[84] Bechara (2009), pp. 17–18.

The first author to use the term "legal good" was Binding, who, with a positivist view, understood that the crime would be the injury to a subjective right of the State, the legal good being what the law established in this sense. Still within the ideals of the positive school, but in a naturalistic-sociological line[85] and seeking to overcome the criticisms of mere formalism in Binding's definition, von Liszt brought the understanding of legal goods as vital social interests, based on concrete social circumstances.[86] In this way, they would not be a consequence of the legal system, but rather previous, resulting from social reality.

From the 1920s onwards, with the neo-Kantian ideology, the liberal bias of the legal good is abandoned, emphasizing its teleological conception, that is, interpreting it from its end, which is seen in community values. This happened because this doctrine based the concept of science of the spirit, like Law, on the method and not on the object, giving rise to an axiological philosophy.[87]

During the period of the German National Socialist regime, the theory of the legal good was criticized because it was understood to be inadequate to the new model of the State due to its individualism and liberalism.[88] Considering the stain brought to Criminal Law by the Kiel School in this anti-democratic and horrific period, subsequently a revaluation of the concept of legal good is noted.[89]

With the end of the world conflict, the humanistic conceptions of Welzel's natural law,[90] initiated in the 1930s, were resumed. The German author seeks to base the delictive system according to ontologism, from the structures logical-objective, or of the nature of things. Human action, which precedes law, is a fundamental logical-objective structure, in view of the human ability to predict the outcome of their actions. "That's why Welzel asserts that the ontological structure of action precedes any regulation, constituting a structure that must be respected when wanting to regulate behaviors."[91]

In this sense, the consideration of the disvalue of action in the delictive analysis stands out in importance. Despite referencing the legal good as a vital interest of the community and the individual, Welzel's finalistic theory does not highlight it in its construction. However, it had the merit of having resumed the idea of its material content, prompting the reflections that followed about the legitimacy of legal-criminal intervention.[92]

---

[85] Bechara (2009), p. 18.

[86] "Liszt argued that the criminal legal good is not created by the legislator, but rather identified by him in the social scenario and, subsequently, protected by the criminal norm. Therefore, one can say that Liszt was the first to expressly defend the idea of a material criminal legal good." Paschoal (2003), p. 33.

[87] Prado (1997), p. 33, footnote 20.

[88] Mir Puig (2005), p. 129; Greco (2006), p. 402.

[89] Silveira (2003), p. 48; Bechara (2010), p. 112.

[90] Welzel (1993).

[91] Reale Júnior (1982), p. 127.

[92] Bechara (2010), p. 114.

In this influx, the understanding of the theme, among sociological, constitutional, or systemic conceptions, began to, mainly,[93] demonstrate support in the Constitution: legal goods would be concretizations of constitutional values related to fundamental rights.[94] This means that the core of the value system is the human person.[95] In the words of Roxin, legal goods are then "(...) realities or ends that are necessary for a free and safe social life which guarantees the human and fundamental rights of the individual, or for the functioning of the state system erected for the achievement of such an end."[96]

The current risk society, with its new problems and needs, has led to a constant rethinking of the theory of the legal good as part of the doctrine. On the one hand, in the sense of its use no longer as a critical and limiting criterion of criminal typification, but, on the contrary, as a justification for increasing the spectrum of incidence of Criminal Law, as done, for example, by Schünemann, in Germany, and Gracia Martín, in Spain.[97] Thus, the expansionist legal-criminal tendency is dogmatically justified.

On the other hand, the reflection on the concept emerges in the sense of abstracting from it as an essential condition for the legitimacy of a criminal prohibition.[98] In other words, a criminalization could have a purpose other than the protection of legal goods. This is the understanding, e.g., of authors like Stratenwerth, Jakobs, Amelung, von Hirsch and, more recently, the position revealed by Roxin.

Proposing the replacement of the notion of legal good by that of life relations themselves,[99] due to the imprecision of the former, Stratenwerth notes:

> Despite multiple efforts, so far there has been no success in clarifying the concept of legal good even approximately. On the contrary, all attempts have failed due to the difficulty, in fact insurmountable, of finding a definition that fits all types of crimes whose legitimacy is beyond question and that, despite this, still expresses something. Instead, the concept only becomes concrete to the extent that it deals with individual interests (life, bodily integrity, freedom, etc.), while, when extended to so-called universal legal goods (such as the community's interest in the correct conduct of a process, respect for religion, the truthfulness of documents, etc.), it only characterizes the basic idea on which the penal provision is

[93] Greco (2006), p. 406. The author reports the alternative responses of Zaczyk, who relies on the philosophy of Kant and Fichte, as well as Kindhäuser, who resorts to the analytical philosophy of language. Greco (2006), p. 406, note 28.

[94] Bechara (2009), p. 20.

[95] da Costa (2010)..., cit., p. 5; Tavares (2002), p. 199; Bechara (2007), p. 169.

[96] Roxin (2007), p. 448 (free translation).

[97] Cf. Schünemann (1999), pp. 627–628; Gracia Martín (2003), *passim*. On the subject, cf.: da Costa (2010)..., p. 8; Bechara (2009), pp. 21–22; Bechara (2010), pp. 123–124.

[98] Greco (2006), pp. 409–410.

[99] Or "relações da vida como tais," as translated from German, p. ex., Dias and Costa. Cf. Dias (2009), p. 614; da Costa (2010)..., cit., p. 18. The thought of Stratenwerth approaches the idea that a criminal type has the objective not to protect legal goods, but to prohibit inconvenient social behaviors. In this sense: Roxin (2009), p. 15.

based. (...) This difficulty could only be overcome if one could start from the premise that the interests of the person are guided exclusively by themselves.[100]

Jakobs, in turn, in his systemic functionalist view,[101] understands that crime is an act of betrayal of the legal order, with the criminal sanction being a response of reaffirmation of the norm vilified by the illicit practice.[102] Thus, the types of crimes, through the system of penalties, protect social expectations of conduct, referenced in the roles of people in a given social context,[103] and not properly legal goods.[104] According to the German author, the punishability must then be guided not by what is contrary to the value per se, but by the social harmfulness of the conduct.[105]

More radically than Jakobs, since for him part of the incriminations that pass through the filter of social harmfulness would be related to the protection of legal goods,[106] which would give factual validity to the corresponding norms, Amelung asserts that the theory of the legal good is simply useless, having to be replaced by the concept of social harmfulness. Influenced by the social systemic theory based on Parsons and Luhmann, the German author believes that the Constitution imposes that only socially harmful conduct should be prohibited, resulting from this that the penal norm can only be applied in a way that results in a contribution to the maintenance of the social system.[107]

In turn, von Hirsch, after analyzing the principle of harm and reflecting on criminalizations such as those related to the environment, as in the case of whale protection, and "conduct crimes" (*Verhaltensdelikte*), as in the case of respect for the dead, concludes that the legal good in itself cannot conform an adequate theory to justify the criminalizing phenomenon, and one should pursue criteria that can go beyond this notion.[108]

---

[100] Stratenwerth (2005), pp. 65–66 (free translation).

[101] On the subject, in national doctrine, all with a critical view, e.g., cf. Reale Júnior (1982), pp. 53–54; Prado (2004), pp. 108–113; Bitencourt (2024), p. 102 e ss.; Tavares (2002), pp. 65–67 e 196 e ss.; de Souza (2024), p. 82.

[102] Jakobs (2009), p. 19 and following, *passim*.

[103] "Pode-se tentar apresentar o direito penal como proteção dos bens jurídicos, mas só de modo bastante forçado. O direito é a estrutura da relação entre pessoas, que por sua vez podem ser representadas como titulares de determinados papéis; a determinação do comportamento não permitido através de diversos institutos da chamada imputação objetiva - hoje, amplamente reconhecida - obriga, a levar em consideração o contexto social, a determinar um papel social, inclusive para os deveres negativos (...). A teoria do direito penal como proteção da vigência da norma demonstra sua validade especialmente na teoria dos fins da pena: o fato *é* uma lesão da vigência da norma, a pena *é* a sua eliminação." Jakobs (2005), p. 51.

[104] Jakobs (2009), p. 61 and ss.

[105] Jakobs (2009), p. 78.

[106] Jakobs (2009), p. 78.

[107] da Andrade (1991), p. 97.

[108] von Hirsch (2007), pp. 37–52. Cf., também, do autor: von Hirsch (2008), pp. 29–42.

In this field, Roxin himself has already mitigated his previous critical understanding,[109] admitting the possibility of an expansion of the scope of criminal law beyond the protection of legal goods. The author does not completely abandon the concept of legal good, but argues that it no longer fits the characteristics of current times, therefore, the use of criminal law should be admitted for the following spheres, where there is no legal good: protection of embryos, protection of plants and animals, and protection of the life of future generations.[110]

Despite the denial of the utility of the theory of legal good, or mere mitigation of this, as a criterion for legitimizing the criminalizing phenomenon, by part of the doctrine, the fact is that Criminal Law represents a violent intrusion into the sphere of fundamental rights of the person, which is why it needs limiting criteria not only formal, but mainly material, under penalty of the consecration of state arbitrariness.

In this influx, the notion of legal good represents a conquest of humanity in the face of the power of the State whose parameter has not been surpassed by any other more coherent proposal. Moreover, the theory's importance stands out as a means of containing the power of the State due to the aforementioned expansionist criminal movement of recent decades.

The proposals for abandonment or replacement of the idea of legal good have so far proved imprecise and disharmonious, permeated by vague and utilitarian concepts, without greater concreteness forming a safe criterion for limiting state arbitrariness. The fact that hypotheses of specific criminalizations do not present a real or convincing legal good[111] of penal stature reveal much more the inadequacy of such penal types than of the theory of the legal good.

A crime without a protected legal good is therefore not admitted, which is the necessary and constitutional foundation both to conceive a duty of protection and to determine the limits to intervention and its precise calculation:

> The determination of the mission of criminal law with the help of the concept of legal good offers the legislator a plausible and practical criterion at the time of making decisions and, simultaneously, an external criterion of proof of the justice of these decisions. This

---

[109] Which affirmed the personal conception of the legal good, even though sometimes related to ends necessary for free and peaceful coexistence—in this way, based on idealizations and not just realities. *See:* Roxin (2008), p. 51 and ss.; Roxin (2007), p. 443 e ss.; Roxin (2009), *passim*.

[110] Roxin (2024), p. 130 and ss.

[111] As in the example of animal abuse crime, which, as we understand, does not seem to possess a legal good of criminal nature, since it is not clearly representative of a measurable fundamental element for free human development in society. In this sense, v. Schünemann (2005), p. 17. The cited text has an exclusive edition in Spanish: Schünemann (2007). On the topic in focus, e.g., cf. also: Manes (2005), pp. 124–126. In Brazilian doctrine, cf da Costa (2010)..., pp. 30–33; Greco (2010), pp. 47–59; Silveira (2010), pp. 372–373; Bechara (2010), pp. 328–340. For this last author, there would be no greater theoretical difficulty in delimiting a legal good in the case, even from an anthropocentric view, aimed at protecting the general relationship maintained between men and animals; however, beyond the identification of a legal good as a criterion for legitimizing the criminal type, as she understands, one should inquire about other criteria, such as compliance with fundamental criminal principles, such as minimal intervention. In this sense, she signals that perhaps it is better for the administrative branch to control the sector. Bechara (2010), pp. 339–340.

> criterion, while usable, should be easily grasped in order to prevent the legislator can threaten with a penalty everything 'that in his opinion should be kept intact and without any change'. The idea of the legal good leads, therefore, to a rational criminal policy: the criminal legislator must measure his decisions with fair and clear criteria, using them at the same time for his justification and criticism. Everything that has nothing to do with the protection of the legal good must be excluded from the scope of protection of criminal law.[112]

Also, in the precise words of Reale Júnior:

> The fundamental values of Justice and freedom demand that the legislator, when constructing the incriminating norms, framework of Criminal Law, have in mind the legal goods considered worthy of protection. The legal good preexists the normative construction, being the object of the choice of the legislator as a value worthy of criminal protection.[113]

This does not mean that criminal legislation should be impermeable to social changes,[114] a result of the highly complex and evolved society of our days, with post-industrial features. The Law is a rational means of facing human challenges arising from intersubjective coexistence.

In this sense, new interests may arise and be protected by Criminal Law. However, respect for clear and secure parameters for delimitation of its contours, such as that achieved through the notion of legal good, is essential for its legitimacy.

It is important to note, without embargo, especially because the theme subject of analysis of this work refers specifically to criminal norms of economic nature, that legal good is not confused with function:

> The necessary link of a state legal good to its origin and personal purpose is a guarantee of the individual that his freedom will not be molested by mere adoption of public policies, in the administrative, economic or social scope, or for electoral purposes. It will be necessary to demonstrate, to validate the choice of this category of legal good, that its injury signifies a damage equally to the person and to his social conditions. Therefore, the notion of function should be discarded from the notion of legal good, which includes state administrative activities, referring to control over a certain sector of life of relationship or of its own organism.[115]

Thus, the reference to the individual, in the sense of protection of his essential living conditions in a society structured on the basis of human freedom, is the justification of a criminal norm.[116] Also to the supra-individual interests there must be a teleological interpretation aimed at identification of the individual

---

[112]Hassemer and Muñoz Conde (1989), p. 105 (free translation). Cf., also, Hassemer (2007), p. 104 and *passim*.

[113]Reale Júnior (1982), p. 28.

[114]In the same sense, e.g., da Costa (2010)..., p. 15.

[115]Tavares (2002), pp. 203–204. Analyzing Tavares' thought, Bechara states: "(...) The function does not have, therefore, an autonomous meaning, consisting of a relationship derived from variables corresponding to reference points of something, without implying a value or interest by themselves." Bechara (2010), p. 235. On the subject, cf. also, *v.g.*: Manes (2005), p. 95 and ss.

[116]Bechara (2009), p. 26.

referent,[117] which, however, it should be emphasized, does not need to be immediate in the structure of the criminal type.[118]

This is the basic premise to guide the present study,[119] a criminal type lacking a legal good, whether this is of an individual or supra-individual nature,[120] is inconceivable. Any attempt to recognize the legitimacy of an economic criminalization—like all others—must, *a priori*, identify the criminally protected legal good.[121]

2.3 Approach to the Concept of Economic Order

For the identification of the legal good deserving criminal protection in the field of economic delinquency, criminal dogmatics must consider, initially, for the purpose of assessing potential points of contact, notions of Economic Law.[122] This is

> (...) the set of legal techniques that the contemporary State uses in the realization of its economic policy. It thus constitutes the normative discipline of state action on the structures of the economic system, whether centralized or decentralized.[123]

The concept of Economic Law emphasizes the idea of an intervention state with a view to the establishment of a normative system intended to regulate the implementation of the adopted economic policy.[124] It should be noted, therefore, that the central notion that gives meaning to this branch of Law is the ordering, or systematization, of the relationship of economic operations, that is, the economic order.[125]

---

[117] In this exact sense is the understanding of Bechara, here adopted: "(...) it is important to highlight that, from the understanding of supra-individual legal goods as collective interests endowed with individual referent, in the qualification of a behavior as a crime it will always be necessary to interpret the penal type teleologically, that is, in attention to this end, and not formally, without being able to verify the existence of an effective affectation of social coexistence." Bechara (2010), p. 235.

[118] Bechara (2010), p. 236.

[119] Similarly, e.g.: Ferrari (2004), p. 260.

[120] On the subject of diffuse legal goods as an object of criminal protection, cf., among others, the in-depth study of Silveira (2003), p. 56 and ss.

[121] "Starting from the assumption that there is no sense in Criminal legislation without the protection of a legal good, it will be essential to know what the value of protection is in economic crimes, based on the concepts of criminal dignity and lack of criminal sanction." Ferrari (2004), p. 260.

[122] Pimentel (1973), p. 6.

[123] *Apud* Pimentel (1973), p. 8.

[124] Pimentel (1973), p. 9.

[125] Pimentel (1973), p. 9.

It should also be noted that the initial idea of Economic Law and, in the same way, of Economic Criminal Law, is linked to the context of state intervention in the economy, which originates when the First World War, especially during the period of following the 1929 crisis[126] and, finally, consolidates after the Second World War.[127] The concept of regulation, or economic ordering, therefore, finds its basis in times of economic crisis.

Criminal Law, in this sense, is inserted within a general idea of economic order, socioeconomic order, or economic model.[128] However, considering that the severe criminal-legal branch is the *ultima ratio* in the protection of values fundamental to social coexistence, the understanding of economic order in its scope cannot be identified with a simple particular form of state intervention in the economy.[129]

Thus, moving away from the contours of Economic Law, the driving idea capable of giving material meaning to Economic Criminal Law is that of an indispensable means of protecting a legal object that aims at the security and regularity of the economic structure of a certain social context.[130]

---

[126] To have an exact dimension of the influence of the Great Depression on the ideals of state interventionism in the economy, it is necessary to remember that the papal encyclical *Quadragesimo Anno*, from 1931, exhorted the regulation of markets based on Christian principles.

[127] Silveira (2003), pp. 20–21 and 64–65.

[128] Such expressions will be used as synonyms in this study—although "economic order" is the most used, including by force, in the Brazilian case, of influence of the constitutional text—as they all generically designate a set of principles and rules that regulate a certain area of social life, which is, in this case, economic relations. Pointing out, however, the ambiguity of the term economic order, its history and scope, cf. Grau (2007), cit., p. 60 and ss. Also, this author differentiates the referred terminology, namely: "*Economic system* as a coherent set of legal and social institutions, in accordance with which the mode of production and the form of distribution of the economic product in a certain society is realized. *Economic model* as a peculiar configuration assumed by the economic order (world of being), affected by a certain *economic regime* (…)." Grau (2007), pp. 192–193, note 14 (original italics).

[129] Cervini (2009), p. 5 and following. Contrary to the above, e.g., cf. Ventura González: "(…) without prejudice to the fact that the economic crime affects the interests of individuals, it is certain that it fundamentally affects the interventionist policy in the socio-economic, which all contemporary states have been forced to adopt to a lesser or greater extent, as a consequence of the insecurity and imbalance inherent to our time. Economic Law is the law of organized economy and the organization is carried out in function of the Economic Public Order. Therefore, the Economic Public Order is the Legally Protected Good." González (1998), p. 29 (free translation).

[130] In a similar sense, Enrique Aftalión understands that the legally protected good in economic crimes is the national economy as a whole. *Apud* González (1998), pp. 31–32.

Without this last conceptual delimitation, but pointing in the direction described regarding the legal object of Economic Criminal Law, the legal good economic order was identified by the XIII Congress of the International Association of Criminal Law (Cairo, 1984),[131] as well as it was doctrinally in Brazil at the dawn of the seventies of the last century by Pimentel.[132]

Rising against this understanding, however, Pérez Del Valle states that the classificatory criterion of designating a legal good or protected interest of economic order provides a certain degree of confusion when finding elements of the crimes that are desired to classify within the study of Economic Criminal Law, as sometimes it would be preferable simply to designate the specific object of attack (such as "industrial property") or even the reference of the *nomen iuris* of the concrete punishable fact ("alteration of prices in public competitions").[133]

Interestingly, however, the author then approaches the thought which sought to refute by, based on Otto, conceptualizing that:

> (…) economic crimes are those behaviors described in laws that harm trust in the current economic order in general or in some of its institutions in particular and, therefore, put at risk the very existence and forms of activity of this economic order.[134]

This latter notion is the one that is accepted here, understanding, on the contrary, that the idea of a list of situations belittles the scientific character of Criminal Law, incapable of giving meaning to the subsystem of Economic Criminal Law.

On the other hand, Martínez-Buján Pérez[135] and Terradillos Basoco[136] also question the idealization that Economic Criminal Law would simply aim to directly

---

[131] Within section II ("Concept and principles of economic and business criminal law, including consumer protection") of the signed document, it was established: "*Terminology*. 4. The term 'economic penal law' is here understood to encompass offenses against the economic order. The term 'business penal law' refers to offenses involving private or public enterprises. Both are closely interrelated in the sense that the offenses violate legal regulations which organize and protect economic and business life. *Protected interests*. 5. In most cases, the use of penal law in this field is concerned with the protection of collective, not only individual, interest. Most of these collective interests, being particularly complex and diffuse, are more difficult to identify and defend than individual interests. Therefore, there is a special need to protect these collective interests. Their protection by penal law should be assumed by the Penal Code." International Association Of Penal Law. Electronic Review of the International Association of Penal Law. Reference: *e-RIAPL 2007*. Available at: <http://www.penal.org/pdf/ReAIDP2007/RICPL%201984.pdf>. Accessed on: August 12, 2024.

[132] Pimentel (1973), p. 9. Currently, in this sense, cf. Rodrigues (2019), p. 29.

[133] Pérez Del Valle (2004), p. 34.

[134] Pérez Del Valle (2004), p. 35 (free translation).

[135] Martínez-Buján Pérez (2007), pp. 119–120, 158 and *passim*.

[136] "Contrary to traditional property crime, crimes against the socio-economic order reveal intangible, institutionalized or spiritualized legal goods, of social or collective ownership. This set of legal goods should not be identified with the 'intervening and regulatory activity of the State in the economy', as suggested by the concept of Economic Criminal Law that the Spanish doctrine has been calling 'strict' (…)." Terradillos Basoco (2003), p. 61 (free translation).

protect the socioeconomic order.[137] These Spanish authors therefore distance themselves from the identification of the legal good in the case as exclusively tied to the notion of intervening and regulating the activity of the State in the economy, understanding that there would be a formalism alien to any harmfulness.[138]

The most suitable solution would thus be, as they understand, the identification of an indirect legal good and another immediate one. The first would necessarily be of a supra-individual or spiritualized nature—the idea of socioeconomic order—while the latter could reveal individual or even supra-individual character, related as it would be with the immediately protected interest, to be considered case by case:

> (…) the broad conception advocated here allows extending the notion to crimes that do not have a supra-individual legal good *supra* - individual as immediate object of protection, also encompassing crimes that protect directly an individual legal good of economic content, but with the particularity that they are oriented to the protection of a mediate legal good *supra* -individual, or if you prefer, that are characterized by the fact that among the motives or reasons that influence the legislator's decision to grant them penal dignity is the existence of collective interests or *supra* -individuals necessary for a correct functioning of the prevailing economic system (e.g., crimes against industrial property, unfair competition crimes, most of corporate crimes).[139]

The ingenious thought, interesting from a didactic point of view, however, in seeking to deny the existence of a legal good tied to economic systematization, also reaffirms it, insofar as it classifies it as a mediate category, and, thus, teleological, little clarifying the situation with the said immediate casuistic interest. Moreover, in seeking to distinguish the economic crime from the merely patrimonial, the understanding is obscure and confuses the interpreter, since certainly in the patrimonial crime one cannot deny the mediate interest of the State, in some way, in the maintenance of the current economic order.[140]

Given the above, the socioeconomic order is notably seen as the supra-individual interest criminally protected by Economic Criminal Law, focusing on the trust, or normative expectation, socially placed in economic trade, capable of injuring or endangering economic life in general,[141] that is, the economic structure[142] of society, representative of a value resulting from individual and social life, indispensable to its maintenance and free development.[143] This last understanding is, thus, the one that,

[137] Understanding, however, majority in the Spanish doctrine, as recognized by the last author cited.

[138] Terradillos Basoco (2003), p. 61.

[139] Martínez-Buján Pérez (2007), p. 119 (free translation).

[140] Contrary to the sense defended here, cf. Martínez-Buján Pérez, p. 120.

[141] Tiedemann (1985), p. 11.

[142] Silveira (2003), cit., p. 32.

[143] Cf. Tavares (2002), p. 202. The final part of the sentence intends to emphasize, based on this last author, that an economic criminal norm should protect a legal good of criminal dignity—thus, with necessary reference to the essential conditions for the peaceful social life of individuals—and not serve a mere state function, which "(…) includes administrative activities of the State, related to control over a certain sector of life or its own organism." Tavares (2002), p. 202. Criminal Law, therefore, does not serve the mere adoption of economic public policies. A norm If it is disregarded in this last aspect, it will be illegitimate.

on the one hand, allows the concretion of the meaning of the legal good in the case, and, on the other, distances the mere individual property damage, typical, e.g., of theft or robbery, from economic delinquency properly said.[144]

In this sense, the concept of Economic Criminal Law refers directly to the protection of the fair balance of production, circulation, and distribution of wealth among citizens,[145] embodying a social control of the market according to the adopted economic model. For this reason, Economic Criminal Law differs, e.g., from Tax Criminal Law[146] and Environmental Criminal Law, in which the pointed reference, although existing, is indirect, closely approaching offenses against free competition, against the capital market, and against consumer relations—which, in turn, are related by the fact that the consumer is the ultimate beneficiary of correct competition in a free market.[147]

2.4 Trust as a Necessary Element for the Reproduction and Circulation of Wealth

In seeking to protect the diffuse interest concerning the economic system, as stated, Economic Criminal Law is used to safeguard the security and regularity of the structure, or base, of society's economy, ultimately safeguard the economic order, all with a view to avoiding damage to the national economy as a whole.

---

[144] Even though the mentioned property crimes may threaten private property, one of the fundamental principles of the economic order, the already suggested thesis of Tiedemann is not accepted here, or in other words, the idea of economic criminality in a broad sense. Cf. Tiedemann (1985), p. 12.

[145] Cf. de Araujo Júnior (1995), p. 36.

[146] Despite the exclusion of tax crimes from the idea of Economic Criminal Law, its function of extrafiscality and consequent state intervention in economic and social life through taxation is well known. Moreover, this function today is gaining ever larger proportions, however, it is assumed here the premise that the primary tax function is the collection and funding of the State. Explaining such aspect, Nogueira writes: "(...) it is, therefore, in the field of Revenue, that the State transforms and modernizes its methods of interference. The tax ceases to be conceived as exclusively intended to cover the financial needs of the State. It is also, depending on the case and the taxing power, used as an instrument of intervention and regulation of activities. It is the phenomenon that today is growing with the extrafiscal nature of the tax." Nogueira (1995), pp. 184–185.

[147] On this topic, cf. Reale Júnior (1982), pp. 159–169. Differentiating the economic crime from the fiscal, for example, in the national doctrine, cf. Pimentel (1973), p. 17 and ss. and pp. 109–110. Regarding the topic, with a different view, cf., e.g., Ferrari: "(...) in a strict view, the economic order should protect the legal regulation of state interventionism in a nation's economy, including as an object of protection the own interest of the State, susceptible of particularized concretion, of which examples are monetary infractions; transactions with the abroad; the fiscal crime, the freedom of the company within the framework of the market economy, free business competition, including within this concept collective interests, of which examples are consumption, the environment, among others." Ferrari (2004), pp. 260–261.

Man, a social being by nature, ends up relating and interacting economically,[148] this being one of the fundamental characteristics of society forged since the end of the medieval period. Starting from Luhmann's sociological conception, especially regarding the formation and structuring of social expectations,[149] one would have, therefore, justified, in terms of the interference of Criminal Law in the economic sphere.[150]

In this sense, the abuse of trust socially placed in the reproduction and circulation of wealth is typical referential conduct in economic delinquency. The *contrario sensu*, it is observed that the economic penal norm aims to consecrate the social trust placed in the intersubjective negotiation of the prevailing capitalist mode of production.

In the exact sense described:

> (…) Criminal law, therefore, when it creates new typical models does not contradict its bourgeois function, it only adapts it to the new reality of social production of wealth, with which it is, ultimately, conditioned. (…) The risk society created the technology that led to the kidnapping of men by their own work. The *world market* arises and with it the elementary untouchables and impassive of any criticism; competition, large-scale and hallucinated consumption, the international financial system, investment pockets, the full volatility of wealth. All these new realities if for some bring benefits and currency circulation, undeniably also realized the need for trust, discipline, compliance with rules of the game, and, exactly at this point, enters the dynamics of criminal law, its managerial typification and, as BERGALLI affirms, its efficiency.[151]

Indeed, a monetized free market system, with a highlighted financial and credit character, fundamentally needs trust for its regular operation. In this sense, it should be emphasized that the functionality of the economy that the State aims to guarantee needs, before everything, the reliability of economic agents, under penalty of resounding failure.

It is for this reason that economic criminalization turns, for example, to immediate interests such as the safeguarding of privileged information in the securities market (*insider trading*), the maintenance of free competition, or the assurance of the truthfulness of the information provided to consumers of a certain product, without which the trust of economic agents in the concrete business reality is compromised.

---

[148] Silveira (2003), cit., p. 29.

[149] Luhmann (1983), p. 53 et seq. and *passim*. For a synthesis of Luhmann's thought, e.g., cf.: Garcia Amado (1999), p. 162 et seq.; Büllesbach (2002), p. 409 et seq. On the subject, *see* also Sect. 2.3, *below*.

[150] Kaufmann (2002), p. 336; Silveira (2003), p. 29; García Cavero (2007), p. 283 et seq.

[151] Salvador Netto (2006), pp. 103–104. Contrarily, but without further depth, understanding that Economic Criminal Law would come to break with the ideology that tends to privilege the interests of the hegemonic classes, cf. de Araujo Júnior (1995), pp. 35–36.

In the same sense, according to Feijoo Sánchez, the primary purpose of criminal sanction in the species is positive general prevention:

> (...) It should be noted, moreover, that while in the first works on the preventive purposes of economic criminal law clearly prevailed negative general prevention (an idea that continues to be basic in the criminal policy of Anglo-Saxon countries), little by little a conception of general prevention is making its way which, more than intimidation, seeks the best way to stabilize the essential norms of economic life, avoiding anomie and the pure law of the strongest, thus maintaining trust in an operation of the economic system in accordance with prescribed by law.[152]

Therefore, trust as a necessary element for the reproduction and circulation of wealth is an important ethical-social value marker capable of particularizing and, in a way, justifying, the economic criminal offense. It is therefore an additional normative element to be assessed in the analysis of the economic criminal type.[153]

By this line of reasoning, it should be highlighted that this parameter represents, moreover, less an argument capable of exclusively justifying the economic criminal expansionism, but rather much more a striking critical element, that is, delimiting, a cited typifying construction. It thus constitutes a value element to be considered in the identification of the legal good economic order. The understanding here adopted of trust as a limiting element of criminal incidence, that is, of a guarantor approach to it, to verify the legitimacy of the economic crime, thus, distances itself, to some extent, from the perspectives of, for example, cited Spanish-speaking authors Feijoo Sánchez and Cavero García. The aim is to achieve greater clarity in identifying a material concept of economic criminal offense.

In other words, it is necessary to clarify at this point that the vilification of economic reliability is a prerequisite, but not sufficient reason, for the criminalization in focus, and a sequence of other dogmatic and political-criminal criteria must be investigated, as will be taken care of throughout this scientific investigation. In this vein, when the prohibited conduct does not even theoretically demonstrate the possibility of undermining such trust, the criminal intervention will be illegitimate.[154]

---

[152] Feijoo Sánchez (2008), p. 844 (free translation).

[153] García Cavero (2007), pp. 284–285. Asserting that the perspective on trust differs according to a criminological or dogmatic analysis, according to the Peruvian author "(...) in criminal law, it is a normative concept that responds not to empirical considerations, but understands that the practice of a crime constitutes a breach of trust in normatively guaranteed expectations, regardless of whether in the specific case there was a breach of trust in those affected. The reestablishment of trust in the norm also does not require, therefore, that the imposed penalty restores factual trust in the economic system. It is clear that normative concepts cannot be sustained without a minimum factual basis (conditions of existence), but it must be clear that the legal analysis of each specific case cannot reverberate to the realm of the empirical. As long as it is not categorically demonstrated that the supposed empirical effects did not occur, the normative disciplines are authorized to suppose them." García Cavero (2007), pp. 284–285 (free translation).

[154] The issue of measuring said impact will be the subject of investigation in this Chapter.

2.5 The Penal Experience of Guaranteeing the Economic System in Current Brazilian Legislation

State interventionism in the Brazilian economy, as mentioned, originates in the Constitution of 1934,[155] with the first criminal offense typification related to it in 1938, with Decree-Law No. 869, which protected the popular economy. Currently, the Brazilian criminal legislation on economic delinquency—as, moreover, in general[156]—reveals the characteristics of expansionism, anticipatory protection, lack of technique,[157] and, truly, confusion. There is, in summary, a lack of systematization and hypertrophy, consecrating a symbolic Criminal Law:

> The theory of positive general prevention is, therefore, a theory of the symbolic function of criminal law, in the sense that the indicated functions relate directly to the expression of the values assumed by the system and with the affirmation of the validity of the norms, this confirmation is symbolic and not empirical, as it is independent of the quantity of infractions and their reduction. Therefore, the defense of legal goods cannot be considered, according to the prevention-integration theory, as a main function of criminal norms. From this point of view, criminal law is not so much an instrument of imposition of the 'dominant morality', but an effective means of representation (symbolic) of this.[158]

As for the form, these laws are enacted autonomously, that is, through special criminal legislation,[159] such as, for example, Laws No. 7.492/86, 8.078/90, 8.137/90, and 10.303/01, among others mentioned *supra.*[160]

In general, materially, subjects are mixed (case, e.g., of Laws No. 8.078/90, 8.137/90, and 8.884/94), conducts of little clarity or great complexity are elevated

---

[155] Article 115 and ss. As a demonstration of the policy then adopted, see the *caput* of Article 115 of the 1934 Charter: "The economic order must be organized according to the principles of Justice and the needs of national life, in a way that enables everyone a dignified existence. Within these limits, economic freedom is guaranteed."

[156] Silva Sánchez (2002b), p. 23 and ss. There was an opportunity to delve into the topic in de Souza (2007), p. 139 and *passim.*

[157] Pimentel (1973), p. 59.

[158] Baratta (1994), pp. 21–22.

[159] Which would not necessarily represent something negative, given the peculiarities of Economic Criminal Law. In this regard, Silveira and Salvador Netto write: "Fundamentally, it can be affirmed that Economic Criminal Law has basic differences from the so-called nuclear Criminal Law. And this, from its first lines. From its typical formation, to the modalities of punishment and quantities of penalty, there are many distinctive filigrees. In it, abstract danger crimes are quite present, forming a true Danger Criminal Law, since it is informed that one could not wait for a harmful effect to the defended economic order. This, however, does not create emerging protection. In fact, the apparent lack of effectiveness of this form of criminal repression has been posed as one of the greatest obstacles to its maintenance as a form of combating crime." Silveira and Salvador Netto (2010), pp. 376–377. Defending a separate regulation from the Penal Code, due to the mutability inherent to Economic Criminal Law, v. Costa (2003), p. 44.

[160] Without prejudice to exceptional specific insertions in the Penal Code (case, e.g., of Articles 168-A and 337-A of the Penal Code) for those who have a broad view of the subject matter covered by Economic Criminal Law. Cf., e.g., Prado (2004), *passim.*

to the category of crimes, and disproportionate penalties are set. The standard typifying form is that of abstract danger crimes, open types, negligent and omissive types, and blank criminal norms, the latter most often to be complemented by administrative norms.

In this way, as will be analyzed *infra*, the principles of legality and harmfulness are constantly vilified, Turning Economic Criminal Law into mere regulatory legislation, of interests of a certain state policy—economic or not—that is, of administrative interests. This scenario consecrates widespread legal insecurity and gives support to arbitrariness, reasons why it is necessary to address the problem.

2.6 Dogmatic Problems of Economic Criminal Law

Economic Criminal Law faces difficulties in effectiveness, which is why it can be strongly criticized. Two orders of problematization are identified as nuances of such obstacles: one of dogmatic construction per se and another of criminal-political, influenced and influencing the previous formulation, of structuring a symbolic criminal law.

There are numerous challenges to the legal-criminal restraint of economic activity, especially today. First, the very dynamism of this human endeavor, constantly evolving and mutating to profit and the conquest of markets in a highly complex free trade society, eager for novelties and boasting of perennial technological renewal, makes the regulatory task quite arduous.[161]

Furthermore, in the face of the constantly expanding global market, the horizon of economic crime is not confined to the borders of national states, but rather, the world.[162] In this sense, beyond practical violation of control, serious problems of territoriality of criminal law hinder its application.[163]

The obsolescence of the norm in the face of the changing color of human ingenuity, the complexity of specific economic activities of a society with a highly evolved capitalist mode of production, with a huge division of tasks and new technologies,[164] the emergence of new business practices and new products, among other characteristics, make it already quite unlikely that Criminal Law, with its characteristics of legality and taxativity, confining itself to only these two fundamentals, is capable of offering real results of prevention and repression of socially harmful economic practices.

[161] Pimentel (1973), p. 31.

[162] Costa (2003), p. 87.

[163] Costa (2003), pp. 101–103.

[164] Costa (2003), p. 88.

Furthermore, the principles of free initiative,[165] free competition[166] and autonomy will increase the difficulty of legal regulation (including extrapenal) even more, since the legal system itself authorizes, or even stimulates, the constant evolution of economic activity. Economic agents seek intensely and continuously the exploration of new markets, the use of unprecedented techniques and practices, the creation of new products or services, etc., all to garner greater profits. This is the logic of our economic system.

In this way, it should be noted that, if reality, in general, is always ahead of the Law, specifically in the case at hand there is a radicalization of such a characteristic, considering that the enormous dynamics of economic factuality engenders a profound abyss with Liberal Criminal Law (reiterate, which consecrates the principles of legality, taxativity, etc., and, therefore, does not reveal a similar dynamism by far). To maintain its own Characteristics concerning economic delinquency, thus, the criminal law will often be ineffective, as it will regulate behaviors surpassed by reality.

On the other hand, as pointed out above, economic crime reveals a huge problem in terms of its accountability, whether in terms of authorship, co-authorship, or participation.[167] This represents another great challenge in the criminal treatment of economic delinquency.

As can be easily inferred from the characteristics of the current stage of capitalist production, today's major economic enterprise is much more related to legal entities than to individuals. The large mergers or acquisitions, the largest accumulations of profits, the most robust transfers of capital, and the largest financial losses, to refer only to a few, but important, paradigmatic situations, most often involve legal entities, not individuals.

---

[165] Article 170 of the 1988 Charter states: "(…) the economic order, based on the valorization of human work and free initiative, aims to ensure everyone a dignified existence, according to the dictates of social justice (…)." About free initiative, cf. GRAU: "It is important to make it clear that the *free initiative* is an expression of freedom titled not only by the company, but also by work. The Constitution, when contemplating the *free initiative*, only opposes it, even if it does not exclude it, to the 'initiative of the State'; it does not privilege it, therefore, as a good pertaining only to the company. It is because the *free initiative* is a mode of expression of work, of free work - as observed by Miguel Reale Júnior - in a free and pluralistic society." Grau (2007), p. 206. On the subject, *vide*, also, e.g., Coelho (2009); Branco (2009), p. 1409; Ferrari (2004), pp. 259 and 302–303.

[166] After, based on Reale, synthesizing the concept of free initiative as "(…) free choice of activity and means of which one must use in the achievement of economic action," Reale Júnior differentiates the concept of free competition, which, in turn, is "(…) a way of unfolding economic activity, raised to the category of principle, alongside private property and social function. Free competition means that economic activity, based on free initiative, should develop according to market laws, without other limits than those established in the Constitution itself, as a means of to prevent competition from turning into abuse, into lack of correctness, into disloyalty, into greed." Reale Júnior (1992), pp. 13 and 15, respectively.

[167] On the tendency towards the indeterminacy of the agents of economic infraction, cf. also Costa (2003), p. 52 and ss.

These, in turn, often boast huge and highly complex divisions of tasks and a large number of partners, administrators and workers and, in this sense, the difficulties of attributing a concrete fact to someone as authorship, co-authorship or participation increase.

Thus, it is often known that the conduct came from a certain legal entity, but it is not possible to particularize the individual author who carried it out.[168] And, abstracting from the position taken regarding the capacity or incapacity of the legal entity, the fact is that unquestionably in our legal system, except for environmental crimes, there is no imputation to it for other forms of delinquency.

In this influx, Economic Criminal Law reveals from the outset a great structural dogmatic incapacity, aggravated by the rampant use of the aforementioned porous constructions of abstract danger crimes, open criminal types, omissive and negligent types, and administrative accessory criminal types, as well as by the incoherence of the discourse legitimizing the ends of punishment, all to substantiate an unprecedented criminal symbolism.

It remains then to examine in detail each of these characteristics in order to endorse the argumentative line developed so far.

2.6.1 Abstract Danger Crimes

The rampant use of the category of abstract or presumed danger crimes in the Criminal Law of post-modern society is undeniable.[169] In the Brazilian economic criminal legal system, the occurrence of this phenomenon is observed with a simple glance at random examples, among many others, such as the crimes provided for in Articles 2,[170] 3,[171] and 4[172] of Law No. 7,492/86 (crimes against the financial

[168] Silveira (2003), p. 74.

[169] Sgubbi (1998), p. 74.

[170] "Art. 2 To print, reproduce or, in any way, manufacture or put into circulation, without written authorization from the issuing society, certificate, caution or other document representative of title or security: Penalty - Imprisonment, from 2 (two) to 8 (eight) years, and fine. Single paragraph. The same penalty applies to anyone who prints, manufactures, disseminates, distributes or causes to distribute prospectus or advertising material related to the papers referred to in this article."

[171] "Art. 3 To disseminate false or harmfully incomplete information about a financial institution: Penalty - Imprisonment, from 2 (two) to 6 (six) years, and fine."

[172] "Art. 4 To fraudulently manage a financial institution: Penalty - Imprisonment, from 3 (three) to 12 (twelve) years, and fine. Single paragraph. If the management is reckless: Penalty - Imprisonment, from 2 (two) to 8 (eight) years, and fine."

system); Articles 63,[173] 64,[174] 66,[175] 69,[176] and 70[177] of Law No. 8.078/90 (crimes against consumer relations) and Article 27-D[178] of Law No. 6.385/76, added by Article 5 of Law No. 10.303/01 (misuse of privileged information).

In response to an idea of risk containment to the system, the legislations abuse the formula, with a view to not even presenting a possibility of injury to certain social interests. The construction of abstract danger crimes, a typical political-criminal option of the risk society, represents, dogmatically, a criminalizing structure relative to a moment prior to an injury.

In terms specifically related to Economic Criminal Law, such use was deemed valid by Resolution No. 8 of the Colloquium of the International Association of Criminal Law of 1982.[179] Nowadays, such construction is so great that economic typification can be tempered as a category of dangerous criminal law:[180]

> The types of economic crimes require less and less the actual injury of a legal good and are structured more on the basis of a danger, so that the criteria of imputation abandon the paradigm of injury crimes and assume a common contour with danger crimes. In a modern society, with a great complexity of causal connections, it is illusory to try to explain the production of a damage by only one factor, and even more to demonstrate its causality in detail.[181]

---

[173] "Art. 63. To omit sayings or ostensive signs about the harmfulness or dangerousness of products, on packaging, wrappers, containers or advertising: Penalty - Detention from six months to two years and fine. § 1° The same penalties apply to anyone who fails to warn, through ostensive written recommendations, about the dangerousness of the service to be provided. § 2° If the crime is negligent: Penalty - Detention from one to six months or fine."

[174] "Art. 64. To fail to communicate to the competent authority and to consumers the harmfulness or dangerousness of products whose knowledge is subsequent to their placement on the market: Penalty - Detention from six months to two years and fine. Single paragraph. The same penalties apply to anyone who fails to remove from the market, immediately when determined by the competent authority, harmful or dangerous products, as per this article."

[175] "Art. 66. To make false or misleading statements, or to omit relevant information about the nature, characteristic, quality, quantity, safety, performance, durability, price or warranty of products or services: Penalty - Detention from three months to one year and a fine. § 1° The same penalties will apply to those who sponsor the offer. § 2° If the crime is committed negligently: Penalty - Detention from one to six months or a fine."

[176] "Art. 69. Failure to organize factual, technical and scientific data that support advertising: Penalty - Detention from one to six months or a fine."

[177] "Art. 70. To use in the repair of products, part or replacement components used, without the consumer's authorization: Penalty - Detention from three months to one year and a fine."

[178] "Art. 27-D. To use relevant information not yet disclosed to the market, of which one is aware and should keep confidential, capable of providing, for oneself or for another, undue advantage, through negotiation, on one's own behalf or on behalf of a third party, with securities: Penalty – imprisonment, from 1 (one) to 5 (five) years, and a fine of up to 3 (three) times the amount of the illicit advantage obtained as a result of the crime."

[179] Silveira (2003), p. 67.

[180] Silveira (2003), *passim*.

[181] Berruezo et al. (2010), p. 75 (free translation).

But, doctrinally, there is enormous divergence regarding this stance, as recognized by Tiedemann himself, its most prominent defender.[182] As Silveira enumerates,[183] one can still highlight in front of a critical discourse Hassemer,[184] in Germany, Silva Sánchez, in Spain, and Reale Júnior, in Brazil, and, in turn, favorably, Schünemann, Gracia Martin, and Martinéz-Buján Pérez, the former in Germany and the latter in Spain.

A more detailed analysis of abstract danger crimes will be carried out *infra*, in two investigative moments: when analyzing specific criminal harm and, later, in view of the study of the theoretical construction of cumulative crimes. This will occur because, precisely, the greatest structural problem is verified, in the first case, in the absence of real contempt for a legal good at the moment of conduct, which fosters considerable criticism of the category of abstract danger crimes, as well as, regarding the construction of cumulative crimes, the observation of a possible dogmatic justification due to the appearance of significant damages originating from a sum of several conducts at first disparagingly inexpressive in themselves. Therefore, it is about court assessments relevant to the discussion of the dangerous crimes in focus, which is why their *topos* differentiated analytical reveals itself more appropriate.

2.6.2 Open Criminal Types

The normative construction of criminal law through vague, imprecise or ambiguous elements, whose meaning can only be extracted by using external contextualizations to the legal text under analysis, is common in risk society.[185] In this influx, it could not be different in matters of Economic Criminal Law, especially when the complex relations which are sought to be protected are often truly misunderstood by jurists, which is why many times the legislative drafting is possibly, according to Pimentel, delegated to economists.[186]

---

[182] Tiedemann (2009), pp. 84–87. In trying to justify the construction of economic criminal types through the technique of abstract danger, the German author even states: "Furthermore, in the case of collective legal goods it is not possible, many times, to encompass the damages worthy of criminal sanction in a rational and constitutional way, that is, in a sufficiently precise way, but rather they must be described as (more) concrete behaviors or as duties (…)." Tiedemann (2009), p. 85 (free translation).

[183] Silveira (2003), pp. 68–69.

[184] And other members of the Frankfurt School. Specifically about this, cf. Sect. 4.1, below.

[185] Although this construction dates back to neo-Kantism (cf., e.g., Bustos Ramírez (1994), p. 147 and ff.), its use was truly exacerbated with the risk society (Cf., e.g., Bottini (2007), p. 105 and *passim*; Salvador Netto (2006), p.113 and ff.; Silveira (2003), p. 121 and ff.; de Souza (2007), p. 126 and ff.).

[186] Cf. Pimentel (1973), pp. 33–34. In a similar sense: Roysen (2003), p. 194. In this vein, referring to the loss of importance of the Legislative Power in the process of typification of Italian economic criminal law, in favor of the Executive, *vide:* Musco (2004), pp.169–182.

It is also noted that overcoming the difficulty of understanding certain protected subjects, or even the solution for the dynamism of the economic reality of the era of economic globalization we live in—which can quickly make legal prohibition superfluous or outdated—is sought through the use of open types.

If on the one hand, the majority doctrine understands the constitutionality of open types—once minimum content guidelines are respected—in the face of the unpredictability of certain situations for the legislator,[187] the fact is that post-modern reality has been highlighting the exaggeration of the formula, through the lack of minimum criteria, generating insecurity in the typification, which, thus, opens the way to state arbitrariness. According to González:

> Another characteristic of Economic Criminal Law is determined by the existence, in many cases, of open criminal types. This is because the criminal figures that the laws describe (Laws of economic content) do not sufficiently define the prohibited conduct, requiring a judicial complementation of their elements. It is the judge, at the time of applying the law, who must exercise the complementation. This can affect the principle of legality (...), as open types sometimes leave an excessive margin to judicial appreciation and constitute an invitation to the application of analogy, which is the negation of the principle "Nullum crimen, nulla poena sine preavia lege," which is the same as there being no crime without typicity.[188]

Among others, in Brazilian legislation there are examples of open economic criminal types —which moreover *in casu* are also of abstract danger—in Articles 3 and 4, of Law No. 7,492/86, and 27-D, of Law No. 6,385/76, added by Law No. 10,303/01, all cited above, and Article 5, items I, III and IV,[189] of Law No. 8,137/90 (crimes against the tax order, economic and against consumer relations).

Indeed, take as a paradigmatic illustration of illegitimate open criminal type in the national order the crime of "reckless management of financial institution" (Art. 4, sole paragraph, of Law No. 7,492/86).[190] If it were not enough the fact that no harm is foreseen in the type—which could, for some, be rebutted by claiming an interest in preventing potentially harmful conduct to social interest—the fact is that the principle of taxativity is openly violated, and therefore, of legal reserve,[191] since it is not known what it is to recklessly manage a financial institution, there being no

---

[187] Zaffaroni and Pierangeli (2008), pp. 386–387.

[188] González (1998), p. 43 (free translation).

[189] "Art. 5° It constitutes a crime of the same nature: I - to demand exclusivity of advertising, transmission or dissemination of advertising, to the detriment of competition; (...) III - to subject the sale of a good or the use of a service to the acquisition of an arbitrarily determined quantity; IV - to refuse, without just cause, the director, administrator, or manager of a company to provide the competent authority or provide it inaccurately, information about the cost of production or sale price. Penalty - detention, from 2 (two) to 5 (five) years, or fine. Sole paragraph. The failure to meet the authority's requirement, within 10 (ten) days, which may be converted into hours due to the greater or lesser complexity of the matter or the difficulty in meeting the requirement, characterizes the infraction provided for in item IV."

[190] Reale Júnior (1982), p. 277.

[191] Cf., e.g.,de Araújo Júnior (1995), p. 155; Prado (2004), p. 230.

minimum guidelines to characterize the precise illicit act, a consideration further aggravated when it is found that any economic activity is naturally fraught with risks.[192] Thus, the penal type in focus translates into mere subjectivism of the judge, a technique that consecrates state arbitrariness.

In this way, the unconstitutionality of such types is noted, and the exacerbated use of said typifying technique is condemnable, which, however, is just one of the insecure formulas daily used, as already pointed out.

2.6.3 Administrative Accessory Criminal Types

The complementation of criminal types through concepts, norms or acts from Administrative Law is manifested in the so-called administrative accessory of Criminal Law.[193]

Also characteristic of environmental, traffic or illicit drug laws, the phenomenon of administrative accessory has been consecrated in Economic Criminal Law. Emblematic examples of this are found in Brazilian Criminal Law, in the following provisions: Articles 7, subsections, II and IV,[194] and 22,[195] of Law No. 7.492/86 and Articles 6, subsections I, II and III,[196] and 7, subsection II,[197] of Law No. 8.137/90.[198]

---

[192] On the permitted risk in economic activities, cf. Silva Sánchez (2022), *passim*.

[193] da Costa (2010), cit., p. 65; Silveira (2003), p. 143 and ff.; García Cavero (2007), p. 137 and ff. and 252 and ff.

[194] "Art. 7° To issue, offer or negotiate, in any way, securities or securities: (...) II - without prior Registration of issue with the competent authority, under conditions different from those Registered or irregularly Registered; (...) IV - without prior authorization from the competent authority, when legally required: Penalty - Imprisonment, from 2 (two) to 8 (eight) years, and fine."

[195] "Art. 22. To carry out unauthorized foreign exchange operation, with the aim of promoting evasion of currency from the country: Penalty - Imprisonment, from 2 (two) to 6 (six) years, and fine. Sole paragraph. The same penalty applies to anyone who, for any reason, promotes, without legal authorization, the exit of currency or foreign exchange to abroad, or keeps undeclared deposits in it to the competent federal department."

[196] "Art. 6° It constitutes a crime of the same nature: I - to sell or offer for sale merchandise, or to contract or offer service, for a price higher than the officially tabled, to the legal control regime; II - to apply a formula for price adjustment or contract indexing prohibited, or different from that which is legally established, or fixed by competent authority; III - to demand, charge or receive any advantage or additional amount of price tabled, frozen, administered, fixed or controlled by the Public Power, including by means of the adoption or increase of a rate or other percentage, incident on any contracting. Penalty - detention, from 1 (one) to 4 (four) years, or fine."

[197] "Art. 7° It constitutes a crime against consumer relations: (...) II - to sell or expose for sale merchandise whose packaging, type, specification, weight or composition is not in accordance with legal prescriptions, or that does not correspond to its official classification; (...) Penalty - detention, from 2 (two) to 5 (five) years, or fine. Single paragraph. In the hypotheses of items II, III and IX, the negligent modality is punished, reducing the penalty and detention by 1/3 (one third) or the fine to a fifth."

[198] Citing part of the listed roll, cf. Silveira (2003), p. 144, note 144.

Even due to the fact that Economic Criminal Law has as its object of protection the economic system and, ultimately, is influenced to some extent by state economic policy, the involvement with Administrative Law is quite close. The norms originating from the Central Bank of Brazil and the Securities Commission, the decisions of the Brazilian Administrative Council for Economic Defense, and the indexing rules established by the government in certain cases are examples of direct influences of the legal-administrative branch in the economic criminal field.

The fact is that the influx of this phenomenon is such that we talk about the administrativization of Criminal Law:

> (…) the term 'Administrativization' indicates that the new criminal types tend to resemble, in their form, more and more, the norms of intervention of public administration, thus distancing themselves from the 'classic' requirements of the law (abstraction and generality). In this way, criminal norms become an instrument of administration of particular situations, of exceptional risks: in other words, an instrument of contingent response to concrete 'emergency' situations (…).[199]

However, administrative assistance cannot mean the transfer of conduct regulation to the Public Administration or to Administrative Law, under penalty of violation of the principle of criminal legality. In addition to characterizing an illegitimate use of Criminal Law, a finding of this nature prompts an important reflection on whether it is possible to fully protect the unwanted facts in the administrative sphere.

2.6.3.1 Blank Criminal Norms

As mentioned, within the context of administrative assistance, there are blank criminal norms. As is known, blank criminal norms are those that require supplementation by other norms, of identical level (homogeneous) or different (heterogeneous). The first to study the topic—and coin the expression—was Binding.[200] For Mezger, the study of the topic lacked significance, as the necessary supplementation always forms part of the criminal type.[201]

Indeed, when it comes to supplementation through a norm of the same level, there is no greater analytical interest, since the referral materially complements the type without violating criminal legality. In this way, the homogeneous blank criminal norm covered by the phenomenon of administrative assistance is not revealed.

However, it is precisely in cases where the complementary norm comes from a body without criminal-legal competence[202] that the question arises as to its

---

[199] Baratta (1994), p. 12.

[200] Pimentel (1973), p. 48; Bacigalupo, Enrique. La problemática constitucional de las leyes penales em blanco y su repercusión en el derecho penal económico. *In:* Bacigalupo (2004), p. 55.

[201] *Apud* Bacigalupo (2004), p. 54.

[202] In this sense, it is reiterated, that such blank criminal norms are within a context of administrative assistance, being a species of this. Cf., about it, García Cavero (2007), p. 254 and ss.

constitutionality.[203] And, considering the rampant use of this typifying technique nowadays and especially in the field of economic delinquency, its accurate study becomes pertinent:

> The use of blank criminal laws is very widespread in economic criminal law precisely because the legal norms in this sector need to adapt to the dynamism of economic life. For this reason, the criminal type makes a very generic description of the criminally prohibited conduct and refers to complementary extra-criminal norms to specify its content. This coupling of the criminal law with the extra-criminal regulation presents, however, serious interpretative problems, because as TIEDEMANN warns, a norm of criminal conduct is produced with the extra-criminal norm, in such a way that economic criminal law assumes a fundamentally auxiliary function in the sense of protection of the extra-criminal regulation. Faced with this situation, the dilemma arises as to whether the complementary norms should be interpreted from an exclusively criminal perspective or maintain their criminal meaning.[204]

On the one hand, some defend this normative modality as the only form of legal discipline of a malleable and agile field like the economic one, maintaining the stability of the fundamental device,[205] there is the understanding of the extreme opposite regarding heterogeneous blank criminal norms, which maintains their invalidity for violating the principle of criminal legality. A conciliatory view intends to analyze each case in particular.

For Bacigalupo,[206] one should analyze which are the rights affected by the mandate or prohibition, the differentiating limit being the infringement of fundamental rights. If so, the legislative competence in criminal matters must be respected.

However, the criterion of the Spanish author seems unclear and difficult to sustain, since Criminal Law necessarily always affects fundamental human rights, as it curtails the freedom of citizens, through the threat or imposition of the most severe state legal response possible, the criminal sanction.

The conciliatory view revealed by the Spanish Supreme Court, however, reveals an interesting construction, which admits to being constitutional:

> the use and judicial application of blank criminal laws, whenever there is satisfactory concretion for the conduct qualified as criminal through sufficiently precise means in the indispensable complement of the norm to which the criminal law refers, thus safeguarding the guarantee function of the type with the possibility of knowledge of the penally threatened action.[207]

Thus, in the indispensable hypotheses for the construction of criminal types, to avoid mere legislative casuistry, through a clear and precise concretion of the complementary norm, the heterogeneous blank criminal norm would be justified. This would be the case for substances prohibited in the anti-drug law or the crime of price table violation, for example. In other cases, although the case-by-case

[203] Bacigalupo (2004), p. 55.

[204] García Cavero (2007), pp. 254–255 (free translation).

[205] Pimentel (1973), p. 50.

[206] Bacigalupo (2004), pp. 56–57.

[207] According to decision no. 127/1990. *In:* Bacigalupo (2004), p. 53 (free translation).

verification criterion may cause some insecurity in the interpreter, the fact is that it seems to be the most appropriate method of understanding for the institute. In any case, the exegete needs to bear in mind that Criminal Law is not an accessory to Civil, Commercial, or Administrative Law, but in the case in focus "fulfills its function through the use of extra-penal complementation or specification criteria."[208] Administrative accessoryship should be something exceptional and, it is worth saying, it cannot mean the transfer of repressive criminal regulation to the administrative sphere.

2.6.4 *Omissive and Negligent Types*

The use of omissive and negligent typifying formulations is also included within the perspective of a Criminal Law of risk society, erecting a preventive-oriented criminal system, aimed at shaping behaviors and punishing the transgression of duties imposed by the State.

In this way, once again, Economic Criminal Law will be permeated by corresponding criminal types, especially in the face of the fact that legal-criminal intervention with this circumvents one of its most serious problems in the economic hypothesis, related to the identification of criminal authorship, due to the greater ease of recognizing recipients of duties, dispensing with the traditional path of causal relation.[209]

Omissive crimes are those in which the agent is punished not because he perpetrates an action, but because he fails to perform what is legally ordered to him,[210] that is, does not comply with what the law imposes on him as necessary. In the case of proper omissions, a common construction in a risk society, the law establishes a specific duty, which, once breached, triggers the sanction. The improper ones are the crimes of result in which those who have the legal duty to avoid it, being able to, do not do it. In any case, there is no factual causality, confining the analysis to duties imposed on the agent, elevated to the condition of the guarantor in the case of improper omissions.

An emblematic example of this modern trend of imposing duties through omissive crimes is found in the aforementioned *Sarbanes-Oxley Act*, which imposed, even extraterritorially to the United States of America, broad duties of information to be provided to administrators and directors of companies, in the name

[208] García Cavero (2007), p. 257 (free translation). The author then concludes: "(…) In this sense, extra-penal norms should be interpreted according to their scope of origin only insofar as they allow to configure the partial decision criteria established by the penal norm or help to specify them in concrete cases. The effects that such norms produce in the extra-penal scope, on the contrary, are not of interest to Criminal Law." García Cavero (2007), p. 257 (free translation).

[209] Machado (2005), pp. 137–138.

[210] Bitencourt (2024), p. 301; de Souza (2024), p. 173.

of trust in business relations. In the specific Brazilian reality, there are cases of economic penalties of pure omissive types, e.g., in Articles 10[211] and 12[212] of Law No. 7.492/86 and 63,[213] 64,[214] and 69[215] of Law No. 8.078/90. Furthermore, the tangle of economic, criminal, and extrapenal norms[216] reveals a trend of establishing guarantors, in the face of the various obligations imposed on economic agents, especially producers and players in the financial market.

Negligent behavior, in turn, is based on the omission of necessary diligence in meeting an objective duty of care.[217] In times of post-industrial uncertainties, the social demand for prevention of potentially harmful behaviors sharpens,[218] which is met with negligent typifications without such results, circumventing, at the same time, the evidentiary difficulties regarding the agent's intentionality[219] and the assessment of a harmful result, giving rise to criminalizations of mere conduct, that is, simple infractions of duties.

Examples of these negligent types in the Brazilian national economic criminal order are found, among others, in Articles 63, § 2, and 66, § 2, both of Law 8.078/90, corresponding, respectively, to negligent omissions regarding the information of product or service risks, and negligent false information or relevant omissions regarding product or service elements. Thus, the common path of omissive and

[211] "Art. 10. To insert a false element or omit an element required by law, in financial statements of financial institution, insurer or institution part of the system of securities distribution: Penalty - Imprisonment, from 1 (one) to 5 (five) years, and fine."

[212] "Art. 12. The former administrator of a financial institution fails to present, to the intervenor, liquidator, or trustee, within the deadlines and conditions established by law the information, declarations or documents of his responsibility: Penalty - Imprisonment, from 1 (one) to 4 (four) years, and fine."

[213] "Art. 63. To omit sayings or ostensive signs about the harmfulness or dangerousness of products, on packaging, in wrappers, containers or advertising: Penalty - Detention from six months to two years and fine. § 1° The same penalties apply to anyone who fails to warn, through ostensive written recommendations, about the dangerousness of the service to be provided. § 2° If the crime is negligent: Penalty - Detention from one to six months or fine."

[214] "Art. 64. Fail to communicate to the competent authority and to consumers the harmfulness or dangerousness of products whose knowledge is subsequent to their placement on the market: Penalty - Detention from six months to two years and fine. Single paragraph. The same penalties apply to anyone who fails to remove from the market, immediately when determined by the competent authority, harmful or dangerous products, as per this article."

[215] "Art. 69. Fail to organize factual, technical and scientific data that underpin advertising: Penalty - Detention from one to six months or fine."

[216] As, e.g., resolutions of the Central Bank of Brazil and the Securities and Exchange Commission.

[217] Reale Júnior (1982), p. 232.

[218] "In this society where risk becomes a necessary ingredient of everyday life, it is evident that the culpable behavior assumes importance, to the point of proposing that it be replaced by an anticipation of criminal protection, giving relevance, especially in vehicle circulation, to the creation of dangerous situations, regardless of any harmful result to someone, transforming the damage into a qualifying circumstance or objective condition of punishability." Reale Júnior (1982), p. 232.

[219] Machado (2005), p. 140.

negligent typifying constructions also contributes to the erection, in postmodern society, of an anticipatory and insecure Economic Criminal Law, aimed at shaping behaviors, which further distances it from the liberal contours of the criminal law branch.

2.6.5 *The Inconsistency of the Discourse Legitimizing the Ends of Punishment*

Given the difficulties of applicability previously pointed out—often the result of poor legislative technique, note—and considering the identification of the economic offender as a possible agent with a greater possibility of escaping punitive jurisdiction, due to his supposed cunning and economic power, one often comes across the defense of severe punishment for economic crime, which could only be achieved through deprivation of freedom.[220] Otherwise, that is, any other type of response, according to this thinking, would enter into the mere consideration of the cost/benefit of illicit economic activity, making a clean slate of any preventive or retributive purposes.[221]

The defense of a more rigorous sanctioning treatment of the economic offender compared to the common offender is thus pointed out by Faria Costa:

> (…) In fact, here, we are dealing with agents of infractions who do not need any resocializing effect, because, if one wanted to be deconstructivist, one could even say that such agents "suffer" from too much socialization. Besides that, even the highest monetary sanctions have no deterrent effect, not only because they cause little discomfort when dealing with astronomical fortunes but also, under certain circumstances, they may only have the consequence of being diluted in the opacity of their repercussion on the prices of the products of the company or companies owned or dominated by the infraction agent. Hence, the short prison

[220] Pimentel (1973), p. 92 and ss. Advocating for maximum punishment in economic crimes, cf., e.g., de Araujo Júnior (1995), p. 38. In European doctrine, advocating for prison response, even if of short duration, stand out Tiedemann, Bajo Fernández, Jescheck and Weingend, and, in the opposite direction, Luzón Peña and Roxin. Cf. Feijoo Sánchez (2008), p. 844.

[221] A significant example of purely utilitarian logic, inspired by Posner, which simply considers that the greater the penalty, the lower the crime rate, ignoring other considerations, is the *Sarbanes-Oxley Act*, American legislation from 2002, which set high prison sentences for economic crimes. Silveira and Salvador Netto (2006), p. 203. On the subject, these authors observe: "The criminal norms contained in the promulgated legislation, given its own inspiring philosophy, mark all the characteristics of a symbolic Criminal Law, oriented towards consequences and, moreover, with a clear preventive-pragmatic character. The premise adopted is the reliability in the market, that is, the instrumentalization of the repressive system in order to maintain, in economic agents, the expectation of truthfulness about the accounting news disseminated by the most diverse companies." Silveira and Salvador Netto ((2006)), p. 201. Subsequently, the authors revisit the topic in: Silveira and Salvador Netto ((2006)), p. 384 and ss. Specifically on the economic analysis of Criminal Law, cf. Posner (2007), p. 343 and ss.

sentence, with a stigmatizing effect, is the one that provides the deterrent and complex effect that every criminal penalty aspires to.[222]

In other words, the study of criminal sanction in matters of economic crime, despite the lack of empirical studies capable of pointing the best way to the legislator,[223] finds considerable political-criminal defenses for a repressive increase for the specific case, under the justification of avoiding impunity[224] or to achieve greater effectiveness of the norm.

In this context, the economic criminal doctrine commonly points out the preventive character of the criminal sanction in economic delinquency, either by a discourse in favor of the intimidating character of the penalty (general negative prevention), with emphasis on Anglo-Saxon literature, or by a general positive preventive defense, rooted in German and Spanish doctrine, which sees in the criminal response in the case a means of stabilizing the essential norms to economic life.[225]

The issue is much more complex than the aforementioned preventive discourse seems to reveal, linking to the idea of the legitimacy of the legal-criminal branch as a whole. This legitimacy is not tied solely from the starting point of the theory of penalties, since the concrete configuration of the Criminal Law system is shown as a product of a dialectical relationship between the interest in eliminating extrapenal social violence and the interest in reducing violence of the penal system itself.[226]

In this sense, mere preventive utilitarianism, quite popular in diffuse criminalization discourses, simple retributive irrationalism, or even the combination of both are not capable of justifying the issuance of economic criminal norms, as well as any others.

The absence of consideration for the precise serious violation of the exact legal good protected (harmfulness), which could not be defended in a less harmful way (subsidiarity); the adequacy of legislative technique for the intended communicative purposes, with precision (taxativity) and sanction proportionality,[227] are essential issues to make sense of the use of the drastic branch of criminal law, in any hypothesis. Furthermore, the consideration of the efficiency of the criminal branch for the protection of the specific interest intended also needs to be made.

Thus, the pursuit of merely regulatory ends, of administrative interests,[228] through Economic Criminal Law without the existence of a valid criminal legal

---

[222] Costa (2003), pp. 92–93.

[223] In this sense, Feijoo Sánchez (2008), p. 843.

[224] Terradillos Basoco (2003), p. 53; Pimentel (1973), pp. 27–29.

[225] Feijoo Sánchez (2008), p. 844.

[226] Silva Sánchez (2002a), p. 186.

[227] Specifically about Economic Criminal Law, Cavero García notes appropriately that there are serious and minor offenses, and that prison sanction should only be reserved for the former. The legislator, thus, should consider the real social harm of economic delinquency for the establishment of its proportional consequence. Cf. García Cavero (2007), cit. pp. 917–918.

[228] See the differentiation between legal good and function made above.

good, is illegitimate and, since it consecrates a greater evil than what is sought to avoid, it must be combated.

The criminal categories, therefore, should not be guided solely according to the ends of the penalty.[229] It is necessary to pay attention to the criminal legal framework that has justifying conditions and practical applicability according to its greater objectives for the criminal protection of the economic order. This appears to be a joint investigation of dogmatic and criminal political nature to endorse or not its reason for existence, which is intended with the present study.

References

Alexander CR (2004) Corporate crime, markets, and enforcement: a review. New perspectives on economics crime. Edward Elger, Northampton

Bacigalupo E (Dir.) (2004) Derecho penal económico. Hamurabi, Buenos Aires

Baratta A (1994) Funções instrumentais e simbólicas do direito penal. Lineamentos de uma teoria do bem jurídico. Trad. Ana Lúcia Sabadell. Brazilian Journal of Criminal Sciences, São Paulo 5: 5–24

Bastos CR (2010) Curso de direito constitucional. Malheiros, São Paulo

Bechara AELS (2003) Delitos de acumulação e racionalidade da intervenção penal. IBCCRIM Bulletin, São Paulo 208:3–5

Bechara AELS (2007) Manipulação genética humana e direito penal. Zouk, Porto Alegre

Bechara AELS (2009) O rendimento da teoria do bem jurídico no direito penal atual. Liberties Journal, São Paulo 1(1):16–29

Bechara AELS (2010) Da teoria do bem jurídico como critério de legitimidade do direito penal. Free Teaching Thesis, Faculty of Law of the University of São Paulo, São Paulo

Bercovici G (1999) A Problemática da Constituição Dirigente: Algumas Considerações sobre o Caso Brasileiro. Legislative Information Review, Brasília, Federal Senate 142:35–51

Bercovici G (2003) Desigualdades regionais, estado e constituição. Max Limonad, São Paulo

Bercovici G (2005) Constituição econômica e desenvolvimento: uma leitura a partir da constituição de 1988. Malheiros, São Paulo

Berruezo R et al (2010) Derecho penal económico. B de F, Montevideo-Buenos Aires

Berstein S et al (2007) História do século XX: volume I: 1900-1945: o fim do "mundo europeu". Trad. Fernando Santos. National Publishing Company, São Paulo

Bitencourt CR (2024) Tratado de direito penal: parte geral. São Paulo: Review of the Courts, Vol. I

Bonavides P (2009) Curso de direito constitucional. Malheiros, São Paulo

Bottini PC (2007) Crimes de perigo abstrato e princípio da precaução na sociedade de risco. Review of the Courts, São Paulo

Büllesbach A (2002) Princípios de teoria dos sistemas. In: Kaufmann A, Hassemer W (Orgs.). Introdução à filosofia do direito e à teoria do direito contemporâneas. Trad. Marcos Keel e Manuel Seca de Oliveira. Calouste Gulbenkian Foundation, Lisbon, pp 409–442

Bustos Ramírez J (1994) Introducción al derecho penal. Temis, Bogotá

Canotilho JJG (2001) Constituição dirigente e vinculação do legislador: contributo para a compreensão das normas constitucionais programáticas. Coimbra, Coimbra

Cervini R (2009) Derecho penal económico democrático: hacia una perspectiva integrada. In: Vilardi CS, Pereira FRB, Dias Neto T (Coords.) Direito penal econômico: análise contemporânea. Saraiva, São Paulo

[229] Silva Sánchez (2002a), passim.

Clinard MB (1969) Black market: a study of white collar crime. Patterson Smith, Montclair
Clinard MB, Yager PC (2005) Corporate crime. Transaction, Somerset
Coelho IM (2009) Princípios da ordem econômica e financeira. In: Mendes GF, Coelho IM, PGG B (eds) Curso de direito constitucional. Saraiva, São Paulo, pp 1405–1415
Coelho YC (2003) Bem jurídico-penal. Mandamentos, Belo Horizonte
Costa JF (2003) Direito penal económico. Quarteto, Coimbra
Cunha MCF (1995) Constituição e crime: uma perspectiva da criminalização e da descriminalização. Universidade Católica Portuguesa, Porto
da Andrade M (1991) Consentimento e acordo em direito penal. Coimbra, Coimbra
da Andrade M (1998) Contributo para o conceito de contra-ordenação (a experiência alemã). In: Institute of economic and European criminal law - faculty of law of the university of Coimbra. Economic and European criminal law: doctrinal texts. Coimbra, Coimbra, vol. I, pp 75–107.
da Costa HRL (2010) Proteção penal ambiental: viabilidade, efetividade, tutela por outros ramos do direito. Saraiva, São Paulo
da Ponte AC (2008) Crimes eleitorais. Saraiva, São Paulo
de Araujo Júnior JM (1995) Dos crimes contra a ordem econômica. Revista dos Tribunais, São Paulo
de Araújo Júnior JM (1995) Crimes against the financial system in the draft of a new special part of the Penal Code of 1994. Revista Brasileira de Ciências Criminais, São Paulo 11:155
de Mondaca LSC (2007) Direito económico. Coimbra, Coimbra
de Sousa SA (2023) Questões fundamentais de direito penal da empresa. Almedina, Coimbra
de Souza LA (2007) Expansão do direito penal e globalização. Quartier Latin, São Paulo
de Souza LA (2024) Direito penal, volume 1: parte geral. Thomson Reuters Brasil, São Paulo
de Toledo GA (2010) Ordem econômica e financeira. In: Martins IGdaS, Mendes GF, Nascimento CVdo (Coords.). Tratado de direito constitucional, vol. II. Saraiva, São Paulo, pp 307–348
Dias JdeF (2009) O papel do direito penal na protecção das gerações futuras. In: Institute of Economic and European Criminal Law - Faculty of Law of the University of Coimbra. Economic and European criminal law: doctrinal texts. Coimbra, Coimbra, Vol. III, pp 603–614
Dias JF, Andrade MC (1998) Problemática geral das infrações contra a economia nacional. In: Institute of Criminal Economic and European Law - Faculty of Law of the University of Coimbra. Economic and European criminal law: doctrinal texts, vol I. Coimbra, Coimbra, pp 319–346
Fabri AQ (2009) Falhas de mercado: por uma nova visão do planejamento econômico. In: Direito econômico – evolução e institutos: obra em homenagem ao professor João Bosco Leopoldino da Fonseca. Forense, Rio de Janeiro, pp 53–64
Feijoo Sánchez B (2008) Sanciones penales y prevención de delitos socioeconómicos. In: Boix Reig J (Dir.), Lloria Garcia P (Coord.) Diccionario de derecho penal económico. Iustel, Madrid, pp 843–852
Ferrari ER (2004) Legislação penal antitruste: direito penal econômico e sua concepção constitucional. In: Reale M, Reale Júnior M, Ferrari ER (eds) Experiências do direito. Millennium, Campinas, pp 253–315
Forgioni PA (2008) Os fundamentos do antitruste. RT, São Paulo
Garcia Amado JA (1999) La filosofia del derecho de Habermas y Luhmann. Universidad Externado de Colombia, Bogotá
Garcia B (2008) Instituições de direito penal. Saraiva, São Paulo, vol. I, tomo I
García Cavero P (2007) Derecho penal económico: parte general. Grijley, Tomo I. Lima
González V (1998) Nociones generales sobre derecho penal económico. Ediciones Jurídicas Cuyo, Mendoza
Gracia Martín L (2003) Prolegómenos para la lucha por la modernización y expansión del derecho penal y para la crítica del discurso de resistencia. Tirant lo Blanch, Valencia
Grau ER (2007) A ordem econômica na Constituição de 1988. Malheiros, São Paulo
Greco L (2006) Breves reflexões sobre os princípios da proteção de bens jurídicos e da subsidiariedade no direito penal. In: Schmidt AZ (ed) Novos rumos do direito penal

contemporâneo: livro em homenagem ao Prof. Dr. Cezar Roberto Bitencourt. Lumen Juris, Rio de Janeiro, pp 401–426
Greco L (2010) Proteção de bens jurídicos e crueldade com animais. Revista Liberdades 3:47–59
Hassemer W (2007) ¿Puede haber delitos que no afecten a um bien jurídico penal? In: Hefendehl R (ed) La teoría del bien jurídico: ¿fundamento de legitimación del derecho penal o juego de abalorios dogmático? Marcial Pons, Madrid, pp 95–104
Hassemer W, Muñoz Conde F (1989) Introducción a la criminologia y al derecho penal. Tirant lo Blanch, Valencia
Hormazabal Malarée H (1992) Bien jurídico y estado social e democratico de derecho: el objeto protegido por la norma penal. CONOSUR, Santiago de Chile
Hungria N (1939) Dos crimes contra a economia popular e das vendas a prestações com reserva de dominio. Livraria Jacinto, Rio de Janeiro
International Association of Penal Law. Electronic Review of the International Association of Penal Law. Reference: e-RIAPL 2007. Available at: http://www.penal.org/pdf/ReAIDP2007/RICPL 1 984.pdf. Accessed on: August 12, 2024.
Jakobs G (2005) O que protege o Direito Penal: os bens jurídicos ou a vigência da norma? Translated by Nereu José Giacomolli. In: Callegari AL, Giacomolli NJ (Coords.). Direito penal e funcionalismo. Livraria do Advogado, Porto Alegre, pp 31–52.
Jakobs G (2009) Tratado de direito penal: teoria do injusto penal e culpabilidade. Translated by Gercélia Batista de Oliveira Mendes and Geraldo de Carvalho. Del Rey, Belo Horizonte
Kaufmann A (2002) Filosofia del derecho. Translated by Luis Villar Borda and Ana María Montoya. Bogotá: Universidad Externado de Colombia
Luhmann N (1983) Sociologia do direito I. Translated by Gustavo Bayer. Tempo Brasileiro, Rio de Janeiro
Lyra R (1940) Crimes contra a economia popular: legislação - doutrina - jurisprudência. Livraria Jacinto, Rio de Janeiro
Machado MRA (2005) Sociedade do risco e direito penal: uma avaliação de novas tendências político-criminais. IBCCRIM, São Paulo
Manes V (2005) Il principio di ofensività nel diritto penale: canone di politica criminale, criterio ermeneutico, parametro di ragionevolezza. G. Giappichelli, Torino
Martínez-Buján Pérez C (2007) Derecho penal económico y de la empresa. Parte general. Tirant lo Blanch, Valencia
Mir Puig S (2005) Derecho penal: parte general. B de F, Montevideo-Buenos Aires
Musco E (2004) El nuevo derecho penal económico entre poder legislativo y poder ejecutivo. In: Terradillos Basoco JM, Acale Sánchez M (Coords.) Temas de derecho penal económico: III encuentro hispano-italiano de derecho penal económico. Trota, Madrid, pp 169–182.
Nogueira RB (1995) Curso de direito tributário. Saraiva, São Paulo
Paschoal JC (2003) Constituição, criminalização e direito penal mínimo. Revista dos Tribunais, São Paulo
Pérez Del Valle C (2004) Introducción al derecho penal económico. In: Bacigalupo E (Dir.). Derecho penal económico. Hamurabi, Buenos Aires, pp 29–52
Pierangeli JH (2001) Códigos penais do Brasil: evolução histórica. Revista dos Tribunais, São Paulo
Pimentel MP (1973) Direito penal econômico. Revista dos Tribunais, São Paulo
Polaino Navarrete M (1974) El bien jurídico em derecho penal. Publicaciones de la Universidad de Sevilla, Sevilla
Posner RA (2007) El análisis económico del derecho. Trad. Eduardo L. Suárez. FCE, México, D.F
Prado Júnior C (1970) História econômica do Brasil. Brasiliense, São Paulo
Prado LR (1997) Bem jurídico-penal e constituição. Revista dos Tribunais, São Paulo
Prado LR (2004) Curso de direito penal brasileiro, volume 1: parte geral, arts. 1° a 120. Revista dos Tribunais, São Paulo
Reale Júnior M (1982) Concorrência desleal e interesse difuso no direito brasileiro. Revista de Direito Penal e Criminologia, Rio de Janeiro 33:159–169

Reale Júnior M (1992) Casos de direito constitucional. Revista dos Tribunais, São Paulo
Reale Júnior M (1999) Despenalização no direito penal econômico: uma terceira via entre o crime e a infração administrativa? Braz J Crim Sci, São Paulo 28:116–129
Reale Júnior M (2009) Instituições de direito penal – parte geral. Forense, Rio de Janeiro
Rodrigues AM (2019) Direito Penal Económico: uma política criminal na era da compliance. Almedina, Coimbra
Roxin C (2007) ¿Es la protección de bienes jurídicos uma finalidad del derecho penal? In: Hefendehl R (ed) La teoría del bien jurídico: ¿fundamento de legitimación del derecho penal o juego de abalorios dogmático? Marcial Pons, Madrid, pp 443–458
Roxin C (2008) Derecho penal: parte general: tomo I: fundamentos - la estructura de la teoria del delito. Trad. Diego-Manuel Luzón Peña, Miguel Díaz y García Conlledo e Javier de Vicente Remesal. Civitas, Madrid
Roxin C (2009) A proteção de bens jurídicos como função do direito penal. Trad. André Luís Callegari e Nereu José Giacomolli. Porto Alegre: Livraria do Advogado
Roxin C (2024) Direito penal: parte geral: tomo I: fundamentos: a estrutura da teoria do crime / Claus Roxin, Luís Greco. Trad. da 5ª edição alemã. Orgs. Luís Greco e Alaor Leite. São Paulo: Marcial Pons
Roysen J (2003) Histórico da criminalidade econômica. Braz J Crim Sci São Paulo, 11(42): 192–213
Salvador Netto AV (2006) Tipicidade penal e sociedade de risco. Quartier Latin, São Paulo
Schünemann B (1999) Sobre la dogmática y la política criminal Del derecho penal del médio ambiente. Cuadernos de Doctrina y Jurisprudencia Penal, Buenos Aires 5(9):627–628
Schünemann B (2002) ¿Ofrece la reforma del derecho penal económico alemán un modelo o un escarmiento? Trad. Lourdes Baza. Temas actuales y permanentes del derecho penal después del milenio. Tecnos, Madrid, pp 185–202
Schünemann B (2005) O direito penal é a ultima ratio da proteção de bens jurídicos! – Sobre os limites invioláveis do direito penal em um Estado de Direito liberal. Trad. Luís Greco. Braz J Crim Sci 53(13):7–34
Schünemann B (2007) ¡El derecho penal es la ultima ratio para la protección de bienes jurídicos! Sobre los limites inviolables del derecho penal en um estado liberal de derecho. Trad. Ángela de la Torre Benítez. Universidad Externado de Colômbia, Bogotá
Sgubbi F (1998) El delito como riesgo social: investigación sobre las opciones em la asignación de la ilegalidad penal. Trad. Julio E. S. Virgolini. Editorial Ábaco de Rodolfo Depalma, Buenos Aires
Shecaira SS (2023) Criminologia. Thomson Reuters Brasil, São Paulo
Silva Sánchez J-M (2002a) Aproximación al derecho penal contemporáneo. Bosch Editor, Barcelona
Silva Sánchez J-M (2002b) A expansão do direito penal – aspectos da política criminal nas sociedades pós-industriais. Trad. Luiz Otávio de Oliveira Rocha. Revista dos Tribunais, São Paulo
Silva Sánchez J-M (2022) El riesgo permitido en derecho penal económico. Atelier, Barcelona
Silveira RdeMJ (2003) Direito penal supra-individual: interesses difusos. Revista dos Tribunais, São Paulo
Silveira RdeMJ (2006) Direito penal econômico como direito penal de perigo. Revista dos Tribunais, São Paulo
Silveira RMJ (2010) Fundamentos da adequação social em direito penal. Quartier Latin, São Paulo
Silveira RdeMJ, Salvador Netto AV (2006) Sarbanes-Oxley Act e os vícios do Direito Penal Globalizado. Revista Ultima Ratio, Rio de Janeiro 1:193–210
Silveira RdeMJ, Salvador Netto AV (2010) A tutela penal do mercado de capitais e o Sarbanes-Oxley-Act: novas considerações. In: Ruiz Filho A, Sica L (Coordenação). Responsabilidade penal na atividade econômico-empresarial: doutrina e jurisprudência comentada. Quartier Latin, São Paulo, 371–396

Sousa Neto (1952) Júri de economia popular: comentários à Lei n° 1.521, de 26 de dezembro de 1951. Forense, Rio de Janeiro

Stratenwerth G (2005) Derecho penal: parte general: el hecho punible. Hammurabi, Buenos Aires

Sutherland EH (2009) El delito de cuello blanco: versión completa. Trad. Laura Belloqui. B de F, Montevideo-Buenos Aires

Tavares J (2002) Teoria do injusto penal. Del Rey, Belo Horizonte

Terradillos Basoco JM (1995) Derecho penal de la empresa. Trotta, Madrid

Terradillos Basoco JM (2001) Empresa y derecho penal. Ad-Hoc, Buenos Aires

Terradillos Basoco JM (2003) Sistema penal y delitos contra el orden socioeconómico. Consideraciones introductorias. In: De La Cuesta Aguado PM et al. Derecho penal económico. Ediciones Jurídicas Cuyo, Mendoza pp 53–78

Tiedemann K (1985) Poder económico y delito: introducción al derecho penal económico y de la empresa. Trad. Amelia M. Villegas. Ariel, Barcelona

Tiedemann K (2009) Derecho penal económico: introducción y parte general. Grijley, Lima

von Hirsch A (2007) El concepto de bien jurídico y el "principio del daño". In: Hefendehl R (ed) La teoría del bien jurídico: ¿fundamento de legitimación del derecho penal o juego de abalorios dogmático? Marcial Pons, Madrid, pp 37–52

von Hirsch A (2008) I concetti di "danno" e "molestia" come criteri politico-criminali nell'ambito della dottrina penalistica angloamericana. In: Fiandaca G, Francolini G (a cura di). Sulla legittimazione del diritto penale: culture europeo-continentale e anglo-americana a confronto. G. Giappichelli, Torino, pp 29–42

Welzel H (1993) Derecho penal alemán. Trans. Juan Bustos Ramírez and Sérgio Yáñez Pérez. Editorial Juídia de Chile, Santiago de Chile

Zaffaroni ER, Pierangeli JH (2008) Manual de direito penal brasileiro. Revista dos Tribunais, São Paulo

Chapter 3
The Concept of Criminal Harmfulness

3.1 Introduction

To investigate the legitimacy of economic criminal law, the interpreter must preliminarily distinguish whether the type reveals itself as a protector of a legal good—in this case, the economic order—or if it simply serves a state function, which, as already stated, encompasses administrative activities of the State, related to control over a certain sector of relational life or its own organism.[1] In the words of Tavares:

> The source of confusion between legal good and function is located, however, in the indefiniteness about the reference object of the norm. The legal good constitutes, at the same time, an object of preference, as a value linked to the purpose of the legal order around the protection of the human person, and an object of reference, as a presupposition of the validity of the norm, as well as its own effectiveness. In the latter case, by subordinating it to the demonstration of injury or endangerment of the legal good.[2]

The distinction proposed by the author stands out in importance in the matter studied, since the simple adoption of a sectoral or momentary economic policy, or the mere administrative convenience in matters of economic regulation, without reference to fundamental human values to the social contract in need of specific criminal legal protection, cannot represent a substrate for valid criminalization.[3] In

---

[1] Tavares (2002), p. 204; Manes (2005), p. 98.

[2] Tavares (2002), p. 205.

[3] In the opposite sense, e.g.: "Economic Criminal Law brings as one of its characteristic notes the instrumental aspect assumed by criminal policy in the face of the various State policies developed within the scope of socioeconomic regulation (e.g., fiscal policy, monetary policy, exchange policy). It follows that a well-founded reflection on the material content of the offense in these territories belonging to secondary Criminal Law must go beyond the dogmatic-penal contours of the typical figure, centering its referential base on the guidelines of the respective political action, to whose regular exception the legal-criminal intervention finds its justification." Feldens, Luciano; Schmidt, Andrei Zenkner. A associação entre o ilícito administrativo e o ilícito penal no exemplo do

L. A. d. Souza, *Economic Criminal Law*,
https://doi.org/10.1007/978-3-031-87236-5_3

other words, the use of Criminal Law as a forceful means of reinforcing the current state economic policy, ignoring its vocation for the protection of legal goods, distorts its characteristic of *ultima ratio* in the protection of human interests essential for peaceful social coexistence, limiting itself to mere penal symbolism[4] thus consecrating, an undue arbitrariness of the State in the private sphere.

Once the protected legal good is identified, namely, the economic order, in the cited sense of the economic structures of a given society, referenced in ensuring the free and peaceful coexistence of its individuals, the principle of harmfulness is the subsequent analytical vector of the relevance of the economic crime:

> In accordance with the principle of offensiveness, in a social and democratic Rule of Law, Criminal Law can only interfere in situations where unbearable injuries to community conditions, essential for the free development and realization of human personality, of which work and economic order are necessarily linked.[5]

The problem becomes much more serious when it is observed that the modern construction of Economic Criminal Law often sanctions the non-observance of rules of convenience of the Public Administration, matters previously of a disciplinary nature, consecrating the phenomenon of the administrativization of Criminal Law,[6] or even, in true anticipatory conduct of criminal legal protection, exacerbates the formulation of abstract or presumed danger crimes, focusing exclusively on the disvalue of the action,[7] thus obliterating any concrete assessment of criminal harmfulness.[8]

In this vein, it is necessary to observe the outlines of the principle of harmfulness to assess structural adequacy in the construction of economic criminal types. For this, it is necessary to analyze the classic, or traditional, thought related to the theme, and the position that questions it, linked to the understanding of harmfulness as a breach of duty—harmfulness at the instance.

---

crime de evasão de divisas. In: Osório, Fábio Medina. Direito sancionador: sistema financeiro nacional. Belo Horizonte: Fórum, 2007, pp. 192–193 (original italics).

[4]Terradillos Basoco (2003), pp. 58–59.

[5]Ferrari (2004), p. 267.

[6]Reale Júnior (1973), p. 21.

[7]Silveira (2006), p. 91 et seq. and 151. The use of abstract danger models is so prevalent nowadays that this author refers to a Criminal Law of Danger, which would be, as he defines with support from Mendoza Buergo, "(…) a Criminal Law suitable for the needs of the current post-industrial society, both as an effective instrument for guiding behaviors and as a means of defense against new risks present today. It aims, therefore, to configure an idea of security in the face of social insecurities." Silveira (2006), p. 99.

[8]For Méndez Rodríguez, for example, democratic Criminal Law does not lend itself to such, making such typifications invalid. Méndez Rodríguez (1993), p. 162.

3.2 Harmfulness in Classic Criminal Thought

According to traditional doctrinal thought, the principle of harmfulness, or offensiveness[9] (*nullum crimen sine iniuria*), consists of the necessary link that must exist between a typical criminal construction and the injury to the legally protected good. This does not mean, of course, that actual damage to the legally protected good must always be required, but rather that at least its relevant affectation is necessary.[10] Thus, "in fact, offensiveness cannot be interpreted naturalistically as damage caused to things, but rather as potential harm to the interest in the thing."[11]

According to Cirino dos Santos:

> the principle of harmfulness prohibits the imposition, application and execution of penalties and security measures in cases of irrelevant injuries, consummated or attempted, against legally protected goods in legal types of crime. In other words, the principle of harmfulness has as its object the legal good determining criminalization, in a double dimension: from a qualitative point of view, it has as its object the nature of the injured legal good; from a quantitative point of view, it has as its object the extent of the injury to the legal good.[12]

The theme goes back to the distinction between formal and material unlawfulness, which arose in Germany at the beginning of the last century as a response to the scientific crisis resulting from the insufficiencies of legal positivism,[13] since the mere contrariness of the conduct carried out with the legal order (formal unlawfulness) proved insufficient to justify a punishment:

> if we assume that criminal law aspires to a purpose of protecting certain interests considered valued by society and, therefore, considered deserving and in need of protection, the relevant behaviors for it (those that it will consider unlawful) will be those that prove harmful to these interests and, therefore, deserving and in need of criminal sanction, this criminal sanction being the means by which criminal law operates in the sense of satisfying this protection assignment.[14]

In this way, as stated *supra*, for a criminal type to be valid not only must a legal good with criminal dignity be identified in its midst, but also the presence of a prohibition of behavior capable of a significant impact on the dear social value protected.[15] This is the essence of the principle, which thus reveals itself as another filter of criminal typification, that is, another limiting criterion of the *ius puniendi*,

---

[9] Ferrajoli (1987), p. 464; Silveira (2006), pp. 161–162; Gomes (2002), p. 11. Based on Garcia-Pablos de Molina and Mata y Martín, Gomes understands that it is synonymous with the expression the principle of the exclusive protection of legal goods. Gomes (2003), p. 88, note 17.

[10] Silveira (2006), p. 163; Gomes (2003), p. 90.

[11] Bechara (2010), p. 236.

[12] Santos (2008), p. 26.

[13] Reale Júnior (2000), p. 89.

[14] Alcácer Guirao (2003), p. 13 (free translation).

[15] Reale Júnior (1973), pp. 21–22.

which is consistent with the general rule of Law that restrictive norm is interpreted restrictively.[16]

Although the scholars of the nineteenth century did not explicitly state the principle of harmfulness, they approached the subject when dealing with the notion of legal good and the purposes of Criminal Law.[17] As a result of the evolution of these reflections, at the beginning of the twentieth century, with von Liszt's material concept of crime,[18] the notion is outlined more clearly. This, along with the thought of Binding and Merkel, characterizes the classic, or traditional, thought of harmfulness: "For v. Liszt, Binding and Merkel criminal law is systematically structured through the concept of legal good, understood as legally protected social interests, whose injuries or exposure to danger the law prohibits."[19]

Although, according to the thought developed since then, this harmfulness is not a factor by itself sufficient to justify the erection of a fact to the condition of a criminal offense,[20] the need for its occurrence for this to happen is verified, which represented an important qualitative leap in the understanding of the general theory of crime, embodying a significant means of demarcating criminal contours.

3.2.1 Principle of Harmfulness and Abstract Danger Crimes

After observing that the criminal expansionism of the risk society occurs, in general, through the use of the delictive category of abstract danger, to control unwanted social risks,[21] Bechara concludes:

> It is precisely in relation to danger crimes that the theory of the legal good and the principle of offensiveness reach the limit of applicability, because, although it does not prevent the legislator from protecting legal goods in early stages of danger when the relationship between both is sufficiently identifiable, caution should be exercised in the critical analysis of proposals for criminalization of conducts that constitute mere preparatory acts or lacking in offensiveness. In these cases, we would be facing criminalizations based exclusively on the disvalue of the action, so as to marginalize the disvalue of the result as a secondary and even dispensable element in the structure of the crime.[22]

---

[16] Maximiliano (2007), p. 167.

[17] Reale Júnior (2009), p. 22.

[18] "In his view, an act would be formally unlawful as contrary to a legal prohibition, and materially unlawful by implying harm or danger to a legal good, that is, formally, unlawfulness is characterized as disrespect for a norm, a prohibition of the legal order; materially, as an attack on vital interests of individuals and the community protected by the norms established by the legislator." Reale Júnior (2000), p. 89. On this topic, see also a detailed explanation by this author in: Reale Júnior (1973), p. 101 et seq.

[19] Reale Júnior (1973), pp. 101–102.

[20] Reale Júnior (2000), p. 95.

[21] Bechara (2010), p. 221.

[22] Bechara (2010), p. 222.

Thus, within the context of the traditional thought of the principle of harmfulness, considering, as stated, the current use of the category of abstract danger crimes, it is necessary to analyze how this is apprehended in the face of that, since they apparently would be in conflict, since the principle of harmfulness requires the significant affectation of a dear social value by the abstractly prohibited conduct, being that there is no need for verification neither of actual damage nor real danger to the legal good in these mentioned crimes.[23]

Based on this last observation, part of the doctrine defends the invalidity of abstract danger crimes, as is done in Brazil, e.g., by Gomes and Bitencourt. According to this thought, there would be a lack of material unlawfulness in the hypothesis, which is why the types would be per se illegitimate.[24] As Bitencourt observes:

> For a crime to be typified, in a material sense, it is indispensable that there is, at least, a *concrete danger*, real and effective of damage to a legally protected good. State intervention in terms of *criminal repression* is only justified if there is an effective and concrete attack on a socially relevant interest, which represents, at least, a concrete danger to the legally protected good. For this reason, all so-called abstract danger crimes are *unconstitutional*, because, within the scope of Criminal Law of a Democratic State, the existence of a criminal offense is only admitted when there is an effective, real and concrete danger of injury to a specific legal good. In other words, the legislator should refrain from typifying as a crime actions incapable of injuring or, at least, posing a concrete danger to the good protected by the criminal norm. Without affecting the legal good, at least putting it at real risk, there is no criminal offense.[25]

According to a parallel developed by Silveira,[26] the attempt to justify the existence of the category of abstract danger crimes is linked to the operative for attempted crimes, as in both there is no requirement for configuration of a concrete harmful result. Let us see.

The justifying theory for the attempt begins with Feuerbach and his objective theory of dangerousness, according to which punishment is valid for the practice of an action that is fraught with dangerousness capable of producing a harmful result.[27] Thus, the prevailing idea-force is the exposure to danger of a legal good, to be analyzed according to an *ex post* perspective.[28]

---

[23] Bottini (2007), p. 203.

[24] Gomes (2002), pp. 41–42 e *passim*.

[25] Bitencourt (2024), p. 30 (original italics).

[26] With support from Cuesta Castor and Sánchez García de Paz, cf. Silveira (2006), pp. 85–91. In Brazilian doctrine, still, e.g., the parallel is mentioned, but without analytical depth, in Silva (2003), pp. 139, 141–142, and 150.

[27] Silveira (2006), p. 87.

[28] Silveira (2006), p. 87.

The developments following Feuerbach's thesis still followed a trend of objective analysis.[29] Thus, von Hippel and von Liszt[30] only added a valuation *ex ante*, relative to the objective dangerousness of the action. Already Binding, Frank and Dohna took only the objective type as an object of investigation, erecting the theory of lack of type, which considers the attempted crime an incomplete objective type criminal offense. In the same way, one could think of this explanation for the danger crime.[31]

It is with Mezger that a first counterpoint to the ideals developed until then arises, since the author accepts a subjectivist thesis, focusing the punitive justification on the criminal will (intent). This theory mainly faced criticism for its authoritarianism, revealing a Criminal Law that punishes mere intentions.

The thought erected next, finalistic, did not present either a break with Mezger's ideas nor was it able to end the doubts raised. Focused on the valuation of the dangerousness of the action and, thus, on the ability to produce a harmful result, the finalistic thought seemed to represent a symbiosis of all the previous development, without, however, providing further clarification.[32]

The Brazilian doctrine, as Silveira refers, usually adopts an objective justifying conception, of a monist or dualist nature, according to an exclusive devaluative consideration of the action or the action and the result:

> (...) By the first, according to the principle of harmfulness, both the legislator and the interpreter of the law are bound. The attempt must therefore be punished as long as a real connection between conduct and result (injury or danger to the legal good) stands out, envisioning only a devaluation of the action. The dualist behavior, on the other hand, is explained by a devaluation of the result, thus showing that the action must provoke a situation of danger indicating a probability of injury to the legal good. For the answer of which danger is being dealt with, some understand it as concrete, while others even accept the abstract. Again, here, the theses *ex ante* and *ex post* will give the direction of criminal application. Whichever is accepted, however, the real distinctive element between the attempt and the crimes of danger is another. In the former, there is a real and factual intent to harm, while in the second, there is not.[33]

Bottini agrees with this last position, without, however, referring to the analysis linked to the attempted crime as an interpretative tool for the consideration relative to the adequacy of the abstract danger crimes in the face of the principle of harmfulness. Analyzing Faria Costa's proposal regarding the structuring of three valid levels of harmfulness (damage/violation; concrete endangerment and care-of-danger),[34]

---

[29] Silveira (2006), p. 87.

[30] "What constitutes the essence of the attempt in the sense of our current conception is the direction of the voluntary act towards an unproduced but represented result; the action seems deserving of punishment, not considered in itself, but for this direction. The reason for the punishability of the attempt lies, therefore, in the dangerous character of the act: although the result that the law does not want was not produced, the act raised the possibility that it could be produced." von LISZT(2003), t. I, p. 314.

[31] Silveira (2006), pp. 87–88.

[32] Silveira (2006), p. 89.

[33] Silveira (2006), p. 90.

[34] COSTA (1992), pp. 642 and ss.

being the abstract danger crime the one that prohibits a conduct capable of offending a legal good (care-of-danger), the Brazilian author understands that the analysis of this must be carried out on two levels, namely, on the legislative and factual (judicial) planes.[35]

In this vein, the mere devaluation of the action, without prior and subsequent consideration about the creation of a situation capable of potentially affecting a palpable human interest, appears to be of questionable validity.[36] Anticipation of criminal protection in these terms ends up losing its limiting potential and its material contours.[37]

3.2.2 Conclusion

Given the above, for classical criminal thought, there is no way to admit, in a Criminal Law of a democratic nature—which has human freedom as a value axis—the simple prohibition of undesired behaviors by a certain state policy, without clearly demonstrating, with the same, a serious affectation of a fundamental human interest for the peaceful coexistence of individuals.

Thus, it is understood as appropriate to prohibit undesired behaviors for their social harmfulness[38] or, still, for their potential of dangerousness to an essential human interest, not outright rejecting the category of abstract danger. But, even if it is not required that the dangerousness be effective, it should at least be tangible, probable, and capable in theory of leading to the realization of damage to a dear social value. If in an analysis *ex ante* or *ex post* it is found that it would be impossible for a harmful result to occur in the case, the punishment will be invalid:[39] in the first

[35] See Bottini: "FARIA COSTA's construction already provides elements to treat abstract danger criminal types as offenses suitable to the principle of harmfulness, at the legislative level, even though it does not clarify how the enforcer of the criminal norm should act to respect such a guideline in the face of conduct that violates the legal text. The harmfulness of abstract danger crimes must be present both at the legal level, through clear and exhaustive provisions that allow the recognition of the interests it aims to protect, and at the factual level, that is, the judge, when applying the norm, must inquire about the harmfulness of the conduct in light of the concrete circumstances surrounding its practice. This verification of the harmful potential of the behavior is done through a judgment of the dangerousness of the action described in the type as abstract danger. Only conduct that exhibits dangerousness has the power to legitimately mobilize criminal law. Actions or omissions that do not imply risks, at least potential, of affecting the legal good, cannot interest the repressive system." Bottini (2007), p. 205.

[36] In a different sense, e.g., understanding that greater consideration should be given to the disvalue of the action in certain cases, highlighting the preventive role of Criminal Law with a view to the future: Silva (2003), p. 138 et seq.

[37] Alcácer Guirao (2003), p. 86.

[38] Reale Júnior (2009), pp. 21–22.

[39] In the sense of the text, e.g., D'avila, Fábio Roberto: "An ex ante judgment of the objective and real possibility of harm to the protected legal good must initially be made, and subsequently a

aspect, in the legislative plan, and, in the last, in the application of the law in the concrete case.

However, it should be noted that this position does not approach the idea of the category of abstract-concrete danger crime, proposed by Horst Schröder and referred to by Francesco Angioni,[40] according to which it would be possible for the legislator to prohibit, in a first form, behaviors considered abstractly dangerous, but with provisions for the law enforcer to ascertain, concretely, elements of this danger, in addition to, in a second form, abstractly dangerous behaviors, but in relation to which the legislator does not inform what the good or goods effectively protected are, to be considered in the concrete case.[41] Such ideology, besides being unclear,[42] in the first intended species seems to associate with the category of concrete danger, while in the second case, it proves to be insecure.

What is now defended, therefore, is that it is valid that, from an *ex ante* perspective, the legislator prohibits a behavior theoretically capable—according to scientific knowledge or normal experience[43]—of offending a legal good, with relative presumption[44] of danger. In this context, the adoption of the precautionary principle[45] in the construction of criminal types is rejected. Following, however, in the application of the law to the concrete case—perspective *ex post*—the judge must verify not if there was an actual damage or realization of danger to the legal good, which would characterize a crime of injury or concrete danger, respectively, but if the relative presumption of danger was rejected by contrary evidence in the concrete situation analyzed, because only in this way does the figure of abstract danger fit the requirement of harmfulness, within a guarantee criminal law.[46]

Therefore, the principle of harmfulness, in liberal terms, but without radicalizations regarding abstract danger crimes, appears, along with the principle of minimal criminal intervention, as a critical criterion that enhances the limiting effectiveness of the theory of legal good for the construction of criminal types.[47] The underlying

negative judgment of the significance of this possibility, under the normative scope of the type." D'avila (2005), p. 404.

[40] Angioni (1994), p. 87.

[41] Silva (2003), pp. 79–80; de Souza (2007), p. 124.

[42] In the same sense: Silva (2003), p. 80

[43] Reale Júnior (2009), p. 276.

[44] This is the position of Rabl, Baumann, U. Weber, E. Gallo, Patalano, and Beristain, cf. Silva (2003), p. 75. This Brazilian author admits the possibility that there may be abstract danger crimes with relative presumption, but not in all cases: Silva (2003), p. 79.

[45] On this, Bottini explains: "The application of the precautionary principle stems from the lack of knowledge about the dangerousness of certain activities: therefore, it derives from the absence of scientific or statistical certainties about any concrete results arising from them, whether harmful or dangerous." Bottini (2007), p. 255.

[46] Reale Júnior (2009), p. 277.

[47] In the same sense, cf. Bechara (2010), p. 243.

idea of this principle, from this point of view, demands the decriminalization[48] of behaviors when not seriously harmful to social order.[49]

3.3 Harmfulness as a Transgression to the Legal System

Currently, part of the doctrine, with emphasis on Jakobs, has been rejecting this traditional conception of harmfulness, postulating as an alternative a material notion of crime as a violation of the norm's validity,[50] as mentioned above. In this influx, the sense of crime as a means of protecting legal goods is replaced by a concept of offense as a breach of duty, thus protecting the validity of the legal system, that is, the legal system.[51]

The position that denies the notion of harmfulness to a legal good as a rule justifying the criminalizing phenomenon, leaning on the understanding of the offense as a breach of duty, however, is not really new, despite different nuances presented in the last century, as briefly described below, before returning to the theory of the author from Bonn.[52]

Hegel can be pointed out as the first author to underpin the thought in focus, based on his understanding that social interest represents a higher value essence than the citizen's interest, as well as that collective morality is the foundation of the state's identity purpose of community cohesion.[53] Furthermore, the idea that the criminal sanction is the denial of the denial of the Law reveals the understanding that it is, in fact, the reaffirmation of this.[54]

Next, combating the liberal-enlightenment ideology of the legal good, the Kiel School advocated that crime represents an act of infidelity, of betrayal to the community, that is, it constituted a breach of duty.[55] According to Amelung:

> the highest value for National Socialist thought is the community, not the individual. Therefore, the highest mission of criminal law is its preservation. However, this end is not identifiable with the protection of its members. The community is more than a sum of individuals living together. It is a living essence of a particular class, which is seated far beyond the individual man: it is the inseparable communion of past, present and future generations bound around blood and soil.[56]

---

[48] Manes (2005), p. 242.

[49] García-Pablos De Molina (2006), p. 542.

[50] Alcácer Guirao (2003), p. 13; Silveira (2010), p. 41; Manes (2005), p. 30.

[51] Alcácer Guirao (2003), p. 14.

[52] Due to the relevance and timeliness of the discussions that this theory entails. For Manes, the only true alternative theory to the protection of legal goods is that of Jakobs. Cf. Manes (2005), p. 12, note 2.

[53] Alcácer Guirao (2003), p. 31.

[54] Alcácer Guirao (2003), p. 32.

[55] Alcácer Guirao (2003), pp. 40–41.

[56] *Apud* Alcácer Guirao (2003), p. 39 (free translation).

Also in Welzel, there is a mitigation of the liberal sense of the material understanding of the crime, since the authentic mission of Criminal Law would be, according to the German author, to protect the validity of the ethical-social values inscribed in the norms.[57] Thus, the disvalue of the result would express an injury to a good, while the disvalue of the action, of greater importance, would reveal an offense to the validity of the value.[58]

Neo-Kantianism, in turn, despite formally referring to an injury to a legal good, in reality, empties its content, as it understands it as an ideal community value. In this way, critical authors of this thought, like Jescheck and Schmidhäuser, approach the notion of duty injury by understanding the legal good not as a factual reality, but as an idealized spiritual value, similar to the disvalue of Welzel's action.[59]

Nowadays, Jakobs' thought, despite rejecting the traditional idea of harmfulness in favor of a formal conception of duty injury, is based on a different critical cut, starting his theory from Luhmann's sociological conceptions.[60] Society is understood as an autonomous social system constituted by a complex tangle of communicative relations.[61] In this sense, the functionality of this system is only possible from the existence of institutional or systemic trust, through which the actors of social relations perform roles[62]—in relation to which the other actors deposit behavioral expectations.[63]

[57] Alcácer Guirao (2003), pp. 44–51.

[58] Alcácer Guirao (2003), p. 45.

[59] Alcácer Guirao (2003), pp. 51–54.

[60] With close ties to Hegel and Luhmann's systems theory, Jakobs bases his construction on the assertion that the purpose of punishment is to "maintain the validity of the norm as a model of social contract. Here are some obligatory considerations on how it relates to the institute of social adequacy. Law, from a Luhmannian perspective, is a structure through which social orientation is facilitated, while the norm acts as a generator of expectations. Society would form and produce itself through Law, with the mission of Criminal Law being to ensure such configuration." Silveira (2010), p. 41.

[61] Alcácer Guirao (2003), p. 60. Cf. Luhmann: "In the social sphere, there is no multiplicity of alternatives to choose from, among them, the operation that defines the social. Communication is the only phenomenon that meets the requirements: a social system arises when communication develops more communication, from communication itself." Luhmann (2009), p. 90.

[62] "The concept of role, while designed to fit the particular human being, alludes to an abstract format, in the sense that the role can be performed by various individuals in a similar manner. The role is guided by indications of skill in the profession and requires meeting a set of requirements, without which it would not be possible to access it. Therefore, the concept of role aims to insert into a theoretical unit the relationship between individual and society, from the moment it is guided both by behavior expectations according to the stimulus/response scheme and by action expectations." Luhmann (2009), p. 254 (original italics).

[63] Alcácer Guirao (2003), pp. 63–64. According to Jakobs: "Just as humans can only deal well with nature to the extent that they can recognize regularities in social contacts - the only ones that matter here - orientation is also only possible when it is not necessary to expect unpredictable behavior from others at every moment. Otherwise, every contact would become an incalculable risk. The fact of engaging in social contact is already a sign that a completely indeterminate outcome is not expected. If the expectation is frustrated, a conflict arises for the frustrated person to which they

According to the argumentative line developed by the professor from Bonn, it does not make sense then to understand crime as something factual related to individuals and their mere private interests but as an injury to the legal system as a whole.[64] Thus, harmfulness would consist of a normative violation act, that is, systemic insubordination or to the instance.[65]

According to this point of view, the social system is shaken by criminal behavior, which is why only the criminal sanction can return it to normality, reaffirming to the social environment that the violated value remains valid. According to JAKOBS: "the function of the penalty is the preservation of the norm as a model of orientation for social contacts. The content of the norm is an opposition at the expense of the offender against the deauthorization of the norm."[66]

Therefore, according to the author, as stated,[67] the criminal types, through the penalty system, protects social expectations of conduct, referenced in social roles. The criminal sanction is, thus, the demonstration of the effectiveness of the violated norm, tending to the stabilization of the order.[68]

Finally, it is worth mentioning the most recent work by Feijoo Sánchez about Economic Criminal Law, in relation to the present *topos*.[69] Questioning the hypothesis that economic crimes constitute infractions of duty, and trying to dismiss the objection of lack of substantial reference of this category, due to positive signaling, the author seeks to harmonize the ideas by attributing material meaning to infractions of duty in Economic Criminal Law by considering that there are criminal types that protect legal goods through the legitimate strategy of guaranteeing the fulfillment of special duties which would have their origin in the performance of legal-economic roles.[70] Examples would be those of the corporate administrator, the executive board member of a company that is listed on the stock exchange, and the taxpayer, since all would not only have a duty not to injure, those the companies and the treasury,[71] having to represent a greater social function.

As the professor from Madrid explains:

> the solution that is offered in this work to many of the problems of imputation that are posed to economic and business crimes goes through a correct material foundation - and not merely

must react, as the frustration reveals that the balance between the events they counted on and those that occurred is no longer in accordance: the orientation models of the frustrated person must be reviewed." Jakobs (2009), pp. 21–22.

[64] Alcácer Guirao (2003), p. 69.

[65] Jakobs (2009), cit., *passim*.

[66] Jakobs (2009), p. 27.

[67] Section 2.2.1.1.

[68] Jakobs (2009), p. 21, *passim*.

[69] Feijoo Sánchez (2009), p. 228 e ss.

[70] Feijoo Sánchez (2009), pp. 231–232.

[71] Feijoo Sánchez (2009), pp. 232 e 245.

formal - of crimes that have to do with special duties of solidarity and collaboration, whose infraction normatively equates to 'injuring or endangering'.[72]

According to the developed thought, it would not be about assuming that the Law protects extrapenal duties with criminal sanctions, but about noting that on certain occasions criminal norms sanction socially harmful facts, based on criteria that would go beyond the mere duty not to cause harm to third parties.[73]

Despite the attempt to provide a greater color to the ideology of legal-criminal infractions of an economic nature as infractions of duty, due to the sense of this branch openly dealing with a search for the stabilization of conduct norms indispensable for the maintenance of social order, in the current economic aspect,[74] highlighting the character of positive general prevention, the thought of Feijoo Sánchez approaches that of Jakobs, thus receiving the same sort of criticisms, developed below.

3.3.1 Critical References and Conclusion

Criminal Law represents the most serious means of formal social control[75] existing, since it restricts the fundamental rights of individuals through the most incisive action of the State. In this way, this branch of Law, since the period of the Enlightenment, simultaneously assumed the roles of protecting interests of indispensable social and guarantee of the citizen against state arbitrariness.

The two fundamental consequences of this liberal postulate are: first, criminal norms should seek to protect the fundamental interests of the citizen related to the essential conditions that allow him to develop his freedom in society;[76] second, the criminal prohibition of behaviors should be aimed at socially harmful actions for social coexistence, excluding, for example, the protection of moral or religious convictions.[77]

For the performance of this dual role, the theory of legal good and the principle of harmfulness represent important guidelines capable of justifying a

[72]Feijoo Sánchez (2009), p. 244 (free translation).

[73]Feijoo Sánchez (2009), p. 232. For the author: "the criminal types that configure the so-called 'modern Criminal Law', of which Economic Criminal Law is a prototype, are often constructed based on the existence of legal relationships or bonds that exceed the most basic or primary duties of respect or non-injury." Feijoo Sánchez (2009), p. 245 (free translation).

[74]Feijoo Sánchez (2009), p. 207.

[75]On the topic of social control, see, e.g., Shecaira (2023), p. 59 et seq.; Reale Júnior (2009), p. 3 et seq.

[76]Alcácer Guirao (2003), p. 77.

[77]Alcácer Guirao (2003), p. 78; Reale Júnior (2009), p. 24; Ferrajoli (1987); Zugaldía Espinar (1993), p. 52 e ss.; Santos (2008), p.

criminalization, as well as, on the other hand, representing a limiting filter of the State's action in curtailing the essential rights of citizens. Simple punishment explained as a response to a violation of duty set by the legal system lacks real content, dating back to the doctrinal period prior to the idea of material unlawfulness.

Trying to overcome the accusations of explanatory emptiness due to the effective lack of offensive concreteness in typifications commonly erected these days, part of the doctrine tries to find justification in the theoretical construction of the spiritualized legal good. In this sense, the existence of harmfulness is identified in the hypothesis on an ideal plane, linked to the disvalue of the action.[78] The injury to a legal good is then seen not as a factual reality, but as a valuation,[79] hence the talk of spiritualized legal good.

Following this point of view, the crime would transmute into an injury or breach of duty and no longer really an offense to a legal good. The valuation in the hypothesis goes back to Hegelian idealization, not appearing as a safe parameter for limiting the power to punish.

As Reale Júnior states:

> The value must be apprehended by the legislator when producing the criminal intervention with the issuance of the incriminating norm, and this recognition and weighing of the value as essential must occur in the face of the circumstances and the spiritual atmosphere of the historical-cultural moment. But the legislator's attention turns to reality to gather the concrete form of the type of behavior that most seriously affronts this value worthy of protection. (…) Thus ZIPF is right to highlight that this contrariness to ethical-social demands is made in the face of the '*concrete social harmfulness of a certain form of behavior*', in understanding seconded by MARIA DA CONCEIÇÃO FERREIRA DA CUNHA, who highlights that alongside the degree of importance of values there is the observation '*of the effects of certain behaviors in the social sphere to these same values*'.[80]

Therefore, the idea of crime as a breach of duty, assurance of apparent functions of the social fabric,[81] or transgression to the order, due to its formalism and abstraction, does not appear adequate to justify or to limit in a safe way the *ius puniendi.* The classic thought on this matter still proves to be the most dogmatically coherent and, in the face of the penal expansionism of recent decades, criminally politically renewed in its importance.

---

[78] Silveira (2006), p. 151.

[79] Silveira (2006), p. 151.

[80] Reale Júnior (2009), p. 23 (original italics).

[81] Silveira (2010), p. 39.

3.4 The Search for the Demarcation of Harmfulness in Economic Crimes

Given what has been developed up to this point, it is necessary to reiterate some specific conclusions reached, which not only serve as benchmarks for the demarcation of harmfulness in economic crimes, but will also serve as an important substrate for the final understanding of the legitimacy or not of Economic Criminal Law.

Initially, let us reiterate the fact that a criminal type is only admitted when aimed at the protection of a legal good of criminal dignity, which is, in the case of Economic Criminal Law, the economic order. This, as explained, transcending mere state interventionist policy in the economic field,[82] refers to the fundamental structures of the economic system adopted by the social model.

However, the mere sense of protection of a legal good is a necessary condition, but not sufficient, to justify criminalization, being necessary to ascertain, among other aspects,[83] respect for the principle of harmfulness. Regarding economic delinquency, this means the possibility of affecting the fundamental economic structure through the prohibited conduct. Transitory, sectoral or regional economic policies, when not directly linked to serious behaviors capable of affecting harmonious social coexistence, not protected more efficiently by other means of social control other than the legal-criminal, do not justify economic criminalization.

In this way, the principle of harmfulness obliges, on one hand, the legislator to avoid criminalizations of merely formal injustices, and, on the other, the interpreter to the theoretical construction of each type integrated into the actual or potential affectation, this through an analytical perspective *ex ante* and *ex post*,[84] of the legal good in focus.[85] This is the general methodological sense with a view to the intended demarcation.

Such affectation may translate, from the thought of Bajo Fernández and Bacigalupo Saggese, into material, immaterial damages and other harmful effects to free social coexistence.[86]

In material terms, the damages characteristic of economic delinquency would be fundamentally financial, although the Spanish authors also recognize the possibility of other material damages of greater social relevance, such as those against life, physical integrity, and health, in the examples of counterfeiting of medicines and

[82] State interventionism in the economy is characteristic of the administrative sphere, occurring directly, as in the cases of energy generation and distribution services, basic sanitation, and the structuring of transport networks, when the State performs the economic activity, or indirectly, consisting of promotion, regulation, monitoring, measurement, supervision, planning, and ordering of the economy. Cf. Marques Neto (2006), p. 74.

[83] To be referred to below.

[84] As referred to above in Sect. 3.2.2.

[85] Cervini (2009), p. 43.

[86] Bajo Fernández and Bacigalupo Saggese (2001), p. 30.

cosmetics, alterations in food, etc.[87] Although easily assimilated, the critical cut of this understanding is actually reduced, since it cannot differentiate in essence an economic crime from another category—such as property crimes, in the first case, and those against life, in the last—as well as it privileges the types with the concrete result, not offering benchmarks to the interpreter, *v.g.*, for cases of danger crimes.

The immaterial damages, in turn, for the authors in focus, are linked to the loss of confidence in commercial traffic, to the distortion of the market balance and to the elimination of competition.[88] Considering that Economic Criminal Law aims to protect the economic structure of society against seriously offensive acts, allowing free human development in terms of wealth reproduction and circulation, within constitutional parameters, this last aspect is an important essential delimiting feature of harmfulness in economic typification.

Thus, more than a transgression to the order, that is, contempt for the legal order, which, as seen, lacks legitimizing content, the violation of the economic agents' confidence in the functionality of the market—since it composes its framework—alongside the structural distortion of this, represents a material justifying and differentiating sense of economic incrimination. A theoretical example of economic confidence shock capable of giving meaning to incrimination occurs with the prohibition of disclosing false information to consumers, while structural distortion of the market, with the protection of free competition, which has the consumer as the ultimate beneficiary of its correct functioning. Concrete cases of such shock occurred with the scandals of the companies Enron and WorldCom, as seen above.[89]

However, note that there is a great difficulty for the legislator and the interpreter in trying, the former, to hypothetically dimension, and the latter, to measure in the conduct concretely analyzed, the shock to the economic order. At first glance, it seems that the contours of criminal technique will hardly be able to erect precise criminal types capable of closely predicting business conduct—which are naturally dynamic—offensive to the legal good in focus. Also, it is hardly credible, in a simple example, that an expired food sold by a butcher to a single consumer represents a sensitization of social confidence in commercial traffic or the distortion of its basic structures.[90]

Nevertheless, the legislative solution to open clauses, to be verified by the law enforcer in the factual hypothesis, such as that which occurs in the aforementioned crime of reckless management of a financial institution (Article 4, sole paragraph, of Brazilian Law No. 7.492/86),[91] is not consistent with Criminal Law,[92] violating the

---

[87] Bajo Fernández and Bacigalupo Saggese (2001), p. 31.

[88] Bajo Fernández and Bacigalupo Saggese (2001), pp. 31–32.

[89] Section 2.1.4.

[90] In this regard, it is necessary to analyze the topic in focus in light of the theory of criminal cumulativeness, which will be addressed in the following chapter.

[91] This pertains to the Brazilian law concerning crimes against the country's financial system.

[92] Reale Júnior (2009), p. 277.

fundamental principle of taxativity.[93] The highlighted criminal offense, establishing a prison sentence of 3 to 12 years, in addition to a fine, simply prohibits the conduct of managing a financial institution in a "reckless" manner, which violates the requirements of a clear and precise law in the Brazilian penal system. What would constitute reckless management, especially in a necessarily risky economic activity? The content of the prohibition is, therefore, imprecise, and it is unacceptable for it to be determined by the judge, as in Brazil this is the exclusive task of the Legislative Branch. The same happens with merely formal types, like those revealed by Articles 17[94] and 18[95] of the aforementioned law[96] of crimes against the financial system, for lack of offensiveness.

In fact, on this aspect, economic doctrine argues that one cannot impose rigor on economic typifications regarding the verification of abusive practices,[97] which, as will be verified *infra*,[98] a better suitability of protection by another branch of Law is emerging. In this sense, the Administrative Council for Economic Defense - CADE, a Brazilian federal agency, regulated by Law No. 8.884/94,[99] aims to guide, supervise, prevent, and investigate abuses of economic power, playing a protective role in the prevention and repression of such abuses, has already expressed itself:

---

[93] Pitombo (2001), p. 51.

[94] Art. 17. Taking or receiving, by any of the persons mentioned in Art. 25 of this law, directly or indirectly, a loan or advance, or deferring it to a controller, an administrator, a member of a statutory board, their respective spouses, ascendants or descendants, relatives in the collateral line up to the 2nd degree, by blood or affinity, or to a company controlled by them, directly or indirectly, or by any of these persons: Penalty - Imprisonment, from 2 (two) to 6 (six) years, and a fine.Sole Paragraph. The same penalty applies to anyone who: I - in their own name, as a controller or in the capacity of an administrator of the company, grants or receives an advance of fees, remuneration, salary, or any other payment, under the conditions referred to in this article; II - covertly promotes the distribution or receives profits from a financial institution.Regarding this criminal offense, see, for example, the critical position of Malheiros Filho: "A loan to a director is, in principle, a risky business, but there is no sense in prohibiting a large institution from offering an employed director financing for the purchase of a home or a car which, in addition to being well secured, is insignificant in amount compared to the financier." Malheiros Filho (1999), p. 5.

[95] Art. 18. Violating the confidentiality of an operation or service provided by a financial institution or a member of the securities distribution system, of which one has knowledge due to their position: Penalty - Imprisonment, from 1 (one) to 4 (four) years, and a fine.

[96] The technical fragility of the law in focus—still in force today—is such that, in a presidential message explaining the reasons for partial vetoes, the President of the Republic asserted that he would soon send a new bill to the National Congress, improving the matter. This is why Araújo Júnior called Law No. 7.492/86 a "provisional law." Cf. de Araujo Júnior (1995), p. 147.

[97] Glória, Daniel Firmato de Almeida. Consumer Law and Competition Law. In: Oliveira, Amanda Flávio de. Direito econômico: evolução e institutos. Rio de Janeiro: Forense, p. 182; BRAZIL. Administrative Council for Economic Defense - CADE. Administrative Procedure No. 08000.020787/96-62. Opinion of Councilor Lúcia Helena Salgado e Silva.

[98] Capítulo 5.

[99] This pertains to the Brazilian law that provides for the prevention and repression of offenses against the economic order.

> (…) it is known that the law establishes in the aforementioned art. 21 merely illustrative forms of indications of anticompetitive practices, not exhausting or limiting the practices subject to punishment. However, only behaviors capable of producing or when they effectively produce the effects provided for in art. 20 will be considered illegal. Thus, the possible abusiveness of such behaviors should be investigated in the economic context in which it occurred, making it necessary to correctly delimit the relevant market, verify the degree of dominant power of the agent and assess the impacts that the behavior under analysis may eventually produce in this market, or if it has already caused some effect on the competitive environment.[100]

In this vein, it is necessary to note that the role of CADE in the prevention and repression of behaviors that violate free competition includes, respectively, the determination of prior limits to the actions of economic agents, e.g., prohibiting mergers and acquisitions,[101] or the imposition of sanctions on companies for anti-competitive acts even if no actual harm is proven.[102] Thus, in accordance with the legal regime established by Brazilian Law No. 8.884/94, criteria for harm are established not only actual, but potential.[103]

This form of protection of the economic order, of relevant preventive nature and significant flexibility, that is, less strict for measuring harm to this dear social interest, as well as with the constant need for contextualized economic analysis, to

[100] BRASIL. Conselho Administrativo de Defesa Econômica - CADE. Procedimento Administrativo n. 08012.004712/2000-89. Vote of Counselor Roberto Augusto Castellanos Pfeiffer.

[101] Regarding this, see the well-known case of the acquisition of the chocolate manufacturer Garoto by Nestlé, Concentration Act No. 08012.001697/2002-89 (in Brazilian Portuguese).

[102] Refer to the content of Articles 20 and 21 of Law No. 8,884/94. On the subject, as already expressed by CADE: "In competition defense legislation in most countries, it is not necessary to prove the harm of a cartel to consumers to condemn it. It is enough to prove its existence to presume its harmful effects. (…) Suppose, for the sake of argument, that a classic cartel has not produced any harmful effect on society. If such a fact occurred, this result was independent of the will of the parties, as they had, by the simple fact of participating in a Cartel, the intention to cause effects that harm consumers: after all, no one takes the risks and assumes the costs of setting up a classic cartel to keep their economic results unchanged. For this reason, I will not consider for the purposes of proof of anticompetitive conduct the SDE studies that aimed to show the harm to society of the practices of the defendants." BRASIL. Conselho Administrativo de Defesa Econômica - CADE. Administrative Proceeding n. 8012.002127/02-14. Vote of Counselor Luiz Carlos Delorme Prado.

[103] See, e.g.: BRASIL. Office of the Attorney General of the Union. Office of the Federal Attorney General. Federal Attorney's Office - CADE. Parecer PROCADE n. 066/2008. Opinion of Prosecutor Marcos Benacchio; BRASIL. Office of the Attorney General of the Union. Office of the Federal Attorney General. Federal Attorney's Office - CADE. Parecer PROCADE n. 365/2009. Opinion of Prosecutor Diogo Thomson Andrade; BRASIL. Conselho Administrativo de Defesa Econômica - CADE. Processo Administrativo n. 08012.002299/2000-18. Opinion of Counselor Afonso Arinos de Mello Franco Neto; BRASIL. Conselho Administrativo de Defesa Econômica - CADE. Ato de Concentração n. 08012.001697/2002-89. Opinion of Counselor Thompson Andrade. Cf. it is paradigmatically verified in this last case (cited Concentration Act involving the companies Nestlé and Garoto), CADE even uses simulations based on econometric estimates, such as John Nash's game theory, to assess the potential harm to the market. Presumptions are expressly admitted in this demarcation by harmfulness.

ascertain, for example, what constitutes a relevant market,[104] dominant position,[105] and abuse of economic power,[106] reveals better suitability of Administrative Law than Criminal Law for its protection.[107]

In this sense, it is not intended to simply totally deny the existence of the criminal legal good economic order, but rather to consider illegitimate the use of this burdensome branch of curtailment of human freedom as a means of shaping behaviors, either to meet social expectations, or for administrative conveniences, or through insecure criteria in precise legal-penal terms. Although undoubtedly the very difficulty of identifying the dear social value involved in the economic penal type indicates that Criminal Law should be used only in extreme cases, it is precisely

[104]"The relevant market is the one in which competition relations take place or the economic agent whose behavior is being analyzed operates. Without its delimitation, it is impossible to determine the incidence of any of the hypotheses contained in the items of Article 20 of Law No. 8,884, of 1994." Forgioni (2008), p. 231. This author further notes that the characterization of the illicit act must be assessed in the specific case, as the concept of the relevant market is flexible, needing to be delimited according to the geographical criterion and the product criterion. Forgioni (2008), p. 231 et seq. In the same sense: "(…) the relevant market is a concept constructed case by case, in order to allow its adaptation to all products and services. To rigidly define it in the law would be a great mistake, as it would prevent its adaptation to new circumstances." Pagotto (2006), p. 157. Thus, if there are already difficulties for Competition Law regarding legal certainty, the distance from this in dealing with the issue through criminal law is much greater, which, as stated, has less flexibility.

[105]Dominant position is briefly characterized as "(…) when there are structural conditions that prevent the establishment of competition." Salomão Filho (2008), p. 53. According to Forgioni, "(…) the dominant position is a consequence and, at the same time, identifies with the power held by the agent in the market, which ensures the possibility of acting independently and indifferently in relation to other agents, impervious to market laws." Forgioni (2008), p. 318.

[106]"On one hand, the abuse of economic power is characterized whenever a company takes advantage of its condition of economic superiority to harm competition, inhibit the functioning of the market, or arbitrarily increase its profits. On the other hand, the abuse of economic power presents itself in various forms. Examples include the trust (pressure from larger companies on smaller ones to command pricing policy), the cartel (agreement between companies in the same sector to control aspects common to their activity), and other practices considered restrictive to the principles of free enterprise and free competition, such as dumping (price discrimination between different national markets), predatory pricing (strategy of deliberately lowering product prices below cost to drive competitors out of the market), tying (practice of conditioning the sale of one good or service on the purchase of another), and selective distribution systems (unjustified restrictions imposed by the manufacturer on the distributor, used to discriminate against distributors, sellers, and consumers, ultimately harming free competition)." Martins (2006), V. II, p. 355 (original italics). It should be noted that the abuse of economic power is not characterized without harm to competition or arbitrary profit increases. In this sense, cf. Forgioni (2008), p. 327.

[107]Furthermore, it is noted that CADE has a strong regulatory role in the economic order, a matter related to Administrative Law. According to, e.g., Di Pietro: "To use the language of Brazilian administrative law, it can be stated, without fear of error, that among the administrative activities under the State's responsibility (public service, promotion, police, and intervention), the regulatory activity encompasses the last three, namely, police, promotion, and intervention in the economic domain." Di Pietro (2003), p. 34.

the task of the criminal scientist to recognize them, to remove from its core any other hypotheses.[108]

Such dogmatic recognition, wrapped in the general difficulties of all collective legal goods, seems to occur through a competition of criteria. The characteristics of intent to profit on the part of the agent, of actual or potential harm to an indeterminate number of people and the need for social control of the market, with direct or indirect reference to the citizen as an economic actor (mainly in his consumer aspect, although also significant in that of entrepreneur businessman) thus embody palpable vectors to guide the legislator and the interpreter. Alongside this, the verification of adequacy or technical legal-penal functionality,[109] taking into account criteria such as subsidiarity, taxativity, and assessment of causality relationship, will serve as a normative differentiator as to the appropriate legal branch for the protection of this human interest.

The sensitization of any of these aspects, shaping a Criminal Law of an exclusively preventive nature, that is, anticipatory, with porous and flexible typifying techniques, as an effective means of combating acts contrary to the current economic order, reveals illegitimacy, denoting legal insecurity. If it is concluded by the choice of the legal-administrative sphere for the protection of the dear social value in focus, nevertheless, its limits and structuring must also be verified.

References

Alcácer Guirao R (2003) Sobre el concepto de delito: ¿Lesión del bien jurídico o lesión de deber? Ad-Hoc, Buenos Aires

Angioni F (1994) Il pericolo concreto come elemento della fattispecie penale – la struttura oggettiva. Giuffrè, Milano

Bajo Fernández M, Bacigalupo Saggese S (2001) Derecho penal económico. Centro de Estudios Ramón Areces, Madrid

Bechara AELS (2010) Da teoria do bem jurídico como critério de legitimidade do direito penal. Tese de Livre Docência, Faculdade de Direito da Universidade de São Paulo, São Paulo

Bitencourt CR (2024) Tratado de direito penal: parte geral, vol. I. Revista dos Tribunais, São Paulo

Bottini PC (2007) Crimes de perigo abstrato e princípio da precaução na sociedade de risco. Revista dos Tribunais, São Paulo

Cervini R (2009) Derecho penal económico democrático: hacia una perspectiva integrada. In: Vilardi CS, Pereira FRB, Dias Neto T (Coords.) Direito penal econômico: análise contemporânea. Saraiva, São Paulo pp 3–60

Costa JF (1992) O perigo em direito penal. Coimbra, Coimbra

[108] In this context, it is important to note once again that the opinion of some scholars that the Constitution contains determinations of criminalizations is not shared, as this is incompatible with the outlines of a Penal Law of ultima ratio. On the subject, and in the sense exposed, cf., among others, in the national literature: Paschoal, Janaina Conceição. Constituição, criminalização…, cit., p. 69 et seq.

[109] Manes (2005), p. 44.

D'avila FR (2005) Ofensividade e crimes omissivos próprios: contributo à compreensão do crime como ofensa ao bem jurídico. Coimbra, Coimbra
de Araujo Júnior JM (1995) Os crimes contra o sistema financeiro no esboço de nova parte especial do Código Penal de 1994. Revista Brasileira de Ciências Criminais, São Paulo 11:145–165
de Souza LA (2007) Expansão do direito penal e globalização. Quartier Latin, São Paulo
Di Pietro MSZ (Org) (2003) Direito regulatório: temas polêmicos. Belo Horizonte: Forum
Feijoo Sánchez B (2009) Cuestiones actuales de derecho penal económico. B de F, Montevideo-Buenos Aires
Ferrajoli L (1987) Derecho y razón: teoria del garantismo penal. Trotta, Madrid
Ferrari ER (2004) Legislação penal antitruste: direito penal econômico e sua concepção constitucional. In: Reale M, Reale Júnior M, Ferrari ER (eds) Experiências do direito. Millennium, Campinas, pp 253–315.
Forgioni PA (2008) Os fundamentos do antitruste. RT, São Paulo
García-Pablos De Molina A (2006) Introducción al derecho penal. Editorial Universitaria Ramon Areces, Madrid
Glória DFdeA. Direito do consumidor e direito da concorrência. In: de Oliveira AF (ed). Direito econômico: evolução e institutos. Forense, Rio de Janeiro, pp 179–207
Gomes LF (2002) Princípio da ofensividade no direito penal. Revista dos Tribunais, São Paulo
Gomes MGdeM (2003) O princípio da proporcionalidade no direito penal. Revista dos Tribunais, São Paulo
Jakobs G (2009) Tratado de direito penal: teoria do injusto penal e culpabilidade. Trad. Gercélia Batista de Oliveira Mendes e Geraldo de Carvalho. Del Rey, Belo Horizonte
Luhmann N (2009) Introdução à teoria dos sistemas. Trad. Ana Cristina Arantes Nasser. Vozes, Petrópolis
Malheiros Filho A (outubro/1999) Crimes contra o sistema financeiro na virada do milênio. Boletim IBCCRIM, São Paulo 83:5–6
Manes V (2005) Il principio di ofensività nel diritto penale: canone di politica criminale, criterio ermeneutico, parametro di ragionevolezza. G. Giappichelli, Torino
Marques Neto FA (2006) A nova regulação estatal e as agências independentes. In: Sundfeld CA (Coord.). Direito administrativo econômico. Malheiros, São Paulo, pp 72–98
Martins EP (2006). Polícia administrativa econômica. Cardozo, José Eduardo Martins et all (Orgs.). Curso de direito administrativo econômico. Malheiros, São Paulo, V. II, pp 344–381
Maximiliano C (2007) Hermenêutica e aplicação do direito. Forense, Rio de Janeiro
Méndez Rodríguez C (1993) Los delitos de peligro y sus técnicas de tipificación. Montano, Madrid
Pagotto LUC (2006) Defesa da concorrência no sistema financeiro. Singular, São Paulo
Pitombo ASAdeMP (2001) Considerações sobre o crime de gestão temerária de instituição financeira. In: Salomão HE (Coord.). Direito penal empresarial. Dialética, São Paulo, pp 51–54
Reale Júnior M (1973) Antijuridicidade concreta. José Bushatsky, São Paulo
Reale Júnior M (2000) Teoria do delito. Revista dos Tribunais, São Paulo
Reale Júnior M (2009) Instituições de direito penal – parte geral. Forense, Rio de Janeiro
Salomão Filho C (2008) Regulação da atividade econômica: princípios e fundamentos jurídicos. Malheiros, São Paulo
Santos JC (2008) Direito penal: parte geral. ICPC-Lumen Juris, Curtiba
Shecaira SS (2023) Criminologia. Thomson Reuters Brasil, São Paulo
Silva ÂRI (2003) Dos crimes de perigo abstrato em face da constituição. Revista dos Tribunais, São Paulo
Silveira RdeMJ (2006) Direito penal econômico como direito penal de perigo. Revista dos Tribunais, São Paulo
Silveira RMJ (2010) Fundamentos da adequação social em direito penal. Quartier Latin, São Paulo
Tavares J (2002) Teoria do injusto penal. Del Rey, Belo Horizonte

Terradillos Basoco JM (2003) Sistema penal y delitos contra el orden socioeconómico. Consideraciones introductorias. In: De La Cuesta Aguado, Paz Mercedes et all. Derecho penal económico. Ediciones Jurídicas Cuyo, Mendoza, pp 53–78

von Liszt F (2003). Tratado de direito penal alemão. Trad. José Higino Duarte Pereira. Russell, Campinas, t. I

Zugaldía Espinar JM (1993) Fundamentos de derecho penal. Tirant lo Blanch, Valencia

Chapter 4
The Construction of Cumulative Crimes

4.1 Notion of Cumulative Criminality

Cumulative criminality, or accumulation delinquency,[1] is linked to the idea of criminal punishment for behaviors that are per se incapable of affecting legal-criminal interests, but that, by political-criminal criteria, are forbidden, since their widespread practice would denote shock (by damage or danger) to a certain legal good. It is, therefore, a dogmatic concept linked to conceptions about the limits of typicity and not properly a legislative technique, since it "reveals before the qualification of certain behaviors as typical behaviors or punishable."[2]

The notion of the institute was brought by the American legal philosopher Joel Feinberg, in 1984, in the studies called *The Moral Limits of the Criminal Law*,[3] when analyzing the limits of the criminal law in the face of the question "What if everyone did the same?" In this sense, the function of the criminal prohibition of conduct, in this case, would be to prevent its repetition in significant numbers within society, fostering a harmful situation due to its accumulation, which Feinberg called *accumulative harms*.

[1] Expressions derived from the term 'cumulative crimes' in German: kumulationsdelikt. In Portuguese literature, the expression 'additive offenses' is also used synonymously. Cf. Dias (2003), p. 304, passim; de Sousa (2006), p. 234, passim.

[2] Dias (2003), pp. 305–306. The author also notes: "(...) It can be said, therefore, that accumulation is a dogmatic concept, which serves for the interpretation of certain types and for the imputation of certain behaviors, and that a sector of the doctrine intends to include it in the General Part of Criminal Law. In this sense, it is a concept that approaches that of social adequacy and distances itself from that of concrete danger – which is also mainly a legislative technique – or that of commission by omission – which is a rule of imputation contained in the General Part of the Penal Code." Dias (2003), pp. 305–306.

[3] In the first volume of such studies (published in a collection called Moral Limits of the Criminal Law Series), which deals with harm to others, cf. Feinberg (1987). It is noted that the work referred to here is a reprint of the one originally published in the mentioned year of 1984.

L. A. d. Souza, *Economic Criminal Law*,
https://doi.org/10.1007/978-3-031-87236-5_4

The American author seeks to go beyond the thought of Stuart Mill, according to whom the State can only curtail someone's freedom against their will when it has to protect the freedom of others, from the parameter of harm to third parties,[4] understanding that the harm principle (*harm principle*) is not the only criterion legitimizing the criminalization of conduct.[5] In this sense:

> (...) Feinberg considers that under certain circumstances the risk of harmful consequences can be equated to actual harm. From such premises, he admits the criminalization of various forms of abstract danger. According to Feinberg's theory, conduct that does not cause harm can be prohibited whenever it may lead to harmful consequences in the future, a situation in which the probability and severity of any damage to occur will be determinant.[6]

After referring to situations such as simple duels as a form of conflict resolution and, also, to tax evasion,[7] in the sense of understanding that a criminal prohibition would not be justified when people in their absolute majority do not act in the undesired way, which, on the contrary, would justify it in cases of low ethical-social motivation,[8] Feinberg analyzes the issue of environmental pollution. The author understands that air and water pollution are paradigmatic cases of cumulative offenses,[9] justifying criminalization mainly due to the importance of the value involved.[10]

Dealing specifically with the criminal environmental field, that is, the crime of water contamination in the German Criminal Code,[11] the concept of accumulation offense was dogmatically developed by German jurist Lothar Kuhlen,[12] professor at the Faculty of Law and Economics at the University of Mannheim, who coined the term *kumulationsdelikt*, and, since then, has been gaining some adherents[13] and,

---

[4]Mill (2000), p. 115 e ss.

[5]von Hirsch (2007), p. 39.

[6]von Hirsch (2007), p. 40 (free translation).

[7]Feinberg (1987), pp. 225–227.

[8]Mendoza Buergo (2001), p. 101; Silva Sánchez (2002), p. 121; Bechara (2003), p. 3.

[9]Feinberg (1987), p. 228.

[10]Feinberg (1987), p. 232.

[11]Provided for in § 324 StGB.

[12]Initially, the German author formulated his initial reflections on the subject in 1986, in an article entitled "Der Handlungserfolg der strafbaren Gewässerverunreinigung," dealing with the action of water pollution, provided for in the German Penal Code. His thoughts were somewhat altered in 1993 in another article, titled "Umweltstrafrecht – auf der Suche einer neuen Dogmatik," which can be freely translated as "Environmental Criminal Law – in Search of a New Dogmatic." Cf. also from the author, not specifically on the subject, but related to it: Kuhlen (2004), pp. 129 et seq.; Also, citing Kuhlen, Silva Sánchez (2002), pp. 121–125.

[13]From different perspectives, the idea of cumulative delinquency is ultimately accepted, according to Bechara's enumeration, in foreign doctrine, by Andrew von Hirsch, Wolfgang Wohlers, Roland Hefendehl, Giovanni Fiandaca, Enzo Musco, Jorge de Figueiredo Dias, and, to some extent, Jesús-María Silva Sánchez. In Brazil, the author points out, e.g., Pierpaolo Cruz Bottini as a proponent. Cf. Bechara (2010), pp. 258 et seq.

mainly, facing major challenges.[14] Even recognizing the existence of debatable aspects of such anticipation of criminal protection, Kuhlen is skeptical about a solution outside of Criminal Law, given in a context of great global risks, thus, not foreseeing another way of protecting said collective interest.[15]

For the German author, it is about "making a contribution to the solution of major problems by prohibiting, under threat of sanction, actions that in sum provide small contributions to the constitution of these problems."[16] In other words, the long-term conservation of nature, whose degradation does not occur only by a singular and precisely identified act, justifies that this act be criminally punished from now on in the name of the relevance of the interest protected. In this way, its foundation is based on utilitarian arguments of criminal policy, being significantly evasive[17] regarding dogmatic criticisms, simply renouncing the liberal theory of legal good, in the name of a so-called realistic prognosis.[18] This is the origin called pragmatic of the concept of cumulativity, which will be better analyzed below, underpinning a systemic bias perspective.[19] However, there is still a philosophical moral perspective,[20] as will also be discussed *infra*.

Although all this ideology relates to collective legal goods, particularly sensitive to environmental and economic issues,[21] and, therefore, is surrounded by interests of high-value load in the social core, the main arguments against such punishment focus on the idea of lack of harmfulness of the punished conduct, due to the absence of injury (or danger) to a protected legal good, in addition to the violation of the principle of culpability, since the punishment is based *ex iniuria tertii*, and, finally, the principle of proportionality, given the mismatch between the prohibited action and the legal response imposed (criminal penalty).[22] Nevertheless, the fact is that this typifying technique found a large expansive field due to the attitude of seeking risk containment in today's society, inserting itself, therefore, in a preventive logic.

---

[14] Silveira (2006), p. 148.

[15] Mendoza Buergo (2001), p. 144.

[16] *Apud* Silva Sánchez (2002), p. 123.

[17] In this sense, Silva Sánchez (2002), p. 123.

[18] See Wohlers (2008), *apud* Dias (2003), pp. 308–309.

[19] Dias (2003), p. 310 e ss.

[20] Dias (2003), p. 310 e ss.

[21] As Dias notes: "(…) The figure was introduced into the dogmatic discourse by Kuhlen regarding the limits of legal-criminal protection of the environment (…), but some proponents of its consecration soon extended it to areas such as the protection of the administration of justice, state tax revenues, or the functional capacity of certain subsystems of the economic system (…)." Dias (2003), pp. 306–307. Also highlighting the possibility of extending the theme to economic crime, cf. de Sousa (2023), pp. 32–34.

[22] See between others, Silva Sánchez (2002), p. 122; Dias (2003), *passim*; Bechara (2003), pp. 4–5.

4.2 The Pragmatic Emergence of the Concept of Cumulativity

Indeed, criminal cumulativity is a theoretical construction resulting from the context of a risk society.[23] As Silva Dias observes:

> The first perspective of foundation, which we will call systemic, gives prevalence to the criteria of global damage or large number, that is, to the probable harmful effects for the social order that will result from the accumulation of singular contributions made independently of each other.[24]

The society of late industrialization, post-industrial or risk, the latter according to the well-known expression coined by Beck, is characterized by the radicalization of its outlines, thus producing, contradictory consequences not desired by the current mode of production. Hence the talk of reflexivity and reflection,[25] the former tied to the idea of the production of unwanted risks[26] and the latter to the ability to recognize these same risks, to overcome them:

> This reflection (knowledge and contact) of the new risks, in turn, ends up causing complex phenomena and difficult solutions in modern society. The awareness of new risks, when widely disseminated, often mistakenly and mediatized, highlights a new form of disenchantment. No longer is there disbelief in the divine world offering traditions and myths, but the collective disbelief of man in dealing reliably with the objects of his own production is imposed. The society, at this moment, moves from the demand for technological production to the need for management. Systems capable of regulating their own contours are sought, reducing the danger of man's action in his surrounding universe.[27]

Thus, the search for industrial production with greater economic viability, that is, with the lowest possible cost and ever-increasing profits, with constantly renewing products, in the face of a competitive market and eager for novelties,[28] culminates in

---

[23] In the same sense, understanding that profound economic and social changes have imposed a new reflection on the function of criminal law, as well as prompted a crisis around the theory of legal goods, cf. de Sousa (2006), p. 238. See also Dias (2003), pp. 310 et seq.; Bechara (2010), p. 257.

[24] Dias (2003), pp. 310–311.

[25] Giddens et al. (1997), p. 11 e ss.

[26] "(...) the process of reflexivity described by the author [Beck] should be understood as a confrontation of the foundations of the modernity paradigm with the consequences of modernization. This confrontation, however, did not arise from a need to oppose the industrial model, nor did it signify a choice that could be accepted or rejected during political disputes. Surprisingly, it derived from the overdevelopment of industrial modernity, which ended up generating effects and threats that could not be assimilated by the rationality of the industrial era. In other words, the confrontation, which is the basis of reflexivity, means the incomprehension and the impossibility of assimilating the reality of the risk society by the system of the industrial society. Cumulatively and latently, the phenomena of the risk society produce threats that question and, ultimately, destroy the foundations of the industrial society." Machado (2005), p. 30.

[27] Salvador Netto (2006), pp. 93–94.

[28] In this sense, highlighting the inherent contradiction of the consumer society, which consists in the proposal to fulfill human material desires while needing them to remain unfulfilled, Bauman's words: "The consumer society is premised on satisfying human desires in a way that no society in

giving rise to widespread environmental degradation and also threatening the very characteristics of the economic system, through practices harmful to competition, consumers, and the State. In the economic field, think, for example, that free initiative, in principle, allows the free choice of means of production, which can in practice result in harmful practices, detrimental to workers, consumers, and competition and, thus, to society as a whole.

Such an unwanted contradictory consequence for a liberal economy system generates a reflection of the search for its overcoming through the attempt of its distancing by numerous regulatory means, such as criminal repression, which becomes an additional element of management law.[29] And, within this transmuted category, naturally, there are also reformulations of understandings, to justify—or ground, or even, validate—this restraining enterprise.

It is in this environment that the political-criminal idealization of cumulative delinquency emerges, as well as other discourses defending penal expansionism in relation to supra-individual legal goods, altering what once were shown as critical criteria to avoid penal incidence into supposed guiding arguments for its expansion. It is a pragmatic logic of risk management, preventively[30] aimed both at protecting current society and future generations.[31] It is understood that only with the expansion of individuals' responsibility towards the social environment is it possible to control the formation of serious risks to human existence and prevent the future perishing of life on the planet.[32]

Nevertheless, a political-criminal ideology as described encounters structural difficulties within the scope of traditional dogmatic criminal construction of an Enlightenment nature. In this sense, it is necessary to consider a supposed philosophical foundation of a moral nature, as well as the confrontation of the new discourse with the categories of danger or harm, as well as in the face of criminal harm, proportionality, and culpability, dogmatic traits of greater vulnerability in the issue, to endorse or not the new discourse.

---

the past could achieve or dream of. The promise of satisfaction, however, will only remain alluring as long as the desire remains unfulfilled; more importantly, as long as there is a suspicion that the desire has not been fully and completely satisfied. Setting easy targets, ensuring easy access to goods suitable for the targets, as well as the belief in the existence of objective limits to 'legitimate' and 'realistic' desires – this would be like the announced death of the consumer society. The non-satisfaction of desires and the firm and eternal belief that each act aimed at satisfying them leaves much to be desired and can be improved – these are the announcements of the economy that target the consumer." Bauman (2009), p. 105.

[29] Silva Sánchez (2002), p. 120. Analisando os contornos da sociedade atual, reveladora de indivíduos que tentam incessantemente calcular e minimizar riscos, cf. Bauman (2009), p. 90 e ss.

[30] Bechara (2010), p. 256.

[31] Alcácer Guirao (2002).

[32] Dias (2003), p. 314.

4.3 Philosophical Foundational Perspective: The Issue of the Free-Rider

In addition to the doctrinal foundational perspective of the additive construction, a result of the contours of risk society, there is another, of a moral philosophical nature, based on the studies of Feinberg and Wohlers.[33] It is the issue of the *free-rider*, or *free-loader*, that is, the "ticketless traveler,"[34] an expression that alludes to the individual who boards a train without having paid the corresponding fare.

According to this thought, the criminal prohibition of behaviors not in themselves harmful to dear social interests would be justified in the face of the reprehensible nature of the conduct of the one who selfishly takes advantage of the honesty of the majority of people, performing an act advantageous exclusively for himself to the detriment of the community. Thus, it would be morally condemnable for someone to wash their clothes in a river just to save on their water bill.

Not punishing this last person would mean, still according to the line defended by these authors, rewarding dishonesty at the expense of honesty, which is why the disvalue of the conduct of the *free-rider* would be in the selfish exploitation of others' solidarity:

> (…) As Feinberg argues, what is morally condemnable in "freeloading" is that the offender gains while the compliers, despite their moral superiority, suffer a loss. This situation turns the moral universe upside down: dishonesty is rewarded and honesty and civility are penalized, or at least not rewarded. The impunity of the "free-loader" behavior will socially prevail the idea that infringing pays off. Wohlers considers that the disvalue of such behavior lies in the violation of the principle that everyone has equal rights and that the legitimacy of the respective criminal sanction lies precisely in the restoration of the disturbed legal equality (…).[35]

Just like in a cumulative construction, the prohibited action does not directly harm the protected good, but, within the mentioned requirement of a realistic prognosis, its widespread practice would entail harmful social consequences.[36] In this context, and because of the frustration of a social expectation of conduct on the part of the *free-rider*, a criminal punishment for his conduct would be justified.

In summary, this is the theoretical scheme that seeks a moral philosophical beacon for the criminal construction under analysis: the exclusive devaluation of a petty, non-cooperative behavior in the face of the social fabric, but which benefits from the cooperation of others, should be curbed by Criminal Law.

---

[33] Wohlers (2008), pp. 125–152.

[34] Dias (2003), p. 316.

[35] Dias (2003), pp. 316–317.

[36] Dias (2003), p. 319, passim. Cf. Sousa: "(…) The prerequisites for the punishability of the free-rider's conduct would be, first, that everyone or a large number of people collaborate in the pursuit of a common goal, and second, that in the face of the free-loader's impunity, their conduct becomes widespread, jeopardizing the pursuit of the collective goal or the preservation of the collective good (…)." de Sousa (2006), pp. 235–236.

Due to its distancing from the liberal criminal-legal construction, which understands that the imposition of criminal sanctions is only justified in the face of behaviors that cause injuries or risks of injury to human interests fundamental to peaceful social coexistence, offering, on the contrary, an ideology legitimizing the revalidation of existing values (moral in this case), the critical analysis of the thought justifying the *free-rider* will take place together with that of the systemic perspective, when verifying the "Cumulativity and the reconstruction of criminal harm."

4.4 Cumulative Crimes as Danger Crimes or Result Crimes

The paradigm of the criminal construction of cumulative offenses is that of security production, promoting risk precaution.[37] In this sense, the very content of what is understood by cumulative offense, as noted, from a diffuse criminal-political point of view, is indifferent to the production of a harmful result.

In other words, essentially the production of damage to the legal good that is protected is not even considered, considering in fact the harmless action. From this, a first observation flows: the cumulative offense is not a result of crime.

On the other hand, neither does the mentioned construction demonstrate the requirement of proof of the production of a danger result to the interest legally criminally protected. This means that, within a traditional doctrinal thought, it is also inferred that we are not facing a category commonly known as concrete danger crime.

In this influx, despite the majority doctrine qualifying the cumulative construction as being of abstract danger, however, as Sousa notes,[38] there are dissonant proposals. Not in the sense of attributing to this new category the delineation of result crime, or of concrete danger crime, but rather identifying some differentiating element in the case, within the category of danger crimes, or even, of denial of the exclusive duality "result crimes" *versus* "danger crimes," simply labeling additive crimes as a subtype of the latter.

Thus, the Portuguese author initially cites Schünemann, who understands that there are three situations of abstract danger: (a) that of crimes that protect spiritualized intermediate legal goods, such as document forgery, in which there would be a devalued mediated result; (b) that of massive actions, prohibited for preventive reasons, in the face of new risks of current society, and (c) that of violations of prohibition due to a subjective duty of care (as in the crime of arson provided for in § 306 of the German Penal Code).[39] Therefore, according to the German scholar,

---

[37] Bechara (2003), p. 3; Bechara (2010), p. 256.

[38] de Sousa (2006), p. 227 e ss.

[39] de Sousa (2006), pp. 229–230.

cumulative offenses would be of the second type described, thus consisting of a precise subtype of abstract danger crime.[40]

Hefendehl, in turn, shows reservations in simply identifying cumulative crimes as abstract danger crimes, considering that "(...) the idea of accumulation serves as material equivalence to the relationship that within harmful causality must occur between action and legal good, making clear the connection between those two realities."[41]

The other authors cited by Sousa,[42] who to some extent signal positively towards the cumulative theoretical construction, such as the Spaniards Alcácer Guirao and Mendoza Buergo, in reality, end up abstracting the classificatory issue and minimizing the harmless character of the criminally prohibited conduct, aligning with the other arguments already discussed.

Given the aforementioned positions, there is no greater justification for the denial of classifying the legislative technique under analysis as abstract danger. In reality, the defenders, to a greater or lesser degree, of the idea in question seem to only want to value the additive construction, fostering a somewhat imprecise thought on the subject. Within a context of risk management, and also taking into account what is traditionally understood as a crime of abstract danger—one in which the actualization of danger to the protected interest is not required—it seems that the category of cumulative offenses is perfectly sheltered in the characterization of crimes of abstract danger. This does not mean, however, that the construction is legitimized.

4.5 Cumulativity and the Reconstruction of Criminal Harm

The very notion of cumulative delinquency shows that in the hypothesis the "(...) punishment does not reach concretely offensive behaviors, instead seeking to protect the social efficiency of certain functions through Criminal Law (...)."[43] In this sense, in the words of Silva Sánchez:

> Well, it is possible to affirm that it is a characteristic of the Criminal Law of post-industrial societies to assume, to a large extent, such a form of rationalizing, that of global harm derived from accumulations or repetitions, traditionally proper to the administrative. This is what is meant when referring to the process of 'administrativization', in which, in our opinion, Criminal Law is immersed. And this could take us even further: thus, not only to affirm that Criminal Law assumes the way of rationalizing proper to Sanctioning Administrative Law, but even that, from there, it becomes a Law of ordinary management of major social problems.[44]

[40] de Sousa (2006), p. 230.

[41] de Sousa (2006), pp. 230–231.

[42] de Sousa (2006), pp. 231–232.

[43] Bechara (2003), p. 4.

[44] Silva Sánchez (2002), p. 120.

Thus, there is no question of harm *in casu*, given the impossibility of establishing a relevant offense link between the minimal individual contributions[45] and the real or potential violation of the protected interest.

In this vein, the defenders of the construction in focus present justifications of a criminal political nature that seek to circumvent this unquestionable dogmatic finding, as noted in authors from Spain, Portugal, Germany, and Brazil, exemplarily listed below.[46]

Silva Sánchez, for communicative reasons linked to the motivating capacity of citizens, that is, privileging positive general prevention, exceptionally admits cumulative offenses, provided that such prohibitions are not punished with deprivation of liberty.[47] Thus, he admits them in a context that he calls the "second speed" of Criminal Law.

Figueiredo Dias, in turn, within the scope of environmental criminal protection,[48] presents a discourse focused on the need for the containment of global risks and the preservation of future generations.[49] The protection of the legal good would thus be indirect, given the empirical observation of a probable accumulation, to generate a danger of harm.[50]

In the same vein is the understanding of Tiedmann, who, also focusing on environmental matters, asserts that the dangers to this essential human interest cannot be understood even approximately.[51] The risks involved, then, would justify the intervention of Criminal Law.

Also, von Hirsch and Wohlers, similarly, seek to legitimize the cumulative construction from the understanding that there is a general duty of cooperation in the social environment, based on the roles played by each individual in the context of society, this should only be conditioned to a realistic prognosis and the consideration of the particularities of each person.[52]

In Brazilian doctrine, Bottini's position stands out.[53] This author agrees with the construction, as long as there is repetition of conduct by the same agent or even if there is prior agreement between several.

In light of the thoughts espoused by such authors, with a gloss on Bechara, a critical reflection is formulated that draws attention to the urgency of consecrating a rationalist criminal law.[54] Initially, regarding the theory of Silva Sánchez, it is noted that the consecration of two non-communicable subsystems would imply a true

[45] Alcácer Guirao (2002), p. 15.

[46] According to the pertinent examples of Bechara (2003), p. 4.

[47] Bechara (2003), p. 4; Bechara (2010), p. 261.

[48] Dias (2001), p. 390 e ss. Also referring to this text: Dias (2003), p. 304.

[49] Dias (2001), pp. 603–614.

[50] Bechara (2003), p. 4; Bechara (2010), p. 260.

[51] Bechara (2003), p. 4; Bechara (2010), pp. 260–261.

[52] Bechara (2010), pp. 258–259.

[53] Bechara (2003), p. 4; Bechara (2010), pp. 261–262.

[54] Bechara (2003), p. 4.

break of the criminal legal system,[55] which would lack sense in the so-called "second speed," since new concepts and institutes would have to be erected, distancing themselves from classical criminal rationality.[56] Moreover, as Silva Franco warns, given the selectivity of criminal law, this unusual duality would likely reflect unfairly on the accused, leading the powerful to answer in the less severe sphere, that is, without the consequence of the penalty of deprivation of liberty, while the helpless would remain in the traditional scope, of a prison nature.[57]

The criminal policy option of Figueiredo Dias, in turn, in the face of the absence of scientific or statistical certainty about effective harmful or dangerous results to a tangible legal good tied to individuals, appears to be linked to the principle of precaution.[58] Thus, this view offered by the professor from Coimbra does not align with the demands of guaranteeing Criminal Law, vilifying the necessary harm to a criminal legal good.[59]

Finally, as Bechara attentively notes,[60] Bottini's reflection[61] displays a mistaken analytical cut, since it confuses the concept of cumulative crime with a causal problem, since a single agent acting repeatedly with a single purpose, or, even, different agents acting with unity of designs, do not represent situations considered by doctrine as cumulative criminality. In these cases, the interpreter is actually facing a cumulative causality.

Indeed, the theory of cumulative crime has not emerged until the present moment as a convincing proposition capable of reconstructing or replacing criminal harm as a critical limiting and legitimating criterion of criminal incidence. Also, when punishing with deprivation of freedom an action in itself harmless, the principle of proportionality is violated.[62] On the other hand, culpability in a broad sense is vilified, since the individual is punished for the actions of others.[63] In this vein, it

---

[55] Bechara (2003), p. 4.

[56] On the subject, a reference has already been made in: de Souza (2007), pp. 63–72.

[57] Franco (2000), p. 134. This text was previously explicitly cited, cf. de Souza (2007), p. 71. The criticisms of the Spanish author's proposal will be resumed in the following chapter.

[58] Cf. referred above, Sect. 3.2.2. On this, Bechara observes: "(…) the adoption of a Criminal Law of behavior, based on social fears and the precautionary principle, even if advocating the indirect protection of supra-individual legal goods, leads to the regression of criminal intervention to the pre-Enlightenment period, and it is not difficult to also approximate this model to the axiological relativism that gave rise to the adoption of authoritarian systems such as the Kiel school. The requirement of the basic principle of offensiveness, achieved in the Enlightenment era, has deeper historical roots than the current Constitution itself and is essential for teleological argumentation in the field of criminal wrongdoing, so that renouncing this principle would mean renouncing the very Democratic Rule of Law and allowing, already in an authoritarian scope, the punishment of mere will or dangerousness." Bechara (2003), p. 4.

[59] Reale Júnior (2009), p. 277.

[60] Bechara (2003), p. 4.

[61] Bottini (2007), pp. 242–243.

[62] Dias (2003), pp. 333–334; de Sousa (2006), p. 237.

[63] de Sousa (2006), p. 237; Bechara (2003), pp. 4–5.

is necessary to observe if a specific analysis in the economic field would have the power to relativize this understanding.

From the point of view of the moral philosophical perspective, that is, that of the question of the *free-rider*, neither better luck emerges in favor of the justification of the cumulative construction. This is because, in the final analysis, criminal punishment for behaviors in themselves not harmful, beyond all the criticism mentioned above, is nothing more than a penal sanction for a breach of duty,[64] deserving to this all the criticisms listed in Chap. 3 of this work.

On the other hand, even if using a thought according to Luhmann's systems theory, as Silva Dias notes, there is no communicative disloyalty justifying a criminal censure, since the *free-rider* does not disregard the norm or even the protected interest, he just seeks an economic advantage for himself:

> (…) The "free-rider" is the selfish one who evades the fulfillment of collective provisions to maximize his own interest, the one who benefits, for example, from the improvement of water quality resulting from the fact that most people refrain from washing clothes in the stream, but renounces doing the same to save costs. His motivation corresponds to that of the "homo oeconomicus," who guides his action by the dictates of an instrumental reason. He acts by choosing the means that allow him to increase profits and decrease costs. He is more or less indifferent whether others respect or not the collective good (…) Thus, his selfish motivation, by itself, does not have the meaning of a communicative disloyalty.[65]

4.6 Cumulative Crimes and Their Justifying Capacity of Economic Criminal Protection

It is necessary to verify, at this moment, if specifically within the scope of economic delinquency, there would be arguments capable of somehow rejecting the criticisms so far offered to the cumulative construction.

Economic activity, as Faria Costa observes, is, in essence, repetitive. In the words of the Portuguese author:

> No one escapes the fact that - contrary to crimes, for example, against people or against life - economic crime has a potential for serial injury infinitely superior to other infractions. Indeed, it is known and immediately perceptible that economic-business activity is, almost by its nature, of repetition. Repetition of processes. Repetition of decisions. Repetition in pursuit of objectives. Now, this trait of repetition extends to all activity and, therefore, also to criminal behaviors. (…).[66]

---

[64] "(…) in addition to the failure to meet the principle of offensiveness leading, in cumulative offenses, to the exaltation of the disvalue of the action to the detriment of the disvalue of the result, thus giving rise to mere disobedience offenses, it also seems impossible to establish what the disvalue of the agent's action is, as it is intended to justify their punishment based on the prognosis of possible harm to third parties." Bechara (2010), p. 263.

[65] Dias (2003), p. 337.

[66] Costa (2003), pp. 58–59.

Thus, the factual economic criminal offense tends to its reiteration, since this is the logic of the current mode of production, revealing the perennial interest in profit by economic agents. Furthermore, not only does the multiplication of action by the same agent take on this same sense, but one must also hypothetically consider the possibility of its imitation by a large number of other agents.

For example, in the Brazilian case, one can think of the crime of "making false or misleading statements, or omitting relevant information about the nature, characteristic, quality, quantity, safety, performance, durability, price or warranty of products or services," inscribed in Article 66 of Law No. 8.078/90, which even prohibits, in its § 2nd, the typically mixed alternative conducts described in the negligent mode. In this way, it is clearly noted that the criminally protected interest, namely, the economic order, which has, as stated, the consumer as the ultimate beneficiary, is not minimally affected by the simple careless omission of a producer or a service provider who forgets the application of a data. In other words, market confidence is not significantly affected by such conduct. This could only happen with the repetition of the act or, remembering Feinberg's maxim, if everyone or a large part does the same. If, e.g., all or the majority of battery or milk producers fail to inform consumers about the quality and durability of products, there could be a generalized collective mistrust in their trades, fostering a shock in the economic order in these sectors.

The simple conjecture formulated presents a hypothesis of prohibition that could be based on the theory of cumulative delinquency, serving the criminal law as an ethical-behavioral motivating instrument in the economic field in situations in which a criminal legal good is not specifically offended, that is, in harmless actions, in which the agent's intentions are not even considered.

A slightly different situation to reflect would occur with, e.g., the crime of "destroying, rendering useless or damaging raw material or merchandise, with the aim of provoking a price increase, for one's own benefit or of a third party," provided for in item VIII of Article 7 of Law No. 8.137/90. Hardly a single act of a small or medium-sized supplier would really cause a price increase. This could only be achieved with the repetition of the conduct or, also, if everyone or a large part does the same. Exactly for this reason, the criminal type in question does not require for its configuration the effective provocation of a price increase but its simple intent. Thus, if on one hand, the type approaches the model of the cumulative crime, on the other, it moves away from the aspect of culpability in a broad sense, since here a special purpose of acting is required. However, in practice, it is hardly possible to prove the mentioned subjective aspect.

In any case, having demonstrated the relevance of the topic in the sphere of Economic Criminal Law, it is therefore questioned whether such a construction would be justified, maintaining the legitimacy of criminal intervention in such cases. To this, the answer is negative.

The institute of cumulative delinquency does not seem compatible with the paradigm of a liberal Criminal Law, based on the force ideas of protecting a legal good fundamental for social existence, as well as grounding in the principles of offensiveness, proportionality, and culpability, limiting criteria of penal repressive incidence. This is the normative framework that constitutes the basis of the validity of the legal-criminal branch in democratic societies and that does not find resonance in additive types,[67] thus reaching its legitimacy, whatever the object that is sought to protect.

In the words of Sousa, quoting the thought of Silva Dias:[68]

> (…) The figure of accumulation would be, from the outset, incompatible with the principle of offensiveness, since each singular action, considered in itself, is devoid of offensiveness, of damage, which the author defines as the loss or decrease in the value of a good for its holder. (…) In cases of accumulation, only the objective sum with other singular contributions can produce this effect of damage. Therefore, the punishability of the cumulative action is based on its dysfunctionality, which points in the direction of the similarity between these crimes and the illicit against-order.[69]

The logic inherent to criminal punishment for conduct in themselves insignificant, whether, in one aspect, due to the lack of technical parameters in legal dogmatics that are intended to consecrate the Democratic State of Law, or, on the other hand, by mere penal disapproval in the name of communicative disloyalty for selfish reasons, only give rise to a theoretical construction of criminal restraint by a model of duty violation, or mere disobedience.[70]

Thus, if on the one hand, the construction of cumulative crimes reveals illegitimacy in the legal-criminal field, characterizing its use as a mere instrument of administrative control,[71] on the other hand, it precisely emerges as more suitable to the scope of Administrative Law, either for its regulatory function or for its aptitude "(…) to function very well as a mechanism to reinforce normative expectations, without the need to resort to Criminal Law."[72]

In this sense, understanding that the theoretical system of cumulative damage is suitable for Sanctioning Administrative Law, Silva Sánchez observes:

> (…) sanctioning Administrative Law is essentially the Law of *cumulative damage* or, also, of the damage derived from *repetition*, which dispenses with an evaluation of the specific fact, requiring only an evaluation about what would be the global transcendence of a certain genre of conduct that came to be considered illicit. In other words, the key question is "what would happen if all the participants in this sector of activity carried out conduct X - when there is, moreover, a serious probability that many of them will do it -, if it were considered lawful?"[73]

---

[67] Dias (2003), pp. 334–335, *passim*.

[68] "(…) The singular conduct is not, as we have seen, offensive to a good, in the sense that it effectively diminishes the utility value of the good for its holders, but dysfunctional in relation to the good, in the sense that it increases the disturbance in the environment of that good (…)." Dias (2003), p. 320.

[69] de Sousa (2006), p. 237. Cf. Dias (2003), p. 339.

[70] Dias (2003), pp. 336–337.

[71] Bechara (2003), p. 3; Bechara (2010), p. 265.

[72] Bechara (2003), p. 5.

[73] Silva Sánchez (2002), p. 117.

References

Alcácer Guirao R (2002) La protección del futuro y los daños cumulativos. Revista Electrónica de Ciencia Penal y Criminología, Granada, n. 4. Disponível em: http://criminet.ugr.es/recpc. Accessed 24 Aug 2024

Bauman Z (2009) Vida líquida. Trad. Carlos Alberto Medeiros. Zahar, Rio de Janeiro

Bechara AELS (2003) Delitos de acumulação e racionalidade da intervenção penal. Boletim IBCCRIM 208:3–5

Bechara AELS (2010) Da teoria do bem jurídico como critério de legitimidade do direito penal. Tese de Livre Docência, Faculdade de Direito da Universidade de São Paulo, São Paulo

Bottini PC (2007) Crimes de perigo abstrato e princípio da precaução na sociedade de risco. Revista dos Tribunais, São Paulo

Costa JF (2003) Direito penal económico. Quarteto, Coimbra

de Sousa SA (2006) *Os crimes fiscais*: análise dogmática e reflexão sobre a legitimidade do discurso criminalizador. Coimbra, Coimbra

de Sousa SA (2023) Questões fundamentais de direito penal da empresa. Almedina, Coimbra

de Souza LA (2007) Expansão do direito penal e globalização. Quartier Latin, São Paulo

Dias JdF (2001) Sobre a tutela jurídico-penal do ambiente – um quarto de século depois. In: Dias JdF et al (orgs) Estudos em homenagem a Cunha Rodrigues, vol I. Coimbra, Coimbra, pp 371–392

Dias AS (2003) "What if everybody did it?": sobre a "(in)capacidade de ressonância" do direito penal à figura da acumulação. Revista Portuguesa de Ciência Criminal 3:303–345

Feinberg J (1987) *The moral limits of the criminal law*: harm to others, vol 1. Oxford University Press, Oxford

Franco AS (2000) Globalização e criminalidade dos poderosos. Revista Brasileira de Ciências Criminais 31:102–136

Giddens A, Beck U, Lash S (1997) *Modernização reflexiva:* política, tradição e estética na ordem social moderna. Trad. Magda Lopes. UNESP, São Paulo

Kuhlen L (2004) ¿Es posible limitar el derecho penal por médio de um concepto material de delito? Trad. Pablo Sánchez-Ostiz Gutiérrez. In: *El sistema integral del derecho penal*: delito, determinación de lapena y proceso penal. Marcial Pons Ediciones Jurídicas y Sociales, Madrid, pp 129–152

Machado MRA (2005) *Sociedade do risco e direito penal*: uma avaliação de novas tendências político-criminais. IBCCRIM, São Paulo

Mendoza Buergo B (2001) El derecho penal en la sociedad del riesgo. Civitas, Madrid

Mill JS (2000) *A liberdade*: utilitarismo. Trad. Isaiah Berlin. Martins Fontes, São Paulo

Reale Júnior M (2009) *Instituições de direito penal* – parte geral. Forense, Rio de Janeiro

Salvador Netto AV (2006) Tipicidade penal e sociedade de risco. Quartier Latin, São Paulo

Silva Sánchez J-M (2002) *A expansão do direito penal* – aspectos da política criminal nas sociedades pós-industriais. Trad. Luiz Otávio de Oliveira Rocha. Revista dos Tribunais, São Paulo

Silveira RMJ (2006) Direito penal econômico como direito penal de perigo. Revista dos Tribunais, São Paulo

von Hirsch A (2007) El concepto de bien jurídico y el "principio del daño". In: Hefendehl R (ed) *La teoría del bien jurídico*: ¿ fundamento de legitimación del derecho penal o juego de abalorios dogmático? Marcial Pons, Madrid, pp 37–52

Wohlers W (2008) Le fattispecie penale come strumento per il mantenimento di orientamenti sociali di carattere assiologico? Problemi di legittimazione da una prospettiva europea continentale e da una angloamericana. In: Fiandaca G, Francolini G (a cura di) *Sulla legittimazione del diritto penale*: culture europeo-continentale e anglo-americana a confronto. G. Giappichelli, Torino, pp 125–152

Chapter 5
Sanctioning Administrative Law

5.1 Introduction

If, on the one hand, there are authors of the most diverse ideological features who defend the penal intervention in the economic field, as a way of equating part of the novel problems resulting from post-modernity, or risk society, among which it is possible to mention Tiedemann, Gracia Martín, Martínez-Buján Pérez, Terradillos Basoco, Faria Costa, etc., on the other hand, paradigmatically, one can point out the members of the so-called Frankfurt School, notably, Hassemer, Naucke, Albrecht, Prittwitz and Herzog, who, with variations of nuances, denote a discourse of resistance to the expansion of the legal-criminal spectrum.[1]

Also with a critical sense, but with very different constructions, there is Silva Sánchez's proposal of double-speed criminal law (limiting at least in terms of a Criminal Law identified as classic or traditional), as well as the ideas of a Sanctioning Administrative Law, whose significant Brazilian exponents on the subject are Reale Júnior, Ferrari, Costa and Osório, who also reflect on studies notably by Spanish authors such as Cerezo Mir, Barbero Santos, Zúñiga Rodríguez and Nieto García, among others, considering that in Spain, unlike what is observed in the doctrine of other European countries, the topic is still to this day the object of in-depth studies.

Although the highlighted idealizations—Frankfurt School, Right of Intervention, Two-speed Criminal Law, and Sanctioning Administrative Law—differ in propositions, they all have in common the search for legitimate solutions in the regulation of harmful social acts resulting from the complexities of post-modernity, distancing themselves from the formulations *de lege lata* underpinning a Risk Criminal Law. In the specific cases of the Frankfurt School, in general, and specifically in the ideology sprouted in its context, that is, from the construction of a Right of Intervention, as well as in the case of defense of a Sanctioning Administrative Law, including,

[1] See, among others, Silveira (2006), pp. 60–61.

L. A. d. Souza, *Economic Criminal Law*,
https://doi.org/10.1007/978-3-031-87236-5_5

fundamentally, it moves away from the very legal-criminal branch as a means of protection.

It is necessary to analyze, then, each thought to, afterwards, in the present doctoral scientific investigation, a taking of stance, either in the sense of justifying Economic Criminal Law, that is, to understand absolutely or partially legitimized the use of the legal-criminal sphere to protect the economic order, or, if its illegitimacy, total or partial, is found, to point out a viable solution to equate socially undesirable economic behaviors.

The emphasis given in this chapter to Sanctioning Administrative Law is justified by the greater amplitude of the proposal relative to the others mentioned, as well as by its relevance to the theme, as will be demonstrated.

5.2 The Frankfurt School and the Discourse of Resistance to the Expansion of Criminal Law

The expression "Frankfurt School" originally refers to a critical trend of philosophical and sociological nature that, from the beginning of the twentieth century, brought together works of intellectuals of Marxist ideology, such as Horkheimer, Adorno, Benjamin, Marcuse, Fromm, Habermas and Neumann, among others, from the creation of the Institute for Social Research of the Frankfurt School.[2] The sense employed in the present work, however, is different, since it is linked to that which Figueiredo Dias attributes as first coined by Schünemann, namely, the one related to a group, that emerged in the second half of the last century, of German penalists of Frankfurt academic origin with markedly liberal thinking, led by Hassemer.[3]

Thus, it is noted that authors such as Hassemer, Naucke, Albrecht, Prittwitz, Lüderssen, and Herzog resist the expansionist legal-criminal movement typical of risk society, starting from the conception that citizens' freedom should be safeguarded to the maximum. As a consequence of this, Criminal Law should be limited to a minimum core, which has the human person as a reference, being certain that this implies that legitimate criminal types are only those that aim at the protection of goods indispensable to peaceful social coexistence, such as, for example, life and property, against the most serious acts that threaten them.

Interestingly, it should be noted that this so-called Frankfurt School does not have its existence explicitly admitted by its identified members,[4] although Hassemer has

[2] See Wiggershaus (2006), passim.

[3] See Dias (2009), p. 605.

[4] Silveira (2006), pp. 60–61, note 113. It is interesting to note that the recognition of a school or legal trend occurs by contrast, as, in the face of specific divergences of thought, it is difficult to identify an affiliation to a current among the authors themselves identified as a group by others. In this sense, see Jiménez De Asúa (2002), pp. 115–117, and, citing the latter, Salvador Netto (2009), pp. 55–56.

already in a certain way offered a signal in this sense.[5] However, the fact is that the criminal doctrine points to this School as a group of German thinkers, who would have in common their place of study in the German city of Frankfurt and a philosophical thought with political guidelines of significant liberal nature.

Regarding Economic Criminal Law specifically, there are severe objections from this line of thought, especially with attention to the anticipation of criminal protection through the construction of types of abstract danger.[6] In other words, it is generally identified the criminal protection of the economic order as an aspect of the penal expansionism of recent decades, which exacerbates the creation of criminal types, especially by constructions, or forms, that are insecure, as is the case of the formulation of abstract danger, which anticipates the criminal response in the sense of not even requiring that a forbidden danger actually occurred, consecrating penal symbolism.

Within the context of the Frankfurt School, given the difficulties pointed out in legislative constructions and also modern dogmatic ones, that is, of Risk Criminal Law, encompassing the discourse that seeks to endorse it, a concrete proposal for equation emerges, offered by Hassemer, namely, the Intervention Law.

5.3 The Proposal of the Intervention Law

Critical of Criminal Law erected under the aegis of risk society, that is, of the unbridled legal-criminal construction that aims at the containment of new social risks, privileging the prevention of undesirable or feared behaviors, especially in the name of combating organized crime, or the powerful, in opposition to what would be mass (traditional, of individual goods crimes), Hassemer reflects on the adequacy of the legal-criminal model forged in this context with that which would be legitimate in a Democratic State of Law.[7] Hassemer starts from the premise that Criminal Law is incapable and does not have the task of managing risks in post-industrial society.[8]

The German author, thus, opposes the Penal Law of risk, advocating that the Penal Law be confined to a nuclear sphere, minimal, limited to the punishment of classic crimes, of individual nature, or even collective, but as long as these are necessarily tied to the individual, that is, have him as a reference:[9]

[5] Hassemer (2004), p. 28.

[6] Silveira and Salvador Netto (2006), p. 197.

[7] Hassemer (1993), pp. 635–646.

[8] As Bottini observes: "The authors of the Frankfurt School point out that criminal law is incapable of containing new risks, and its function is merely symbolic and insignificant for addressing current problems. Today's criminal law, with its expansive tendencies, is seen as a criminal law of counter-illustration." Bottini (2007), p. 99.

[9] "The new tones sounded very different. Think of the fragmentary nature of criminal law and especially the principle of the protection of legal goods: better gaps than excessive criminalization and, at least, no threat of punishment without solid demonstration of the need for criminal protection

> I think that Penal Law has to give up these modern parts that I examined. Penal Law should return to the central aspect, to the formal Penal Law, to a field in which it can function, which are the goods and individual rights, life, freedom, property, physical integrity, finally, rights that can be described accurately, whose injury can be the subject of a normal criminal process. (...) I believe it is necessary to think about a new field of law that does not apply the heavy sanctions of Penal Law, especially the sanctions of deprivation of freedom and that, at the same time can have lesser guarantees. I will call it Intervention Law.[10]

Given the incompatibilities verified from the confrontation between the penal dogma fruit of the Enlightenment development and the new social interests criminally protected, Hassemer proposes that such interests be regulated by a new branch of Law, namely, the Intervention Law. This novel sanctioning system advocated, according to his understanding, would be situated between Civil or Administrative Law and Penal Law.

There would not be, in this way, such a burdensome and rigid discipline for the typical interests of post-modernity, thus leading to a broad decriminalization of conducts. But, on the other hand, so that there is no verify the absence of effectiveness of the protection by the civil or administrative branches, these would be reinforced, through a punitive intensification that would transmute them into a new branch, which the author calls Intervention Law. This, more flexible than the Penal Law and with the possibility of greater preventive function with a view to the management of new risks resulting from social development, would not, however, impose prison sentences. The price paid for the mitigation of the guarantee would be, thus, the impossibility of adopting the prison sanction.

Although full of meaning and sense, given by the tone of the criticism aimed at the symbolic Penal Law of post-modern society, the fact is that Hassemer's proposal lacks greater precision, since the author does not outline the contours of what would effectively be the Right of Intervention. Therefore, the proposed ideal remains vague, without greater concreteness, losing its strength due to a lack of a more in-depth delimitation:

> (...) Even though it presents itself as a viable alternative of legislative organization, it does not seem sufficiently mature to be applied to Brazilian law. The lack of precision of the contours of the intervention law, assumed by Hassemer, could lead to the practice of arbitrariness, in the name of effective risk containment. The exclusion of the prison sentence does not mean that the other sanctions can be applied without a rigid system, which respects the principle of legality and due legal process. For this, a deeper and more reflective discussion is necessary about the parameters for the incidence of intervention norms,

of a threatened human interest." Hassemer (1994a), p. 36. Regarding the thought of the Frankfurt author, Machado observes: "Opposing all trends of risk criminal law, Hassemer advocates the reduction of criminal law to a nuclear criminal law, formed only by offenses against classic individual legal goods or supra-individual legal goods strictly linked to the person, serious and evident concrete danger offenses, and rigid imputation rules and classic guarantee principles. Thus, the protection of supra-individual legal goods in the face of new technological risks would be definitively removed from criminal law, avoiding any attempt to expand criminal protection – and it would also not simply be left to administrative law (...)." Machado (2005), p. 197.

[10] Hassemer (1994b), p. 49.

> about the limits of the flexibility of this system and about the conducts on which its norms are applied.[11]

Bottini also refers to the criticisms that Hassemer's proposal receives for supposedly creating two classes of Penal Law, since the most serious core, with the imposition of prison sentences, The traditional delinquents, members of marginalized classes, would be turned to, while the new branch would be an escape valve for the powerful, that is, the white-collar criminals, who would be immune to imprisonment.[12] Interestingly, among such critics is Silva Sánchez,[13] who proposes the system of bipartition of Criminal Law into two categories, in a sense quite close to Hassemer's idealization.

5.4 The Proposal of Two-Speed Criminal Law

In the same sense as Hassemer, that is, in the face of the mismatch verified from the confrontation between traditional criminal dogmatics and the new interests of risk society, often complex and little settled, but criminally protected, Silva Sánchez develops a particular proposal, namely, the creation of a Two-Speed Criminal Law:

> The conflict between a broad and flexible Criminal Law (turned into an undesirable *soft law*) and a minimum and rigid Criminal Law - certainly impossible - must thus find a solution in the "middle ground" of dualistic configuration. Indeed, it does not seem that current society is willing to admit a Criminal Law oriented to the paradigm of "minimum Criminal Law." But this does not mean that the situation leads us to a model of maximum Criminal Law. The rationalizing function of the State on the social demand for punishment can give rise to a product that is, on the one hand, functional, and on the other hand, sufficiently guaranteeing. Thus, it is about safeguarding the classic model of imputation and principles for the untouchable core of crimes, to which a prison sentence is assigned.[14]

Thus, according to this ideology, the legal equation of the difficulties arising from postmodernity would still be within the category of Criminal Law, with its stigmatizing power. However, the criminal-legal branch should be bipartite. For the novel problems, notably diffuse, a less guaranteeing Criminal Law would be used, of a flexible nature, or relativized, but that would not impose a custodial sentence; for traditional interests, classic individual legal goods, such as life and property, the liberal guarantee vector would prevail, with all its technical rigor.

According to the Spanish author, then, the dualistic solution uses the intimidating capacity of Criminal Law—which no other subdivision of Law has—but without the sacrifice of individual rights. The symbolic function of Criminal Law would justify its use in place of any other legal branch.

---

[11] Bottini (2007), pp. 100–101. In the same sense, see Bechara (2010), p. 223, note 45.

[12] Bottini (2007), p. 101.

[13] Silva Sánchez (2002), p. 143. Explicitly citing him, see Bottini (2007), p. 101, note 36.

[14] Silva Sánchez (2002), pp. 145–146.

The ideology of Silva Sánchez, in this way, on the one hand, approaches to some extent the proposal of Hassemer, in the sense of not using the prison sanction[15] to curb the new social risks on the other, it moves away from it in essence, as it maintains the protection of unprecedented diffuse interests within the criminal-legal scope. That is, the Spanish author does not advocate for the reduction of Criminal Law to a minimum level.[16] For this reason, Silva Sánchez's theory is understood as expansionist, that is, it believes that Criminal Law should face harmful situations within the new social complexities.[17]

It should also be noted that in the second edition of his work on the expansion of Criminal Law, Silva Sánchez adds at the end of a chapter that discusses a possible "third speed" of criminal law, identified by the author as an "emergency" Criminal Law, related to the issue of "Enemy Criminal Law."[18] This new speed would be the hypothesis of having, in situations of absolute necessity, subsidiarity, and effectiveness, in an emergency context, an expansion of the criminal frontier, imposing a deprivation of freedom in competition "with a broad relativization of political-criminal guarantees, rules of imputation and procedural criteria."[19] Although the author criticizes the legislative posture when it is done in a comfortable and unreflective way, which he prognosticates as a trend, he ends up admitting it as a necessary evil in exceptional cases.

With regard to Economic Criminal Law specifically, the author proposes a controlled relativization of the rules of imputation and political-criminal principles:

> (...) regarding Economic Criminal Law, for example, a controlled flexibilization of the rules of imputation (namely, criminal liability of legal entities, expansion of the criteria of authorship or commission by omission, of the requirements of the defeasibility of error etc.), as well as of political-criminal principles (for example, the principle of legality, the mandate of determination - that these principles admit a graduation or demonstrate the different taxativity of some and other criminal types, the different scope of normative references, the greater or lesser recourse to evaluative elements etc. - or the principle of culpability).[20]

[15] For Silva Sánchez, "(...) the problem is not so much the expansion of Criminal Law in general, but specifically the expansion of Criminal Law with regard to imprisonment." Silva Sánchez (2002), p. 139.

[16] "(...) Silva Sánchez does not advocate for the reduction of criminal law to a minimum level, as proposed by the Frankfurt School, but defends a system that addresses new risks while respecting the principles of a Democratic State of Law: the two-speed criminal law. For this author, the expansion of current criminal law should be accompanied by a reduction in the severity of sanctions: thus, the flexibilization of traditional principles will be admitted when accompanied by the generalization of pecuniary penalties, deprivation of rights, or penal reparation, instead of imprisonment." Bottini (2007), p. 102.

[17] de Souza (2007), pp. 62 et seq.

[18] Silva Sánchez (2002), pp. 148–151.

[19] Silva Sánchez (2002), p. 148.

[20] Silva Sánchez (2002), pp. 145–146.

The proposal of the professor from Barcelona represents, however, a systemic break,[21] in addition to consecrating the typical penal expansionism of the risk society. For Bechara, "(...) it constitutes a euphemistic discourse, which, through the exchange of labeling, ends up intending to justify the flexibilization of the repressive state intervention, converting it into an authoritarian instrument of social control."[22]

The distortion of the liberal contours of Criminal Law, representative characters of its essence, as understood here, such as the rules for attributing a fact to its author (imputation) and the basic principles that compose it, such as legality, taxativity or culpability, end up demanding something different from Criminal Law.

Furthermore, as Costa rightly points out, indicating that the criminal prosecution is already infamous in itself:

> The most serious defect of his proposal lies in identifying the application of the deprivation of freedom penalty with the system of guarantees of criminal law. The guarantees of criminal law are not based solely on the fact that through them the deprivation of freedom penalty can be applied. Such guarantees are directed at the entire penal system, which as a whole represents an attack on fundamental rights. The police investigation, the precautionary measures, the criminal process itself and the application of any penalty, whether it is deprivation of freedom or not, already constitute a burden on fundamental rights. For this reason, one cannot agree with the author when he states that the problem is the expansion of criminal law of the deprivation of freedom penalty, and not simply of criminal law.[23]

Similarly to Hassemer's construction, this doctrinal proposal seeks a solution for the direction of Criminal Law in the risk society, therefore having the merit of the necessary reflection that the important topic requires.[24] However, if the ideology of the Frankfurt professor can be criticized for the lack of depth of the proposal or, even, for possibly giving rise to a two-class Criminal Law, endorsing a social injustice, that of the Spanish author certainly perpetrates this last criticized characteristic,[25] with the aggravating factor of consecrating penal expansionism, which curtails human freedom not only in its aspect of coming and going.

As for the possible third penal speed, its admission, although somewhat timid by the Spanish professor, besides revealing itself in a certain way contradictory with the proposal defended until then,[26] lacks further justification, being truly vague.

---

[21] Bechara (2003), p. 4. See also Costa, who observes: "Abandoning a single theory of crime – one of the greatest guarantees developed by the tradition of criminal law – certainly means a huge anachronism." da Costa (2010), p. 192.

[22] Bechara (2010), p. 226.

[23] da Costa (2010), p. 214.

[24] "The proposals of Hassemer and Silva Sánchez are unequivocal demonstrations of the jurist's perplexity in the face of new risks." Bottini (2007), p. 103.

[25] For Franco, the adoption of Silva Sánchez's conception would consecrate this inequality, as "the powerful would receive a reward, despite the minimization of the guarantee process, and the weak, a custodial sentence, even though they have full guarantees..." Franco (2000), p. 134.

[26] For it precisely removes, albeit exceptionally, everything that had hitherto been the alleged object of concern to preserve (criminal guarantees in the face of imprisonment, in a risk society context). In

Moreover, the same criticisms directed at Jakobs' extreme functionalist proposal are directed at it, in the sense of vilifying the liberal contours legitimizing an incrimination.

5.5 The Administrative-Sanctioning Reading

5.5.1 Introduction

The main ideas related to Sanctioning Administrative Law[27] in the Brazilian context are due, notably, to Reale Júnior, Ferrari and Costa, as well as to the administrative law scholar Osório.[28]

The thoughts revealed by the aforementioned national authors have in common the liberal methodological coherence and the awareness that Sanctioning Administrative Law is a normative ideology under construction, whose adoption, however, generates important consequences for the horizontal limits of Brazilian Criminal Law.

Starting from the premise that there is no substantial difference between the criminal norm and the administrative-sanctioning one,[29] a discourse is made *de lege ferenda*, defending, in general terms, in the economic field, in the face of penal subsidiarity, a first use of Administrative Law in the protection of economic order, but with specific nuances—hence the specification of "sanctioning"—since greater independence of the repressive organs of the Executive, mainly, and Legislative,[30] as well as the restrictive delimitation of the repressive action form is necessary.

In this sense, indeed, very little would be said with the simple assertion of mere decriminalization of conducts and transfer of guardianship to Administrative Law of economic delinquency.[31] In fact, if adopted, such thought could prove enormously

---

the opposite direction, Costa believes that the dual rigid system paves the way for a third form: da Costa (2010), p. 214.

[27] Administrative Sanctioning Law is understood as the "(...) set of legal norms that regulate the exercise of sanctioning power by the Public Administration," according to the definition by Pereña Pinedo (2005), p. 117 (free translation).

[28] Among the main works of the authors cited regarding the topic in focus are: Reale Júnior (1999), pp. 116–129; Reale Júnior (2007), pp. 93–100; Ferrari (2004), pp. 253–306; Ferrari (2003), pp. 1185–1203; da Costa (2010), pp. 215–245; Osório (2010), passim.

[29] Reale Júnior (2007), pp. 93 et seq.; Ferrari (2004), p. 261; Osório (2010), p. 102; da Costa (2010), p. 202.

[30] The defense of greater independence of the Legislative Power is justified, in the Brazilian case, due to, for example, the way of appointing members of the Administrative Council for Economic Defense—CADE—who are questioned by this Power. See Ferrari (2004), p. 303.

[31] What is actually not supported by the cited authors. Regarding environmental crimes, Costa writes: "On the other hand, it is not suggested a mere transfer of conduct from criminal law to administrative law. A global strategy must be adopted, which also reflects on the effectiveness of

difficult, considering that the state arbitrariness fostered by Criminal Law would only change its labeling[32] or even would engrave in certain cases,[33] only not imposing a prison sentence.

In other words, it is noticeable that the mere administrative punishment of socially undesirable behaviors, without guarantees such as those revealed by the legal-criminal branch, such as those brought by the principles of legality, proportionality, culpability, etc., can in certain situations even be more burdensome to citizenship than criminal repression,[34] as it has the power to arbitrarily curtail the freedom of citizens in all other aspects that are not related to the right to come and go, which, notably, is not the only one susceptible to being affected by the penal response. This, in fact, is the critical sense of certain Portuguese authors these days, in the face of the distortion that occurred in that order regarding the offenses of mere social ordering.[35]

Aware of this possibility of transmutation of the address of arbitrariness, the national authors in question defend, on the contrary, a certain use of Administrative Law, combining efficiency with broad respect for individual guarantees, independence of action, and assurance of similarity to Criminal Law in what pertains to its construction, creating, for example, among other propositions, a General Part for the Sanctioning Administrative Law, and delimiting a precise interpretative methodology.

Thus, far from being an ideology lacking in greater concreteness, as one could critically formulate regarding proposals like the Right of Intervention by Hassemer, based on foreign experience, the Brazilian doctrinal idealization proves to be robust and consistent with an Enlightenment trend, of effective protection of the economic order without losing sight of the guarantees to the dignity of the human person, vectors provided for in the Constitution of the Federative Republic of Brazil.

Thus, in this *topos*, details of this relevant national proposal will be taken care of, which, without losing sight of the solid foreign reference, whether in doctrinal or legislative terms, specifically reflects the national legal system, to substantiate itself in a prominent construction with significant consequences in respect to Brazilian Economic Criminal Law.

preventive measures. It is no coincidence that the principles of precaution and prevention operate in environmental law (...)." da Costa (2010), pp. 185–186.

[32] In this sense, Santana Vega (2000), p. 121, note 82; Zúñiga Rodríguez (2001), p. 1441. Also, citing the former, see Bechara (2010), p. 245, and the latter, da Costa (2010), p. 207, and Reale Júnior (2007), p. 96.

[33] For Bechara, "(...) administrative sanctioning law can, if poorly elaborated and interpreted, constitute a pre-Beccarian repressive law." Bechara (2010), p. 245.

[34] Reale Júnior (2007), p. 95.

[35] See, among others, Brandão (2009), pp. 721 et seq.

5.5.2 Differentiation Between Administrative Offense and Criminal Offense

First, according to the fundamental assumption of the Brazilian authors in focus, it is necessary to verify whether there would be an ontological, normative, or merely formal difference between the administrative offense and the criminal offense. This verification is essential to the issue, considering that, if the differentiation is ontological, it is necessary to ascertain which material characteristics have the power to separate one construction from another, or, on the other hand, if the distinction is of a normative bias, it is necessary to ascertain the formal and material requirements for a valid legislative elaboration. Finally, if the criterion is merely formal, it is not only necessary to identify it, but also to reflect on the consequences of adopting this criterion.

The debate around the issue begins in the second half of the nineteenth century, in German lands. Although the Penal Code of the Empire (*Reichsstrafgesetzbuch*), of 1871, made no distinction, identifying only what would be a crime, German doctrine was already debating the topic. The evolution of this debate generated, at the beginning of the last century, an emblematic work, by James Goldschmidt, entitled *Das Verwaltungsstrafrecht*,[36] which identified a qualitative differentiation between entities. In this sense, in general terms, the criminal offense would be the action that causes offense to a legal good, while the administrative offense would correspond to non-compliance with an administrative prescription.

Despite the debate generated from this last work, under the influence of Eberhard Schmidt, the formal criterion ended up prevailing in the German economic criminal law of 1949,[37] which was followed in subsequent laws, from the 50s, 60s, and 70s. Finally, nowadays, despite different doctrinal positions—with emphasis on Naucke, who makes a qualitative differentiation—quantitative theories predominate. The constitutional jurisprudence of Germany, however, adopted the position that the administrative offense is part of Criminal Law, thus consecrating a mixed theory, much criticized.[38]

In Italy, the 1981 legislation produced extensive economic decriminalization,[39] based on formal criteria, this being the understanding that prevails in the doctrine of that country.[40] In this sense, this specific legislative change signals the absence of a relationship with the importance of the legal good, confining the distinction to legislative policy criteria.[41]

---

[36] The title of this work can be freely translated as The Administrative Criminal Law.

[37] Dias (1998), p. 21; da Costa (2010), p. 193; Bechara (2010), p. 249.

[38] da Costa (2010), pp. 193–196.

[39] Ferrari notes as a great advantage of this Italian legal change the possibility of holding legal entities accountable for economic infractions, see Ferrari (2004), p. 297.

[40] da Costa (2010), pp. 193–197.

[41] "The decriminalization processes that occurred in Italy and France clearly demonstrate how the choice of the criminal or administrative route has nothing to do with the importance of the legal

In Spain, on the other hand, the debate remains rich, with great doctrinal production to this day.[42] The majority thesis in the country is that there is a general *ius puniendi* of the State, the difference between administrative and criminal offenses is found in the sanction (quantitative thesis, which has as a doctrinal exponent, e.g., Cerezo Mir).[43]

Among the Spanish-speaking authors, diverging from this position, for example, are Silva Sánchez[44] and García Cavero,[45] understanding that the distinction is not

good, but rather is a choice based on the political convenience of one path or the other, aiming to better achieve the preventive and retributive ends of a punitive law that increasingly becomes unique (...)." Reale Júnior (2007), p. 93. The author then observes: "As Alejandro Nieto points out, indeed Italian doctrine and jurisprudence consecrate the mere normative difference between offenses, as clearly explained by the 1980 decision of the Ravenna Court, according to which the distinction between crime and administrative offense is only normative and not structural, for although the choice between placing a certain fact in one sphere or another may result from the severity of the aggression, the option derives 'from the discretionary decision based on legislative policy criteria'." Reale Júnior (2007), p. 94.

[42] As a recent notable work, see, e.g., Rando Casermeiro (2010).

[43] Rando Casermeiro (2010), pp. 87 et seq.; da Costa (2010), pp. 197–201. In the same sense, Gómez Tomillo observes: "The currently predominant thesis argues that both phenomena have the same nature, whether or not the quantitative thesis is accepted without reservations. Regardless of the reservations that may be formulated to such a point of view, the conclusion inevitably associated with it, which we must maintain here, is that criminal offense and administrative offense would be essentially, materially, substantially identical." Gómez Tomillo (2008), pp. 68–70 (free translation).

[44] "The perspective that focuses only on the unjust and its conformation to distinguish the scope of criminal and administrative law is, in my judgment, erroneous. That is why the classical theory of ethical basis was erroneous. But the modern theory of (merely) quantitative differentiation is also incomplete. Indeed, the decisive factor of the said differentiation is not (only) the configuration of the unjust, but the criteria from which it is viewed, the criteria of imputation of that unjust, and the various guarantees (formal and material) that surround the imposition of sanctions on it. In this respect, it is evident that subjection to a judge is a qualitative difference, as is the impossibility of the administration imposing custodial sanctions. Such special guarantees, which surround criminal law and have to do with the communicative-symbolic repercussion of the assertion that a 'criminal offense' is involved, converge favorably to the idea that it is appropriate to introduce a perspective of qualitative differentiation that should be reflected, above all, in the way of understanding the harmfulness of one and the other class of offenses and in the criteria used for their imputation." Silva Sánchez (2002), p. 116. The author then concludes that the decisive factor of the distinction is the teleological criterion, since Criminal Law pursues the concrete protection of legal goods, while Administrative Sanctioning Law aims at "reinforcing the ordinary management of the administration." Silva Sánchez (2002), p. 116.

[45] García Cavero (2007), pp. 123 et seq. For the author, "(...) In our understanding of legally protected economic goods, for example, it should be clear that economic criminal law should not restore all disruptions of expectations derived from the structures of the economic system, but only those expectations whose validity is indispensable for maintaining the essential identity of society in the economy. On the other hand, for maintaining the functioning of aspects that simply give order to the global economic system or accessory issues of the system, the re-stabilization mechanisms of the economic system itself or the extrapenal legal devices of administrative sanctioning law will suffice. The essential nature of the expectations restored through criminal law marks a qualitative difference with administrative sanctioning law, which explains, among other things, that the latter

merely quantitative, but qualitative, and Nieto García,[46] for whom the difference is normative.[47]

It deserves particular mention, still in the context of verifying the prevailing understanding in countries closest to our doctrine, of the Portuguese reality, both for the particularity of the legislative experience and for the significant doctrinal production on the subject.

Influenced by German law, studied by Eduardo Correia, a professor from Coimbra who became Minister of Justice in 1979, an opportunity in which he directly contributed to the enactment of Decree-Law No. 232/79, the Portuguese legislation promoted extensive economic decriminalization, creating the regime of mere social ordering law, or of offenses. According to Dias:

> The offense of mere social ordering, as I said, was legally consecrated among us for the first time in Decree-Law No. 232/79, of July 24, still here by direct action of Prof. Dr. Eduardo Correia as Minister of Justice. This diploma, it should be emphasized, even went further than what was the legislation of West Germany between 1952 and 1975 (date on which the new Penal Code began to be in force there). Because while this, alongside the extra-penal category of *Ordnungswidrigkeiten*, maintained until 1975 the specifically penal category of *Übertretrungen*, Decree-Law No. 232/79 completely eliminated the category of offenses punishable with fine, by establishing in art. 1°-3 that "offenses or transgressions provided for by the current law to which pecuniary sanctions are applied are equivalent to offenses." However, soon after, Decree-Law No. 411-A/79, of October 1, repealed the aforementioned art. 1°-3 of Decree-Law No. 232/79, thus preventing the preconized transformation, in block and automatic, of the offenses in force and punishable only with a fine into offenses.[48]

Despite a few months after its enactment Decree-Law No. 232/79 was amended to partially limit the scope of its discipline, it was only abrogated in 1982, with the promulgation of Decree-Law No. 433, still in force, but with amendments made in 1989, 1995, and 2001. These latest modifications, note, in search of a greater assurance of the fundamental rights of the accused, ended up truly disfiguring the model established in 1979, having, in many aspects, a return to the penal model.[49]

---

fundamentally resorts to cognitive re-stabilization mechanisms such as seizure, preventive security measures, etc." García Cavero (2007), p. 124 (free translation).

[46] Nieto García (2008), pp. 152 et seq.

[47] Silva Sánchez and Nieto García are also cited by Costa, see da Costa (2010), pp. 198–200. Additionally, Silva Sánchez and García Cavero are referred to on the topic by Gómez Tomillo (2008), p. 58. On the topic, expressing that it is a problem of legal policy, see Rando Casermeiro (2010), pp. 35 et seq. It is also interesting to note in the thought of this latter author the defense that, considering that ius puniendi is one, it would also be necessary to apply the principle of harmfulness in the determination of administrative offense. See Rando Casermeiro (2010), pp. 160 et seq.

[48] Dias (1998), p. 24.

[49] "(...) DL 232/79 was later repealed and replaced by DL 433/82, of 27-10, which established the new general regime of mere social order law and its respective process. This decree was later reformulated – in insignificant points – by DL 356/89, of 17-10, and subsequently by DL 244/95, of 14-9, and by L 109/2001, of 24-12. The reformulation of these latter decrees aims to cover the need for a more consistent defense of the rights and guarantees of the defendants, but in many points, it unfortunately approaches a 'counter-revolution against social order offenses', suggesting a return to

Although Portuguese law differentiates the penal offense and the offense in a formal way, since Article 1 of Decree-Law No. 433 establishes that "Every illicit and reprehensible fact that fulfills a legal type in which a fine is imposed constitutes an offense," in doctrinal terms, since the studies of Eduardo Correia, and until today, with emphasis on the thought of Figueiredo Dias, the understanding prevails that there would be a material distinction between the offenses.

Thus, Correia argued that the differentiation would be on an ethical-legal plane, directly foundational to the penal offense.[50] In the case of the offense against the order, in turn, we would be facing an ethically neutral command.[51] In a similar sense, Dias understands that the disvalue of conduct points, on one side, to the identification of a penal offense, an axiologically-socially relevant action, while that, on the other, for the recognition of an offense of mere social ordering, an axiologically-socially neutral action.[52]

In national doctrine, the understanding prevails that there is no substantial difference between the penal norm and the administrative-sanctioning one,[53] since there is an *ius puniendi* general of the State, which is revealed by the penal or administrative facet.

---

the past times of the (criminal and procedural criminal) model of contraventions." Dias (2007), pp. 158–159.

[50] Correia (1998), p. 9.

[51] Correia (1998), p. 10.

[52] According to the professor from Coimbra: "It has been thought – and continues to be thought, predominantly in Germany – to deny the possibility of material determination of criminal offense and mere social order offense on the basis of not being able to recognize the existence of an ethically and socially indifferent offense, even if it is of 'mere' social order. Those who support this impossibility are, in our view, correct. But they are not correct when they intend to conclude from this the impossibility of material delimitation between the two offenses. It is necessary that the perspective of 'ethical-social indifference' is directed not immediately to the offenses – which already assume the legal valuation – but to the conduct that integrates them. There are indeed conducts to which, before and independently of the disvalue of illegality, corresponds, and conducts to which does not correspond a broader moral, cultural, or social disvalue. The conduct, independently of its legal prohibition, is in the first case axiologically and socially relevant, in the second case axiologically and socially neutral. What in mere social order law is axiologically and socially neutral is not the offense, but the conduct itself, divorced from the legal prohibition; without prejudice to, once connected with it, it becoming a suitable substrate of an ethical-social disvalue. This is the decisive criterion that underlies the normative principle that grounds the material distinction between criminal offense and mere social order offense." Dias (2007), pp. 161–162 (original highlights).

[53] Ferrari highlights that "In our view, there is no ontological difference between the economically protected goods by the administrative scope compared to the criminal field. Both protect the economic order and the regular development of the market, making it clear that the two best preventive means for greater feasibility of economic development are information and administrative organization." Ferrari (2004), pp. 261–262.

Thus, protection through criminal or administrative means does not rest on the eventual importance of the legally protected good[54] but rather, generically, on criteria of political convenience and social efficacy.

Costa,[55] in Brazil, as well as Nieto García,[56] in Spain, rightly observes that crime does not exist as a reality, being a product of a definition—which, however, is not made arbitrarily. In this sense, the same happens with the administrative offense, which is created, thus, normatively.

The category "illicit," regardless of its species, is something normative, which is why ontological theories have a fundamentally mistaken assumption, according to the Brazilian author cited:

> (...) qualitative theories that are based on supposed ontological differences fail because they adopt a mistaken starting point. They also sin by ending up accepting the existence of a hard core of behaviors that would need to be sanctioned through criminal law, establishing, therefore, spaces of mandatory criminalization, which does not fit with a fragmentary and subsidiary criminal law.[57]

For this reason, the author, following a similar position to Reale Júnior,[58] argues that the differences must be investigated normatively,[59] which, certainly, has the power to justify the best option for each concrete situation. In other words, "(...) the choice for the qualification of a behavior as a criminal or administrative offense is nothing but legislative policy, aiming primarily at the pursuit of greater social efficacy."[60]

In the same vein, reflecting specifically on the economic field, Ferrari observes that the effectiveness of the sanction matters much more, with a view to the smooth running of the economy than the modality of this punitive response.[61]

---

[54] In the opposite direction, D'Avila (2006), pp. 9 et seq. The author is also cited by Reale Júnior, who summarizes the author's ideas as follows: "In the opposite direction, recently, the study by Fábio Roberto D'Avila, which proposes a material difference. For the author, the criminal offense requires the protection of a criminal legal good, endowed with criminal dignity, of axiological consistency, from which the analysis of the offense can be concretized. Offensiveness is the main identifying factor of the criminal offense, as it requires damage or danger to the criminal legal good, which distinguishes it from infractions of simple disobedience, as it requires a not insignificant possibility of damage to the legal good." Reale Júnior (2007), p. 94 (original italics).

[55] da Costa (2010), pp. 201–203.

[56] According to the Spanish author: "(...) The offense does not exist in reality, being created by the norm, so without a norm there can be no offense. Without a norm that establishes a prohibition, no prohibition can be violated (...)." Nieto García (2008), p. 154 (free translation).

[57] da Costa (2010), pp. 202–203.

[58] Reale Júnior (2007), p. 95.

[59] da Costa (2010), p. 203. In the same sense, Bechara (2010), p. 253.

[60] Reale Júnior (2007), p. 95.

[61] Ferrari (2004), p. 262.

5.5.3 Reasons Alleged for the Use of Sanctioning Administrative Law

Having verified the absence of an ontological distinction between the species of offenses, a position adopted in the present investigation, it is necessary to verify, then, the possible justifications, or reasons, for which the legislator can validly adopt one or the other path. That is, if the construction in question is normative, it is necessary to ascertain what the requirements are for a legitimate restrictive regulation.[62]

In search of the verification of the suitability of the instrument[63] to be used, Costa,[64] citing Hassemer,[65] states that, to conclude for a valid criminalization, it is necessary to employ the fundamental criterion of assessing penal dignity, composed of the elements of justice and appropriateness to the ends. Justice is used in the hypothesis with the sense of verification in the specific prohibition intended of injury or danger of injury to a penal legal good, through respect for the essential principles of Criminal Law.[66] And, appropriateness to the ends, understood as the feasibility of the means employed (criminalization) for the achievement of the end (protection of the penal legal good).[67]

Due to its greater severity, the author notes that the criminal offense requires more requirements for its configuration than the administrative offense. Thus, she proposes as requirements of a differentiating criterion that can legitimately characterize criminal legal protection the conduct being essential for free human development in society, the constitutional provision of protection of interest, and the verification of adequacy regarding its technical functionality.[68]

Thus, in penal terms, it should be emphasized that the interpreter finds as essential guidelines for their conclusions the verification, case by case, of the concurrent presence of a penal legal good, respect for the fundamental principles of Criminal

[62] According to Reale Júnior: "Normatively, the criminal offense requires meeting a series of requirements to be fulfilled, while the administrative offense is limited by some criteria different from those adopted in criminal law. The systems also differ in terms of the technique of operation." Reale Júnior (2007), p. 95.

[63] Reale Júnior (2007), p. 95.

[64] da Costa (2010), p. 203.

[65] "Winfried Hassemer alludes to a qualitative difference between criminal offense and administrative offense, represented not by different legal goods, but by the different technique of their protection, understanding that administrative criminal law and criminal law are legitimized by the prevention of dangers or injuries to legal goods. However, administrative criminal law protects the same legal goods in a qualitatively different way from criminal law, using sanctions and establishing a distinct procedure. It typically acts as a form of early protection of classic legal goods, repressing conduct not immediately aimed at injuring or endangering the legal good, but rather standardized danger situations." Bechara (2010), p. 252.

[66] da Costa (2010), p. 203.

[67] da Costa (2010), p. 203.

[68] da Costa (2010), pp. 203 et seq.

Law, as well as the efficiency in the use of the criminal legal system for the intended prohibition of conduct.[69]

Thus, for example, even if faced with a legal good of a criminal nature, with respect to the master rules of this legal branch, but, even if an inefficient criminalization is found, there will be a just, but inadequate, norm that should be removed from the legal system, for lacking sense. The opposite, that is, an efficient, but unjust norm, completely vilifies the primary notions that are held of the Rule of Law:

> Justice and adequacy are two elements that relate in a dynamic way. Efficient, but unjust, criminalization transforms the law into terror, violates the fundamental rights of the person and ends up tearing, in the long run, the very strength and credibility of criminal law. Thus, it fails to achieve the purpose of the penalty and shows itself, in the end, inefficient. On the other hand, a just, but inefficient penalty corrodes trust in the application of norms, in addition to generating inequality, since the inefficiently applied penalty increases even more the selectivity of criminal law, producing execution deficits. The violation of the principle of equality, after all, ends up perverting the very justice of incrimination.[70]

The Sanctioning Administrative Law can then protect a legal good of a criminal nature if it demonstrates to have more yield for so. There is no harm to citizenship in this measure. On the other hand, the penal type lacking a legal good worthy of such protection, with the mere function of conforming rights, limiting or restricting them, proves to be illegitimate.[71]

These parameters should therefore guide the interpreter of the economic criminal law. However, before the consolidation of this reflection, it is necessary to describe the significant proposals for the improvement of Sanctioning Administrative Law, inscribed in the national doctrine from the thought of Reale Júnior. Once such ideas are adopted, in the name of greater legitimacy and technical functionality, it certainly facilitates the eventual defense of the protection of the economic order by the administrative branch.

5.5.4 Proposals for the Improvement of Sanctioning Administrative Law

As mentioned, the doctrinal studies in focus not only defend significant decriminalization of behaviors that threaten the economic order or the environment, for example, but also aim to offer a viable idearium of legal protection to social interests of large relevance—which, it should be noted, may even have criminal dignity, but often should be treated by another legal branch, due to, among other reasons, better efficiency. In this sense, the national authors cited formulate propositions *de lege ferenda* to build a valid and effective discipline in the Democratic State of Law.

---

[69] On the topic of efficiency, see the critical position of Rando Casermeiro (2010), pp. 513 et seq.

[70] da Costa (2010), p. 204.

[71] See referred above, Sect. 2.2.1.1.

Justifying the creation of the mentioned proposal of a General Part of Sanctioning Administrative Law, in search of greater yield in the protection of the interests disciplined by this branch, and, fundamentally, to move away from any possibility of consecration of state arbitrariness, writes Reale Júnior:

> In our view there should be a *General Part in the laws typifying administrative-criminal infractions*, which contains the principles guarantors of Criminal Law applicable to administrative-criminal infractions, as well as the principles *ordering the normative set*. These allow, on the one hand, to give effectiveness to infractional norms, expanding the scope of incidence - which occurs, as we will see, in the case of joint liability, in the form omissive commission - and, on the other hand, limit its incidence, which happens in the admission of the error of type or the extinction of punishability.[72]

Next, the Brazilian author, emphasizing that he does not intend to exhaust the theme, systematizes seven suggestions[73] for the outline of his proposal for the mentioned novel General Part, namely: (a) the adoption of the principle of legality; (b) the flexibility of the assessment of the element subjective in the hypothesis, with a presumption of intent; (c) the establishment of solidarity between the company and its director in the imputation of the practice of infraction to the economic order; (d) the establishment of norms related to diriment causes based on the inexigibility of another conduct; (e) the provision of the error of type and force majeure, to exclude the sanction; (f) the precise regulation of the individualization of the sanction; (g) the contemplation of causes of extinction of punishability and prescriptive sanction.[74]

Also, the observations, highlighted by Costa and Ferrari, in the sense of the need to offer an adequate procedural system[75] to Administrative Law Sanctioning, highlighting guarantees to the involved agencies.

It is necessary, therefore, to observe each of the referred proposals.

---

[72] Reale Júnior (1999), p. 125 (original italics). Analyzing specifically environmental infractions, Costa also advocates the construction of a General Part of Administrative Sanctioning Law: "(...) it is not possible to dispense with, in administrative law, general rules, organized in a General Part, which define, in accordance with constitutional precepts, the fundamental principles, the assumptions for the configuration of the offense, the way in which responsibility will be imputed, the applicable sanctions, and the procedural rules and guarantees of administrative environmental offense. These general parameters should be applied to all administrative infractions in the environmental sphere." da Costa (2010), pp. 216–217.

[73] These points are also addressed by da Costa (2010), pp. 220 et seq.

[74] Reale Júnior (1999), pp. 126–128.

[75] On the subject, see also Osório (2010), pp. 383 et seq.

5.5.4.1 Adoption of the Principle of Legality

The topic occupies a central position in the delimitation of the administrative offense,[76] as Costa affirms, being well established in Administrative Law.[77] Regarding this aspect, Reale Junior believes that there should be a prohibition of analogy *in malam partem*, in addition to the provision of the retroactivity of the more benign law, of the consecration of a strict interpretation,[78] respecting the verification of the typicity of the conduct, adhering to the technique of taxative construction, which, consequently, avoids the use of generic expressions, open or the referral to extrajudicial concepts.[79] Also as a consequence of the adoption of the principle of legality, the imposed sanctions must be certain and previous.[80]

Respect for the principle of legality by the administrative sanctioning branch—that is, compliance with the rule that state restriction of conduct in the administrative field is done using a formal, previous, and certain law[81]—constitutes a basic guarantee of limitation of state power in the face of citizens' freedom, essential in Criminal Law, in Tax Law[82] and Administrative Law. Thus, even though there is undoubtedly greater flexibility in administrative repression than in criminal,[83] it is necessary to establish formal and material limits[84] capable of rejecting arbitrariness.

[76] The subject is prominent in Spanish doctrine. Gómez Tomillo, e.g., in an extensive analysis, briefly understands that its corollaries are: the mandatory reservation of law, respect for the principle of specificity, the prohibition of analogy in malam partem, the non-retroactivity of unfavorable norms and the retroactivity of favorable norms, and respect for the principle of non bis in idem material. Gómez Tomillo (2008), pp. 99–227. On the subject, see also for example: Pereña Pinedo (2005), pp. 123–171; Meseguer Yebra (2001), pp. 15–20.

[77] da Costa (2010), p. 219.

[78] A crucial aspect, since restrictive norms are interpreted restrictively.

[79] Reale Júnior (1999), p. 126.

[80] Reale Júnior (1999), p. 126.

[81] da Costa (2010), p. 220.

[82] da Costa (2010), p. 223.

[83] A demonstration of this is found in the concurrent legislative competence between the Union, States, and Federal District for the creation of administrative offenses, established by the Constitution, as well as the possible need for law supplementation by administrative regulations, which, while it should be avoided, in many situations appears inevitable and, in any case, more tolerable than in the criminal sphere. See da Costa (2010), pp. 221 et seq.

[84] "It is important to introduce material considerations to the administrative offense. In administrative law, offenses that do not harm or endanger criminal legal goods are admitted. This does not mean, however, that the administrative offense should be devoid of material content. In the environmental case, the material delimiting criterion should be the collective interest realized in the protection of the environment. It is an open formula, but it can certainly minimize many arbitrariness." da Costa (2010), p. 223. Similarly, regarding the specific object of investigation of this work, the collective interest realized in the protection of the economic order can be adopted as the material delimiting criterion of the economic offense.

5.5.4.2 The Flexibility of the Assessment of the Subjective Element in the Case, with a Presumption of Intent

The need for flexibility in the determination of the subjective element in administrative offenses is the solution, possible within the scope of Sanctioning Administrative Law, for a huge problem of structural difficulty of Economic Criminal Law, namely, that of the "proof of effective participation of administrators with awareness and will in the practice of the fact."[85]

In this way, one of the crucial aspects for the lack of effectiveness of the criminal protection of the economic order, the possible instigator of impunity, can be addressed by the administrative sanctioning branch, being a primary differentiating factor between the criminal and administrative offense.[86] However, the author goes further in the search for the efficiency of the administrative system, noting that it is possible to admit a relative presumption of intent.[87]

5.5.4.3 The Establishment of Solidarity Between the Company and Its Director in the Imputation of the Practice of Infraction to the Economic Order

The establishment in the General Part of the Sanctioning Administrative Law of solidarity between the company and its director regarding abusive acts aims to avoid impunity in the specific case through the stipulation of a duty to act as a guarantor on his part:

> (…) This solidarity must be extended based on stipulation, to be included in the General Part, that there is, on the part of the director or manager, a duty to act as a guarantor in preventing actions of abuse of economic power, this duty being limited by the power to act within the decision-making scope of the company. Thus, whether in the commission form, or commission by omission, solidarity is established between the company and its director in the imputation of the practice of infraction to the economic order.[88]

5.5.4.4 The Establishment of Rules Related to Diriment Causes Based on the Non-demand of Another Conduct

If the two previous items are embodied in elements of greater flexibility in relation to the penal system with a view to greater punitive effectiveness in the administrative field, the present, like the next ones, rescues the idea, just like the principle of legality

[85] Reale Júnior (1999), p. 127.

[86] Reale Júnior (1999), p. 127.

[87] Proposal not referred to, e.g., by Costa, for whom the responsibility of the natural person is always subjective and, in turn, regarding the legal person, a minimum of fault must always be assessed. da Costa (2010), p. 224.

[88] Reale Júnior (1999), p. 128.

referred to above, of consolidation of more significant legal certainty, in favor of the security of the Sanctioning Administrative Law. It is perceived, thus, that Reale Júnior seeks to outline more effectiveness to the rules, but without ever losing sight of the prohibition of state arbitrariness, a source of injustice.

In this sense, the author proposes the establishment of rules related to the diriment causes based on the non-demand of another conduct, such as the "irresistible coercion and the state of necessity, situations that can present themselves as possible, as in the case of concerted actions of uniform price fixing, under pressure from other competitors."[89]

5.5.4.5 The Provision of the Error of Type and Force Majeure, to Exclude the Sanction

Another important aspect, shaped by the penal dogmatic, is the discipline of error in the General Part of the Sanctioning Administrative Law. There is no need to punish the individual who did not have a plausible possibility of knowing his duties.[90] In the same way that in what concerns the normative complexity environmental duty allows the application of the discipline of error in the administrative branch,[91] so too must it proceed, for reasonableness, in the economic field, in which the regulation is even more extensive and intricate.

Illustrating the possibility of the occurrence of force majeure in an economic infraction, justifying the exclusion of the sanction, Reale Júnior writes:

> (…) if, by chance, the fact occurs due to force majeure, in the case, for example, of refusal to sell goods under normal payment conditions (art. 21, XIII) due to a lack of energy that prevents the loading of the merchandise, this does not establish a objective responsibility, as the act must be carried out with the aim of limiting competition.[92]

5.5.4.6 The Precise Regulation of the Individualization of Sanction

The need to establish clear regulation about the individualization of punitive response is an essential point in order to avoid the consecration of injustices in the administrative-sanctioning field, either by the possibility of practical assessment of impunity or of exaggerations in the sanction set. Therefore, the establishment of aggravating or mitigating circumstances,[93] causes of increase or decrease of the

---

[89] Reale Júnior (1999), p. 128. In the same sense, Costa, who also observes that "At this point, it is interesting to mention that the German system of administrative offenses also adopts the idea of culpability, but provides that, in some cases, when a legal person practices typical and unlawful conduct, but not culpable, some non-punitive measures may be applied." da Costa (2010), p. 226.

[90] da Costa (2010), p. 225.

[91] da Costa (2010), p. 225.

[92] Reale Júnior (2007), p. 99.

[93] Reale Júnior (1999), p. 128.

punitive measure, rules for cases of material, formal, or continuity of infractions,[94] among others, bring legal security and have the power to appropriately particularize the sanction in each specific case,[95]

As an example of an inadequate norm to be avoided, Reale Júnior refers to Article 27 of Law 8.884/94 (Brazilian Antitrust Law):[96]

> **Art. 27**
> In the application of the penalties established in this law, the following will be taken into consideration:
>
> I - the severity of the infraction;
>
> II - the good faith of the offender;
>
> III - the advantage gained or intended by the offender;
>
> IV - the consummation or not of the infraction;
>
> V - the degree of injury, or danger of injury, to free competition, to the national economy, to consumers, or to third parties;
>
> VI - the negative economic effects produced in the market;
>
> VII - the economic situation of the offender;
>
> VIII - recidivism.

Note that the simplicity of the discipline of the application of the penalty in the referred diploma gives room to the discretion of the judge. The legal terms are too generic and there are no other articles in the body of the diploma that deal with the theme, so the minimum notion of legal security in the species is compromised.

Therefore, the precise delimitation of the application of administrative-sanctioning sanctions and, before that, of them themselves, as Costa affirms,[97] constitutes an also essential point for the full validity and effectiveness of the matter. In this aspect, the author properly observes the impossibility of imposing a prison sentence or community service.[98]

In addition to the fine, Article 24 of the Antitrust Law brings other examples of sanctioning possibilities in the economic field, some very serious: I—the publication, in half a page and at the expense of the offender, in a newspaper indicated in the

---

[94] Regarding the last three examples, see: Osório (2010), pp. 331 et seq.

[95] "If each human being is an individual, each offender must receive individualized, particular treatment, with the possibility of knowing the concrete and specific reasons for the sanctioning act, being able to challenge or accept it. This individualization applies to legal entities, equally endowed with relevant peculiarities, from the perspective of ensuring proportional sanctions." Osório (2010), p. 374.

[96] Reale Júnior (1999), p. 128.

[97] da Costa (2010), pp. 228 et seq.

[98] da Costa (2010), p. 229.

decision, of an extract of the condemnatory decision, for two consecutive days, from one to three consecutive weeks; II—the prohibition of contracting with official financial institutions and participating in bidding for acquisitions, disposals, carrying out works and services, granting of public services, with the Federal, State, Municipal and Federal District Public Administration, as well as indirect administration entities, for a period not less than 5 years; III—the registration of the offender in the National Consumer Defense Register; IV—the recommendation to the competent public bodies that: (a) a compulsory license of patents owned by the offender be granted; (b) the offender is not granted a payment plan for federal taxes owed by him or that tax incentives or public subsidies are canceled, in whole or in part; V—the division of a company, transfer of corporate control, sale of assets, partial cessation of activity, or any other act or measure necessary to eliminate the harmful effects on the economic order.

Therefore, precise regulation regarding the punitive aspect of administrative infractions is elementary for the achievement of a non-penal control system in accordance with the higher principles of a Democratic State of Law.

5.5.4.7 The Consideration of Causes of Extinction of Punishability and Prescriptive Sanction

Also from the perspective of legal certainty,[99] it is necessary to contemplate the causes of the extinction of punishability and the prescriptive sanction in the general administrative-sanctioning discipline.[100]

The predictions of consequences for the death of the agent, extinction of the legal entity,[101] payment of indemnities to consumers or a more advantageous exchange for them of defective products, among other possibilities of extinguishing causes of administrative punishability in the regulation of economic infractions, must be inscribed with a view to the justice of concrete solutions.

Also, specifically regarding prescription as a cause of extinction of punishability, Osório observes appropriately:

> The constitutional justification for the institute of prescription is, without doubt, the principle of legal certainty. No one can be at the mercy of judicial or administrative actions for indefinite or, what is worse, perpetual periods. It is an individual guarantee, but with intense social transcendence. Social relations need security and the Law seeks, in one of its ends, to ensure stability in life of relations. It is not possible an absence of limits for someone to sue the other for alleged material damages to the treasury, in search of the imposition of censure.[102]

---

[99] In the same sense regarding prescription: Osório (2010), pp. 426–427.

[100] Reale Júnior (1999), p. 128. Costa also mentions the need to establish a prescription period: da Costa (2010), p. 226.

[101] On the hypotheses of the agent's death and the dissolution of the legal entity in the case of administrative infractions, see Gómez Tomillo (2008), pp. 563 et seq.

[102] Osório (2010), p. 427.

5.5.4.8 Erection of an Adequate Procedural System, with Organic Independence

The administrative-sanctioning intervention constitutes a serious interference in the sphere of freedom of individuals, often with the practical possibility of proving to be even more burdensome than a criminal response, as stated. Furthermore, the Public Administration cannot be considered as a neutral element in the procedural relationship with the defendant, since it has a direct interest in the outcome of the process.[103]

Thus, the construction of Sanctioning Administrative Law must be guided by applicability criteria that aim to neutralize this imbalance, for the consecration of a fair application. This means that, in a Democratic State of Law, an adequate administrative procedural system must be erected, guided by the protection of the disadvantaged party and the correct application of the law.

In other words, this goal can only be achieved through a technical-legal scheme of guarantees for the administratively processed individual, as well as maximum impartiality of judgment. This is the meaning of ideas developed in our doctrine by the authors in focus.

According to the legal order outlined by our Political Charter, in summary, the need to respect the principles of due process, contradiction, ample defense, publicity, motivation, and appealability[104] is mentioned. Also, according to the principle of presumption of innocence, it is highlighted that the burden of proof is on the Administration, illegitimate evidence such as wiretaps or breaches of confidentiality without judicial authorization being prohibited, and the accused being allowed the right to produce evidence, such as expert opinions and presentation of written statements.[105]

It is also asserted that the Administration can use precautionary measures, which, in turn, can be reviewed judicially.[106] In fact, regarding this aspect, Costa highlights the constitutional hypothesis of the possibility of recourse to the Judiciary, regarding administrative precautionary measures or final decisions.[107]

Finally, an important aspect to be referenced is the indispensability of restructuring administrative bodies, whether for investigation or judgment, with a view to their impartiality and independence.

In this vein, Costa argues that the body that investigates the administrative infraction must be different from the one that judges it.[108] Ferrari, on the other hand, sensitive to the national reality, also highlights the importance of the stability of wages and the position and the structuring of the body's staff, among other essential points:

---

[103] da Costa (2010), p. 231.

[104] da Costa (2010), pp. 232 et seq.; Osório (2010), pp. 383 et seq.

[105] da Costa (2010), pp. 233 et seq.; Osório (2010), pp. 383 et seq.

[106] da Costa (2010), p. 235; Osório (2010), pp. 407–408.

[107] da Costa (2010), p. 235.

[108] da Costa (2010), p. 232.

By giving the members of the Administrative Judging Body the guarantees of independence and stability of wages, including with the enunciation of a quarantine period, its members should be composed of people independent of the Legislative and Executive Powers, with prerogatives of the Judiciary, with mandates that ensure a minimum of stability for specialized and impartial judgment, advocating Administrative Criminal Law for an investment not only structural but, specifically, personal, creating an administrative and economic structure in the framework of the judges' assistants, specializing them in the scope of the administrative-economic field, representing an attempt to strengthen the administrative structure, without the necessary bureaucracy currently existing in the Judiciary, allowing that in a single instance one can appeal to the Judiciary, in the mold of the Arbitration Law.[109]

Given the above, it is noted that the non-exhaustive suggestions of the Brazilian authors cited boast, by their own outlines, wide feasibility in achieving an improved administrative system, not distorted in any of its objectives, for the effective protection of dear interests to the economic reality. They do not represent any systemic break in the sphere of Administrative Law, respecting the contours of a liberal political system. For these reasons, they must be seriously considered in relation to orders such as the Brazilian one.

References

Bechara AELS (2003) Delitos de acumulação e racionalidade da intervenção penal. Boletim IBCCRIM 208:3–5

Bechara AELS (2010) Da teoria do bem jurídico como critério de legitimidade do direito penal. Tese de Livre Docência, Faculdade de Direito da Universidade de São Paulo, São Paulo

Bottini PC (2007) Crimes de perigo abstrato e princípio da precaução na sociedade de risco. Revista dos Tribunais, São Paulo

Brandão N (2009) Questões contra-ordenacionais suscitadas pelo novo regime legal da medição de seguros. In: *Direito penal económico e europeu*: textos doutrinários, vol III. Coimbra, Coimbra, pp 721–735

Correia E (1998) Direito penal e direito de mera ordenação social. In: Instituto De Direito Penal Económico E Europeu - Faculdade De Direito Da Universidade De Coimbra. *Direito penal económico e europeu*: textos doutrinários, vol I. Coimbra, Coimbra, pp 3–18

D'Avila FR (2006) Direito penal e direito sancionador: sobre a identidade do direito penal em tempos de diferença. Revista Brasileira de Ciências Criminais 60:9–35

da Costa HRL (2010) *Proteção penal ambiental*: viabilidade, efetividade, tutela por outros ramos do direito. Saraiva, São Paulo

de Souza LA (2007) Expansão do direito penal e globalização. Quartier Latin, São Paulo

Dias JdF (1998) O movimento da descriminalização e o ilícito de mera ordenação social. In: Instituto De Direito Penal Económico E Europeu - Faculdade De Direito Da Universidade De Coimbra. *Direito penal económico e europeu*: textos doutrinários, vol I. Coimbra, Coimbra, pp 19–33

Dias JdF (2007) *Direito Penal*: parte geral: tomo I: questões fundamentais: a doutrina geral do crime. Revista dos Tribunais/Coimbra Editora, São Paulo/Coimbra

[109] Ferrari (2004), p. 294.

Dias JdF (2009) O papel do direito penal na protecção das gerações futuras. In: Instituto De Direito Penal Económico E Europeu - Faculdade De Direito Da Universidade De Coimbra. *Direito penal económico e europeu*: textos doutrinários, vol III. Coimbra, Coimbra, pp 603–614

Ferrari ER (2003) A ilegitimidade da criminalização de condutas atentatórias ao meio ambiente. In: Andrade MC et al (eds) Liber discipulorum para Jorge de Figueiredo Dias. Coimbra, Coimbra, pp 1185–1203

Ferrari ER (2004) Legislação penal antitruste: direito penal econômico e sua concepção constitucional. In: Reale M, Reale Júnior M, Ferrari ER (eds) Experiências do direito. Millennium, Campinas, pp 253–315

Franco AS (2000) Globalização e criminalidade dos poderosos. Revista Brasileira de Ciências Criminais 31:102–136

García Cavero P (2007) *Derecho penal económico*: parte general. Tomo I. Grijley, Lima

Gómez Tomillo M (2008) *Derecho administrativo sancionador*. Parte general. Teoría general y práctica del derecho penal administrativo. Aranzadi, Navarra

Hassemer W (1993) Crisis y características del moderno derecho penal. Trad. Francisco Muñoz Conde. Actualidad Penal 43(2):635–646

Hassemer W (1994a) História das idéias penais na Alemanha do pós-guerra. Trad. Carlos Eduardo Vasconcelos. Revista Brasileira de Ciências Criminais 6:36–71

Hassemer W (1994b) Perspectivas de uma moderna política criminal. Trad. Cezar Roberto Bitencourt. Revista Brasileira de Ciências Criminais 08:41–51

Hassemer W (2004) La autocomprensión de la ciencia del derecho penal frente a las exigencias de su tiempo. Trad. María del Mar Diaz Pita. In: Muñoz Conde F (Coord) La ciencia del derecho penal ante el nuevo milenio. Tirant lo Blanch, Valencia

Jiménez De Asúa L (2002) Introducción al derecho penal, vol 1. Jurídica Universitária, Ciudad de México

Machado MRA (2005) *Sociedade do risco e direito penal*: uma avaliação de novas tendências político-criminais. IBCCRIM, São Paulo

Meseguer Yebra J (2001) La tipicidad de las infracciones en el procedimiento administrativo sancionador. Bosch, Barcelona

Nieto García A (2008) Derecho administrativo sancionador. Tecnos, Madrid

Osório FM (2010) Direito administrativo sancionador. Revista dos Tribunais, São Paulo

Pereña Pinedo I (Coordinación) (2005) Manual del derecho administrativo sancionador. Ministerio de Justicia: Aranzadi, Navarra

Rando Casermeiro P (2010) *La distinción entre el derecho penal y el derecho administrativo sancionador*: un análisis de política jurídica. Tirant lo Blanch, Valencia

Reale Júnior M (1999) Despenalização no direito penal econômico: uma terceira via entre o crime e a infração administrativa? Revista Brasileira de Ciências Criminais 28:116–129

Reale Júnior M (2007) Ilícito administrativo e o *jus puniendi* geral. In: Prado LR (Coord) *Direito penal contemporâneo*: estudos em homenagem ao professor José Cerezo Mir. Revista dos Tribunais, São Paulo, pp 93–100

Salvador Netto AV (2009) *Finalidades da pena*: conceito material de delito e sistema penal integral. Quartier Latin, São Paulo

Santana Vega DM (2000) La protección penal de los bienes jurídicos colectivos. Dikinson, Madrid

Silva Sánchez J-M (2002) *A expansão do direito penal* – aspectos da política criminal nas sociedades pós-industriais. Trad. Luiz Otávio de Oliveira Rocha. Revista dos Tribunais, São Paulo

Silveira RMJ (2006) Direito penal econômico como direito penal de perigo. Revista dos Tribunais, São Paulo

Silveira RMJ, Salvador Netto AV (2006) Sarbanes-Oxley Act e os vícios do Direito Penal Globalizado. Revista Ultima Ratio 1(0):193–210

Wiggershaus H (2006) *A Escola de Frankfurt*: história, desenvolvimento teórico, significação política. Trad. Lilyane Deroche-Gurgel e Vera de Azambuja Harvey. Difel, Rio de Janeiro

Zúñiga Rodríguez L (2001) Relaciones entre derecho penal y derecho administrativo sancionador ¿Hacia una "administrativización" del derecho penal o una "penalización" del derecho administrativo sancionador? In: Nieto Martín A (Coordinador) Homenaje al dr. Marino Barbero Santos in memoriam. Ediciones de la Universidad de Castilla-La Mancha: Ediciones de la Universidad de Salamanca, Cuenca, pp 1417–1444

Chapter 6
Criminal Law and Economic Offenses

6.1 Introduction

This concluding chapter aims to establish a position on the legitimacy or not of Economic Criminal Law. For such a stance, it is necessary to synthesize the discourses of diffuse criminalization, previously pointed out, which seek, by the most diverse arguments, to support economic criminal protection, pointing out the purpose and efficiency of Criminal Law in the economic field, in addition to the concrete technical structuring of this legal-criminal branch. Beyond the ends of Criminal Law, analyzing the structural compatibility of economic criminal typification is necessary.

Thus, the most suitable solutions will be made explicit to equate the economic behaviors undesired by society, in the context of a Democratic State of Law, that is, the most suitable legal regulation for economic delinquency will be pointed out.

In this sense, the characteristics of rights conformation, flexibility of protection, and preventive bias, as will be seen, point to Administrative Law as the most suitable legal branch to deal with most economic infractions. But this field of Law must be rethought, strengthening its sanctioning bias, without losing sight of the outlines of a democratic system, necessarily guaranteeing. Therefore, the proposals *de lege ferenda* considered most pertinent to the hypothesis must be emphasized. This is the intended original contribution of this thesis to Brazilian legal science.

6.2 The Discourses of Diffuse Criminalization

Diffuse criminalization discourses are understood as doctrinal thoughts that aim to endorse the criminal protection of new interests posed by risk society. Assuming that "these new risks are almost always the result of, at least in theory, human decisions, it was concluded that perhaps Criminal Law was effective for its protection,"

L. A. d. Souza, *Economic Criminal Law*,
https://doi.org/10.1007/978-3-031-87236-5_6

erecting a so-called "Criminal Law of Risk Society."[1] In this sense, part of the doctrine seeks to justify, or understand as legitimate, the legal-criminal expansionism verifiable in practice by the legislative tone of various countries around the world in recent decades.

Given this understanding that multiple current problems stem from human decisions, according to Beck's thought, a legal system aimed at preventing and controlling sources of danger is sought.[2] Regarding the precise theme of this investigation, in this line of reasoning, it would be based on the fact that significant decisions of diffuse consequences are carried out in the business sphere, hence the importance of Criminal Law in the economic field would be highlighted, justifying the expansion of its horizons over this specific field.

Throughout this scientific work, various understandings have been referenced which can be identified, by interconnected aspects, or even by quite different ones, according to a discourse of diffuse criminalization. By the most diverse arguments, what they all have in common is the understanding that Criminal Law, to a greater or lesser extent, must have a share of participation in the face of post-industrial challenges, that is, it must protect typical interests of risk society.

It is therefore necessary, at this point, to reference them, in a general overview, considering that the ideals of the Frankfurt School, Intervention Law, and Sanctioning Administrative Law, studied in the previous chapter, show themselves as possible theoretical alternatives to them. Although the construction of Two-Speed Criminal Law also largely reveals itself as an alternative to this discourse of diffuse criminalization, as stated, it ends up being inserted in the same category, as it reaffirms the answer within Criminal Law. That is, although with a mitigated delineation, Silva Sánchez's theory is a proposal encompassed in an expansionist legal-criminal ideology, as we understand it.

First, albeit generically, a significant part of the criminal doctrine is observed, to a greater or lesser degree, valuing the political-criminal aspect in the construction of Criminal Law, which is shown as something quite sensitive in a risk society context and ends up influencing thoughts as diverse as authors such as, among numerous others, in a European context, Roxin, Jakobs, Schünemann, Silva Sánchez or Dias.

In other words, this means that, from the paradigm of the risk society, there is a relevant trend of orientation of the most diverse dogmatic-criminal discourses towards the reality of social problems, present or future.[3] Political-criminal assumptions are thus considered relevant, or even determinant, for the delineation of the contours of Criminal Law.

This precise political-criminal link in the configuration of crime is, e.g., the basis of Roxin's penal functionalism, developed from his prominent work on *Criminal Policy and Criminal Law System*, from 1970. Among others, Schünemann observes that the broad renormativization of systematic legal-criminal thought that has been

[1] Silveira (2006), p. 97.

[2] Silveira (2006), p. 97.

[3] Machado (2005), p. 92; Coelho (2006), passim.

imposing itself in Germany since 1970 is closely linked to the aforementioned programmatic study by Roxin.[4]

It is noted, in this influx, in a relevant part of contemporary doctrine, notably that identified with penal functionalism, of mitigation, or even denial of the idea of legal good as a material referent of Criminal Law. It was thus previously cited[5] Roxin's own recent controversial thought on the theory of legal good, admitting the crossing of criminal-legal boundaries beyond the protection of legal goods, in the name of defense of ethereal interests typical of our generation, which would not fit convincingly with the ideology of the legal good.

Also in line with an ideal of abandoning the theory of the legal good, but incisively, is Jakobs' thought,[6] which endorses the anticipation of criminal protection to prevent undesirable social behaviors, as in the economic field, thus supporting, among other aspects, the use of the typifying technique of abstract danger crimes.[7] According to this systemic normativist position, the scope of Criminal Law would not be mere protection of legal goods, but rather to ensure the maintenance of the normative system, reaffirming the validity of the norm through criminal sanctioning of human interferences in the creation of unwanted risks in the social environment.[8] The crime would be, thus, the violation of a duty.

It is necessary to observe, at this point, that, although multifaceted, there is in common in all positions considered as discourses of diffuse criminalization, or of Criminal Law of Risk Society, a process of spiritualization (or dematerialization), or even of true denial, of the traditional concept of legal good.[9] The anthropocentric ideal, particularized, with an individual reference, aimed at the erection of a critical element limiting the grievous criminal-legal intrusion into the fundamental rights of

---

[4] See Schünemann (1991), p. 703.

[5] Section 2.2.1.1.

[6] Also addressed in Sect. 2.2.1.1. Cf. Jakobs (2009), pp. 61 et seq.

[7] Jakobs (2009), p. 79. On the subject, see also Silveira (2006), p. 98.

[8] "In a systemic functionalist line, it is intended to justify the penal expansion from the so-called phenomenon of erosion of social norms, identified with the reduction of normative expectations, due to the adoption of different standards typical of pluralism, multiculturalism, and socioeconomic differences in general. Faced with a more complex and less reliable society in terms of its expectations, the State is demanded to assume the protection of norms that begin to weaken. The purpose of criminal law resides, according to this approach, in the conservation and self-referential reproduction of systemic values. Such construction, however, leads to the suppression of the possibility of value dissent, avoiding, from the non-correspondence to institutionalized expectations, any analysis or critique of political content, which leads to the depreciation of the very concept of democracy." Bechara (2010), p. 211.

[9] Sgubbi (1998), p. 70; Machado (2005), pp. 103 et seq.; Bechara (2010), pp. 211, 221, passim; Silveira (2006), pp. 150 et seq. This last author observes: "The creation of meta-individual legal goods is, without a doubt, one of the political-criminal techniques of anticipation of criminal protection. With antecedents in the creation and broad development of issues such as health and heritage, then, it moves to the generic rule of typifying broad conduct of the risk society. It is often justified that this is done in a direct attempt to create a supra-individual legal good in an orbit outside the individualized plan." Silveira (2006), p. 151.

the citizen only in indispensable situations for harmonious social coexistence thus begins to be abandoned, in the name of another model, namely, risk management, that is, of pretended social security.[10]

Trying to outline the understanding of a so-called spiritualized intermediate legal good, Schünemann understands it as the supra-individual good of an immaterial nature that plays a role in representing final goods belonging to individuals, which would give rise to autonomy and its own protection, the latter conceived in abstract terms.[11] Thus, the author does not deviate from a theory of the legal good, a hypothesis that he considers to be a setback,[12] but effectively transmutes his traditional ideal of a critical, limiting criterion, to what can be understood as a justification for the increase in the spectrum of criminal incidence in the face of the new difficulties of postmodern society. Advocating for the operation of globalized Criminal Law in the economic field, the German author even states that "when the globalized economy can no longer be controlled by state law, this situation is called anarchy."[13]

In the face of the difficulties of detecting any harmfulness through typical individual actions in spiritualized goods, which would not justify, but would remove the incidence of Criminal Law in economic infractions, the ideology of the Spaniards Martínez-Buján Pérez and Terradillos Basoco was also mentioned[14] who, in search of the legitimization of Economic Criminal Law, offers a theory that identifies the existence of a mediate legal good and another immediate one. The immediate good would necessarily be that of a spiritualized bias—such as economic order—while the immediate one would have an individual or diffuse nature, related to the immediately protected interest, to be considered case by case.[15]

Stratenwerth, in turn, understanding the notion of legal good to be imprecise, given the impossibility of characterizing an ideal that fits all situations of legitimate criminal protection, proposes its substitution by the notion of protection of life relations as such, or in themselves, which would better justify universal interests.

[10] The thought of Andrew von Hirsch was also mentioned, according to which the justification of the criminalizing phenomenon must go beyond the concept of legal good. von Hirsch (2007), pp. 32 et seq.

[11] Silveira (2006), p. 152; Silveira (2003), pp. 14–15; Corcoy Bidasolo (1999), p. 260; Bechara (2010), p. 233.

[12] Schünemann (2007), p. 31.

[13] Schünemann (2005), p. 4.

[14] Section 2.3.

[15] "(...) the broad conception advocated here allows extending the notion to crimes that do not have a supra-individual legal good as the immediate object of protection, also encompassing crimes that directly protect an individual legal good of economic content, but with the particularity that they are oriented towards the protection of a mediate supra-individual legal good, or if you prefer, that are characterized by the fact that among the motives or reasons that influence the legislator's decision to grant them criminal dignity is the existence of collective or supra-individual interests necessary for the proper functioning of the prevailing economic system (e.g., crimes against industrial property, unfair competition crimes, most corporate crimes)." Martínez-Buján Pérez (2007), p. 119 (free translation).

In this way, new criminal dogmatics would be inscribed, and positioned in defense of anticipated and preventive situations of possible danger to social stability and guaranteeing the expectations and security of the correct functioning of interaction contexts.[16]

Starting from this understanding, Dias intends a conciliatory view in which he does not deny the concept of legal good, but seeks to justify the immediate punishment of certain unwanted behaviors, in the name of the protection of collective goods, to present and future generations:

> In this measure we end up approaching in a certain way, it is true, the idea of Stratenwerth according to which the protection of great risks and future generations can in certain cases go through the assumption of a *criminal law of behavior* in which pure *life relations as such* are penalized and punished. However, this is not an alternative to the criminal law of legal goods: even here **the immediate punishment of certain types of behaviors is done in the name of the protection of collective legal goods** and only in this measure is it legitimized. In this way, fidelity to the enlightenment criminal law paradigm that accompanies us and is expected to continue to be a source of development and progress; and can thus continue to assume its irreplaceable role in containing the mega-risks of post-industrial society and in the protective function of interests also of future generations.[17]

From the reflections of Feinberg and Kuhlen, the theoretical construction of cumulative offenses, in turn, also reveals itself as a result of the context of risk society, considering that, as analyzed, the ideal of criminal prohibition to undesired behaviors, which by themselves are incapable of affecting a legal good, but that, once disseminated, could denote a shock to a certain social interest, represents clear criminal policy adoption of a risk management criterion.

Regarding Silva Sánchez's thought, even though it seeks to reveal itself as a possible alternative to the Criminal Law of Risk Society—criticized by the author—it ends up endorsing penal expansionism in the face of new diffuse interests, since it assimilates the solution within the criminal law sphere, even if partially modified due to the proposal of prohibition of imprisonment. Despite the theoretical effort of the Spanish author to ensure criminal guarantees in traditional cases, the fact is that his proposal is for diffuse criminalization, understanding it to be the role of Criminal Law to protect, even without prison sanction, the unprecedented interests of risk society.

Aside from the important particularity of the systemic break pointed out formulated by Silva Sánchez, the essential criticism presented here to each of the cited

[16] Bottini (2007), p. 104. This author also observes with propriety that similar considerations are offered in Spain by Gracia Martín, who also departs from classical criminal law: "According to the author, facing these situations [new challenges of the risk society] cannot be done efficiently only through formal and quantitative changes in criminal legislation, but requires a material, substantial rupture in relation to liberal criminal law. The new regulations of criminal law should be based on a system that transforms into criminal offenses the totality of harmful actions, perpetrated by powerful classes (...)." Bottini (2007), p. 105. Gracia Martín advocates a penal system aimed both at protection against new risks and at ensuring the maintenance of social trust. Cf. Gracia Martín (2003), p. 64.

[17] Dias (2007), p. 154 (original highlights).

understandings points to the same path, namely, the need to maintain the concept of criminal legal good as a material reference for the construction of Criminal Law. This understanding is a conquest of the Enlightenment representative of a clear and safe limit, therefore, a pertinent and rational critical element, against the state arbitrariness, not yet surpassed by any other more coherent proposal.

The same argumentative line applies to criticism of García Cavero's reflections in his outstanding work on Economic Criminal Law. For the author, the starting point for assessing the legitimacy of Economic Criminal Law is in Silva Sánchez's proposal, with just a change of focus. Thus, the creation of a dual criminal law system, preserving, on the one hand, the guarantees for traditional interests and, on the other hand, flexibilizing the rules of imputation and the criminal principles in diffuse cases, such as economic infractions,[18] would be the most rational, but not because of a justification based on the criminal sanction, that is, on the legal consequence, but essentially because of the punishable fact. For the professor at the University of Piura:

> (…) Flexible criminal law is based, in our opinion, on the social need to guarantee the enforcement of certain essential social expectations regardless of the appearance of an individualized harmful result. (…) The protection of the current configuration of the economy can only be achieved satisfactorily by ensuring the enforcement of normative expectations at levels that certainly do not yet imply an individualized injury. Despite this resulting in a reduction of traditional criminal guarantees linked to the requirement of a concrete injury, there is no other alternative to normatively maintain the current configuration of the economic system (…).[19]

The oppositions that can be presented to this thought of the Peruvian author are similar to those directed both to the one taught by Silva Sánchez and to that by Jakobs. In addition to an unacceptable systemic fissure of the proposed ideology, a criminalizing justification anchored in the protection of social expectations of conduct—as Jakobs does—lacks concreteness and, in this way, is insecure, opening up space for state arbitrariness.

Furthermore, García Cavero's thought gives rise to a very serious "third penal speed," as it admits in theory the same penal responses for classic and diffuse interests, thus allowing, in the final analysis, the occurrence of cases of imprisonment of individuals in the name of the normative maintenance of the economic system configuration. Although the Peruvian doctrinaire makes the caveat that imprisonment should only be used for cases of economic infractions with "sufficient gravity,"[20] the criterion offered, besides being unclear, does not change the fundamental argument that criminalization is based on the mere need to safeguard social expectations of conduct. In the name of this function, to substantiate the need for protection of the economic order, it moves away from the theory of the legal good,

[18] Silva Sánchez (2002b), pp. 145–146.

[19] García Cavero (2007), p. 108 (free translation).

[20] García Cavero (2007), p. 918.

with which it does not agree, as stated, due to the absence of a clear and reliable filter against the drastic repressive legal-criminal means.

It is important to stress, at this point, that the defense of maintaining the theory of the legal good as a material criminal criterion does not mean, however, a necessary attachment to a minimum and immutable core of criminal legal goods, since society evolves, and the Law, consequently, should follow it.

Thus, even though it does not fail to insert itself to some extent in a context of diffuse criminalization discourse, although much less prone to a radical change of classic dogmatic paradigm compared to the others mentioned, there is an understanding that does not deny the traditional theory of the legal good, but seeks to shelter within its scope the protection of part of the diffuse interests, in view of the modification of the historical context now experienced.[21] That is, the theory of the legal good is understood as a material interpretative reference of Criminal Law, however, without limiting this legal branch to a list of classic interests of exclusively individual bias, as advocated by the Frankfurt School.

Thus, Corcoy Bidasolo observes that in the twenty-first century, there are other interests that the citizens value as indispensable to effectively exercise their fundamental rights in social life, and therefore, Criminal Law cannot limit itself to fundamental legal-criminal goods of an individual nature, such as life, health, freedom, and property.[22] For the professor at the University of Navarra:

> (…) The situation of helplessness in which the citizen finds himself in the face of new technologies and the complexity of both consumer products as of institutions and organizations, both public and private, determines that control by Criminal Law of these areas of activity is necessary and legitimate.[23]

In this sense, the possibility of Criminal Law protecting supra-individual or diffuse interests is not denied, as long as they prove essential for the free human development in society and have constitutional anchorage.[24] Moving away from the view of universal risk management, present or future, or of regulation of administrative functions, the verification of this binomial is found according to a liberal theory of legal good, limiting the penal boundaries, without the need for a Copernican turn of theorization.

The economic order fits into this possibility of protection, substantiating itself, as adopted here, in the economic structure of society, representative of a value resulting from individual and social life, indispensable for its maintenance and free development. Insofar as this structure will enable the means of subsistence of the citizen, as

[21] Bechara notes that, although the idea of legal good derives from the liberal political context, representing a guarantee of citizenship against state arbitrariness, the evolution of the State implied the protection of collective interests, aiming at the free development of the individual, cf. Bechara (2010), pp. 229–230.

[22] Corcoy Bidasolo (1999), p. 369, passim.

[23] Corcoy Bidasolo (1999), p. 369.

[24] da Costa (2010), p. 16. In Brazilian doctrine, also admitting the criminal protection of diffuse interests, but with limits, cf., e.g.: Silveira (2006), passim; Bechara (2010), p. 231.

well as his personal fulfillment through work and, why not, through consumption, it clearly shows itself as a fundamental value *susceptible* to criminal protection.

With the contours of the global risk society, the value of the economic order becomes increasingly important, ensuring, in part, a priori, the legitimacy of Economic Criminal Law:

> Economic Criminal Law has its legitimacy ensured by the very globalized risk society. The importance assumed by Economy, in this context, seems undeniable. It seems right to accept a criminalization of conducts in a prior context, in order to ensure its protection. But there is still the question of what would be the limits to be imposed for the formatting of this new Law. If it is certain that the limits normally found in classical Criminal Law should be here obeyed, some differences and distances found in situations of abstract danger.[25]

It must be emphasized, then, that this does not mean that Economic Criminal Law will always be legitimate, with all and any protection with this preliminary purpose backed in the name of the important interest that surrounds it. In other words, not every economic criminal manifestation is in itself legitimate. Indeed, in the absence of a comprehensive understanding of the very notion of legal good, the possibility of a categorical prior affirmation of the legitimacy of a criminal proposition is compromised, offering, instead, a negative criterion of delegitimization.[26]

The limits of economic criminalization will then emerge, beyond the identification of the dear value at stake, with constitutional support, in the typical structure used and the effectiveness of this protection mechanism, elements whose assessments most of the time will demonstrate illegitimate criminal types,[27] recommending the use of another means of protection, such as Sanctioning Administrative Law.

6.3 The Protection of the Economic Order: Purpose and Efficiency—Delegitimization of Criminal Law

The difficulties encountered by the doctrine for the Criminal Law of risk society, present in Economic Criminal Law, present two major blocks of challenges, which make us reflect on its legitimacy and effectiveness, one of a structural nature and another conjunctural.

---

[25] Silveira (2006), p. 159.

[26] Bechara (2010), pp. 384 et seq., passim.

[27] "Although the assertion that criminal law cannot remain indifferent to everything that is happening in the world seems correct, the current formulations of Economic Criminal Law, where social control is sought, mainly through abstract and anticipatory terms, divergent from the entire liberal construction, seem somewhat risky." Silveira and Salvador Netto (2010), p. 379.

6.3.1 Structural Problems of Economic Criminal Law

The first essential challenge is structural, that is, the General Theory of Crime presents, a priori, a wide mismatch with the Economic Criminal Law.

The evolution of the General Theory of Crime, mainly from the end of the nineteenth century, by German authors, was based on the paradigm of the intentional crime of action, of material result, with individual authorship, or a limited number of individuals, to whom direct execution is attributed of a fact. This theoretical model was put into effect in a generalizing, abstract way, and according to the philosophical thought of successive periods, starting with causal-naturalism.

The General Theory of Crime, also known as the theory of punishable fact, is important for the identification and delimitation of the general assumptions of punishable action and the corresponding requirements of imputation. The General Theory of Crime is, therefore, the theory of a teleological attribution of meaning to a fact of a subject.[28] Throughout its trajectory, therefore, generalizing dogmatic solutions are sought for the cases presented.

Economic Criminal Law, for its part, conflicts with this entire model. It arises, at least initially, in moments of exception, of serious crisis, for the concrete solution of specific cases, as clearly noted at the beginning of the twentieth century.

Thus, Economic Criminal Law is not, in principle, endowed with a generalizing nature. Moreover, for this reason, it does not have greater concerns of philosophical support, although, for some time now, it has fallen into the graces of normativism, which seeks to give it coherence, such as through the overall valuation of the fact and the referral to extrapenal normative.

The current evolution of Economic Criminal Law, moreover, contrary to the tradition of the General Theory of Crime, which remains, is not German, but Anglo-Saxon. We used to talk about *Tatbestand*, today about *compliance*, *whistleblowing*, and *willful blindness*. The elaboration of new economic-criminal types intensifies the tension regarding the basic institutes of the traditional Theory of Crime.

Economic Criminal Law, although not only, usually focuses on unwanted economic behaviors perpetrated in the business environment, that is, it refers to an organized group of people, inserted in a complex structure. Thus, reversing the logic of the General Theory of Crime, there is a dissociation between action and responsibility, due to a broad hierarchical structure, which sensitizes topics such as error, coercion, imputation, autonomy, and the subjective element of the type.

And yet: the division of labor often leads to the fragmentation of the practice of the elements of the type, often shaped by a series of neutral actions or wrapped in error. Consequently, criminal responsibility, according to the construction arising from the evolution of the General Theory of Crime, is violated.

In this context, the typical model of crime of the General Theory of Crime, namely, homicide, shows a wide discrepancy with a subsystem focused on ethereal, supra-individual interests, of an economic nature, shaped by an open, variable model

[28] Silva Sánchez (2002a), pp. 192 et seq.

of protection, perpetrated by an often indeterminate group of individuals with different degrees of awareness and will, or even with their absence. Moreover, the typification of accumulation crimes and authorization clauses is frequent in this context.

Difficulties in this sense can be identified regarding imputation. For objective imputation, traditionally thought by the figure of permitted risk,[29] it is verified the extrapolation of the limits accepted by the doctrine of abstract danger through the weakening in the relationship between conduct and the legal good object of protection of the penal type. As for subjective imputation, there is a reduced scope for the appreciation of intent and error.[30]

Thus, the traditional paradigms of the General Theory of Crime do not they find consonance in Economic Criminal Law, which has been developed, for example, in the sense of the criminal liability of legal entities, one of its dear themes. Permeated with discord, the subject has a central connection with the problem of imputation, whether in terms of authorship, co-authorship, or participation.[31]

In the face of the current stage of capitalist production, it is verified that today's economic enterprise of greater magnitude is much more related to legal entities than physical ones. The large mergers or acquisitions, the largest accumulations of profits, the most robust transfers of capital, and the largest financial losses, to refer to a few paradigmatic situations, most often involve legally not physical persons, but legal ones.

In turn, these often present enormous complexity of task divisions and a large number of partners, administrators, and workers and, in this sense, make it difficult to attribute a concrete fact to someone as authorship, co-authorship, or participation.

Thus, it is often known that the conduct came from a certain legal entity, but it is not possible to particularize the physical person or author who carried it out.[32] And, abstracting from the position taken regarding the capacity or incapacity of the legal entity, the fact is that unquestionably in our legal system, apart from environmental crimes, there is no imputation to it for other forms of delinquency.

The theme, therefore, deserves particular mention in the economic criminal field.

6.3.1.1 Criminal Liability of the Legal Entity

The criminal liability of the legal entity is included in the context of expansion of criminal law, widening the subjects that can suffer the imputation. In foreign

[29] Permitted risk means risk not disapproved by criminal law, either for quantitative reasons (low probability of injury ex ante), or qualitative (absence of criminal devaluation of a conduct of probable or even certain harmfulness), all according to the adopted social model. In this sense, Silva Sánchez (2022), p. 20.

[30] Dias (2001), pp. 179 et seq.

[31] On the tendency towards the indetermination of economic offense agents, see also Costa (2003), pp. 52 et seq.

[32] Silveira (2006), p. 74.

legislation, it appears as one of the central axes of current Economic Criminal Law.[33]

Introduced in Brazilian legislation through Law 9.605, of February 12, 1998, known as the Environmental Crimes Law, and characterized by a legislative deficit in its elaboration,[34] the criminal liability of the legal entity has been developed in Brazil mainly by the jurisdictional action of the Superior Court of Justice (STJ).[35] Characterized by a law with several gaps, the Court's action has been in the sense of creating parameters for its application.[36]

With dogmatic difficulties to be overcome, the STJ has already recognized the existing challenge in dealing with the theme of the criminal liability of the legal entity, establishing, from the judgment of an appeal filed against a decision issued by the TRF of the 4th Region in the case of Writ of Mandamus 2002.04.01.013843-0/PR,[37] some criteria for its application. Explicitly, the requirements were defined[38] that "the violation results from the deliberation of the collective entity" and "that the material author of the infraction be linked to the legal entity," and implicitly it was established the obligation of "that it be a private law legal entity," "that the author acted under the protection of the legal entity," and "that the action occurs in the sphere of activities of the legal entity."

This judgment, while refusing any impediment to the application of penalties to legal entities, even if not expressly stated, has shaped the jurisprudential understanding of the hetero-responsibility model in Corporate Criminal Law, in which the constitution of criminal responsibility of the legal entity can only occur if a natural person also figures in the passive pole. This position, repeated by the courts in other rulings, was changed with the judgment of the Federal Supreme Court[39] in Extraordinary Appeal 548.181/PR.[40]

The rapporteur Minister Rosa Weber recognized, in this judgment, the possibility of a legal entity being criminally pursued exclusively, even when there is no action against natural persons. This understanding, marked by the absence of dogmatic

---

[33] On the subject, cf. de Sousa (2023), pp. 89 et seq.

[34] Salvador Netto (2018), p. 299.

[35] The Superior Court of Justice (STJ) is a Brazilian judicial body established by the Federal Constitution of 1988 with the purpose of standardizing the interpretation of federal law in the country. Its jurisdiction encompasses the definitive resolution of civil and criminal cases that do not involve constitutional matters or specialized courts (such as military crimes or labor disputes).

[36] Tangerino (2017), p. 351.

[37] The Brazilian Federal Judiciary is one of the branches of the country's Judicial Power, comprising federal judges, who represent the first instance, and the Regional Federal Courts (TRFs), which are second instance bodies. In criminal matters, the Federal Judiciary has jurisdiction over the adjudication of tax crimes, money laundering, international drug trafficking, among others.

[38] Salvador Netto (2018), p. 302.

[39] The Supreme Federal Court (STF) is the highest court in Brazil, acting as the superior instance or the final instance of the country's judiciary. It has original jurisdiction or serves as the ultimate judicial body for appeals when there is a violation of the Brazilian Constitution in a specific case.

[40] STF, Recurso Extraordinário 548.181/PR, 1ª T., rel. Min. Rosa Weber, j. 06.08.2013, DJe 30.10.2014.

arguments and based on considerations of a political-criminal nature,[41] led to a change in the position of Brazilian jurisprudence.[42-43]

In any case, it is clear that the topic, besides representing a complete modification of the traditional foundations of criminal science, truly lacks better legislative discipline in the Brazilian case, being subject to changing judicial interpretations. Moreover, in the absence of corporate accountability, the discipline of *criminal compliance* is partially compromised in its rationality.

6.3.1.2 Criminal Compliance

In this context of mutation of Criminal Law archetypes, the topic of *criminal compliance*[44] also develops. As Silva Sánchez warns,[45] the insecurity, characteristic of the current moment, authorizes state apparatuses to promote surveillance or prevention parameters that have characteristics that go beyond traditional criminal mechanisms. For this reason, among others, offenses are established in the form of duty infractions, because, of course, it is easier to identify duty bearers than doers of concrete facts.

This leads to the stipulation of legal compliance programs, cooperation, or simply, compliance rules, leading to the adoption of ethical and legal measures for the corporate structure. Thus, the idea that the corporate entity itself should be socially responsible is reinforced, creating mechanisms of good governance and reinforcement of business ethics.[46] Compliance officers are often established and designated for the prevention of events, who often prove to be not only promoters, but also responsible for such practices, assuming a true guarantor position, which can easily also be used in the criminal sphere.

This, in fact, is a concern still open in criminal dogmatics, showing how criminal contours quickly leave their traditional aspects, widening their borders without greater theoretical support. The business risk, also known as the risk of the business,

[41] Salvador Netto (2018), pp. 304–306.

[42] Although Brazil does not adopt the Common Law system, the body of court rulings, whether from higher courts or not, but especially from the STF and the STJ, has played an important role in guiding or even compelling lower courts to adopt certain positions. This means that, in the current framework, the importance of jurisprudence as a source of Criminal Law, at least in a complementary sense, is highlighted.

[43] STJ, Agravo Regimental no Recurso em Mandado de Segurança 48.085/PA (2015/0087565-0), 5ª T., rel. Min. Gurgel de Faria, j. 05.11.2015, DJe 20.11.2015; STJ, Recurso em Habeas Corpus 53.208/SP (2014/0283383-0), 6ª T., rel. Min. Sebastião Reis Júnior, j. 21.05.2015, DJe 01.06.2015.

[44] Understood as "the result of the evolution of the well-known corporate conduct codes, with supplementary premises for the implementation of a criminal nature" by Silveira and Saad-Diniz (2015), p. 65, and which would express the positive disposition of the company to stay out of the delinquent scope, according to the understanding of Gómez-Jara Díez (2005), pp. 255 et seq.

[45] Silva Sánchez (2016), pp. 153 et seq.

[46] de Sousa (2023), p. 143.

expands through the preventive logic in which the company must answer for the risk of non-compliance with legal regulations.

The very importation of the term and mechanism of *compliance* into the Brazilian legal system has raised a series of questions, not only about its meaning, but especially because of the consequences that non-compliance with duties can entail.

Concretely, one can identify the absence of a greater political-criminal and dogmatic reflection on the topic. Both the hypothesis of an increase in guarantee positions in the face of a crime of duty infringement (which is what actually happens with the *Bribery Act* English, from 2010, for example), and the need to obey the principle of subsidiarity.

Therefore, the obligation and the ability for self-regulation are consolidated in order to curb the practice of illegal acts within its internal structure. The supposed freedom to self-regulate is progressively replaced by the obligation to organize and monitor its internal activity according to certain parameters.[47] Otherwise, it may be held responsible for defects in its organizational structure.

The interest of Criminal Law in internal structures appears when an organizational deficit causes a typical conduct, leading to criminal imputation to the company.[48] For the assessment of culpability, measuring the level of commitment to the organization undertaken by the company allows for determining the degree of reproach.

The logic of preventing delinquent behaviors is also present in money laundering legislation, or *money laundering*, regulated in Brazil by the Money Laundering Law, Law 9.613/1998.

A topic already within the criminal field of several European countries, such as Germany, Austria, Belgium, Spain, France, Italy, Luxembourg, and Sweden, the national laws brought as part of their methodology the obligations to collect, inform and collaborate with authorities through: (a) duty to identify and store data from their clients, logic known as *know your client*; (b) register transactions whose amount exceeds the limit set by the competent authority; (c) obligation to create and maintain the customer register at the regulatory or supervisory body; (d) meet the requirements presented by the Council for Control of Financial Activities (Coaf);[49] (e) report to Coaf operations that denote indications or infringement of money laundering legislation, and (f) obligation to report normal or atypical transactions.

It is noted that the Brazilian regulation[50] of the subject of money laundering has determined the adoption of practices aimed at prevent the commission of this crime, imposed on the private sector, such as stock exchanges, insurers, insurance brokers,

---

[47] Salvador Netto (2018), p. 221.

[48] Ortiz De Urbina Gimeno (2013), pp. 264 et seq.

[49] The Financial Activities Control Council (COAF, in Portuguese) is an agency of the Ministry of Economy whose main function is to monitor and analyze financial information to prevent and combat illicit activities such as money laundering, terrorism financing, corruption, and other crimes related to the financial system.

[50] In addition to Law 9.613/1998 and Law 12.683/2012, other frameworks were issued to regulate the matter, aiming to establish rules and procedures for the effective fight against money laundering.

financial institutions, commercial boards, accountants, etc.[51] If they do not comply with such requirements, they are subject to administrative penalties. Also acting in the other direction, regulation has opened the possibility of offering *rewards*[52] when the private entity cooperates with public authorities, through the so-called "integrity programs."

Transferring part of the preventive activity to the private sphere, the State gradually delegates its investigative function.

The broadening trend of responsibilities and duties continued after the issuance of said laws through resolutions of the body. The Res. Coaf 24 and 25, of 16.01.2013, as well as Res. Coaf 30,[53] established new rules for customer registration, transaction recording, and information provision. The first established the obligation of individuals or legal entities providing advisory, consulting, accounting, auditing, counseling, or assistance services in certain activities to report transactions and proposals that lead to the payment or receipt of an amount equal to or greater than R $ 30,000.00. Similarly, Res. 25/2013 brought regulations for people who trade in luxury or high-value movable goods or who carry out intermediation in their trade, even through auctions.

With the issuance of Res. 30, of 04.05.2018,[54] by the same body, new rules are set that must be observed by individuals or legal entities that promote, intermediate, market, broker, or negotiate transfer rights of athletes or artists. Thus, transactions of equal or greater value to R$ 30,000.00 must be registered with the body.[55]

It is observed how, due to the wide variety of economic activities touched by the resolutions, the low set values, or even the obligation to report mere proposals (Res. 24/2013),[56] the imposed regulations result in being very expansive, likely to reduce the dynamism of economic activities and remaining subject to state arbitration.

In any case, it is noted that the current trend in the field of economic criminal law is to increase preventive control, transferring duties and responsibilities to individuals. Another vector in the same influx is noted with the so-called plea bargaining.

Among them, we can mention: Circular Bacen 3.461/2009; Carta-Circular Bacen 3.430/2010; Instrução CVM 301/1999; Circular Susep 445/2012 and Resolutions 24, 25, and 30 of Coaf.

[51] Feldens and Diettrich (2016), p. 47.

[52] As provided in Law 12.846/2013—Lei Anticorrupção.

[53] The resolutions of COAF are determinations of the Brazilian governmental body for the control of financial information for the purposes of preventing and combating illicit activities, as mentioned above.

[54] This Brazilian governmental regulation provides for the procedures to be observed by individuals or legal entities engaged in the promotion, intermediation, commercialization, agency, or negotiation of transfer rights of athletes or artists.

[55] Around 5000 US dollars, in December 2024.

[56] This resolution regulates the procedures to be adopted by individuals or legal entities not subject to the regulation of their own regulatory body who provide, even occasionally, advisory, consultancy, accounting, auditing, counseling, or assistance services, in accordance with the Brazilian Money Laundering Law.

6.3.1.3 Plea Bargaining

The so-called plea bargaining, or plea deal, also fits into this context of Economic Criminal Law focused on minimizing prohibited risks, often applied through leniency agreements. Initially, in political-criminal terms, this must be reflected in ethical terms. The relevant discussion about the consecration of a lack of ethics on the part of the State in encouraging plea bargaining is a fundamental prerequisite for its adoption. This is a dear topic, for example, in countries that suffered the hardships of Nazi state terror, like Germany and France.

Collaboration, in the sense that it has been established mainly from the North American and English legal systems, known as *whistleblowing*,[57] a questionable political-criminal strategy, is fundamentally the one that occurs within the corporate structure, typically by an employee, with the superior, the supervisory body (such as *compliance officers*) or the authorities, including through financial incentive.

The main Brazilian law detailing the functioning of plea bargaining is the so-called Criminal Organization Law (Law 12.850/2013), which regulates the reduction or exemption of punishment for the offender who denounces his accomplices, provided the legal requirements are met. In general terms, the institution represents the adoption of a simply pragmatic path, recognizing the insufficiency of state persecution.[58]

In any case, such institutes, namely, criminal liability of the legal entity, duty infringement offenses, *criminal compliance,* and *whistleblowing* reveal, as asserted, the mismatch of the General Theory of Crime with Economic Criminal Law.

6.3.2 Conjunctural Problems of Economic Criminal Law

It is not only in the general theoretical framework that the difficulties of Economic Criminal Law. There is also a mismatch of the characteristics of modern criminal types with their basic concepts. Topics such as private corruption, environmental crimes, crimes against consumer relations, social security crimes, associative crimes of criminal organization, stock market offenses, among others, have been involved in the field of Economic Criminal Law, making it difficult to construct a coherent and harmonious theorization with the idea of the legal good or the traditional rules of imputation.

In this influx, Economic Criminal Law, in addition to revealing from the outset a great structural dogmatic incapacity, shows itself to be conjuncturally compromised, either by novel protected interests, or by the rampant use of the aforementioned porous constructions of abstract danger crimes, open criminal types, omissive and

---

[57] Strategy that encourages people inside and outside the company to report criminal practices they are aware of, according to Ragués I Vallès (2013), pp. 29 et seq.

[58] In a critical sense, e.g., Bitencourt and Busato (2014), pp. 116 et seq.

negligent types and types of administrative accessory crimes, as well as by the incoherence of the legitimizing discourse of the ends of punishment, all to substantiate an unprecedented penal symbolism.

If on the one hand it is noted that the economic order is a legal good with criminal dignity, for the reasons stated, which necessarily leads to the conclusion that the expansion of Criminal Law is not always dysfunctional, on the other hand, it is verified that the economic criminal legislation effectively produced in the context of risk society encounters serious difficulties of validity and effectiveness, abusing the symbolic character of Criminal Law, and should therefore be rethought. In practice, what is assessed in countries like Brazil is the administrativization of Criminal Law in the economic field, which is a negative characteristic, since it sanctions the illegitimate use of this burdensome means of state intervention.

More concretely, what is noted *de lege lata* is the wide use of the legal-criminal branch for the purpose of ordering administrative interests, seeking to force behaviors or curb by this drastic means unwanted economic behaviors, which is not the role of Criminal Law.

A prodigious example of this posture is found in Brazilian legislation regarding crimes against the financial system, Law No. 7.492/1986, a diploma in which in numerous criminal types the objective type is made with the simple non-compliance with rules of the Central Bank of Brazil or the legislation pertaining to the securities market, regardless of the concrete assessment of a patrimonial loss. Among other articles of the law in focus, for example, the following primary norms signal in this direction: Article 7, II: "To issue, offer or negotiate, in any way, securities or securities: (...) II - without prior registration of issuance with the competent authority, under conditions divergent from those of the register or irregularly registered; (...)," Article 10: "To insert a false element or omit an element required by legislation in financial statements of a financial institution, insurer or institution part of the securities distribution system," and Article 12: "To fail, the former administrator of a financial institution, to present, to the intervenor, liquidator, or trustee, within the deadlines and conditions established by law the information, declarations or documents of his responsibility." It is important to note that, despite the strong administrative bias, except for the crime provided for in Article 21, all the other criminal types of Law No. 7.492/86 are punished with imprisonment, causing serious criminal restraint for non-compliance with prescriptions of interest to the Public Administration.

First, it should be noted that "(...) the criminal type cannot protect mere disobedience to the administration, it should always check if there is, concurrently, affectation of the legal good."[59] In this influx, the first and fundamental incompatibility of administrative accessory with the typical construction of Economic Criminal Law is assessed.

In this way, in the creation of the economic criminal norm, most of the time it starts from a mistaken and therefore illegitimate assumption, the aggressor of the

[59] da Costa (2010), p. 153. In the same sense, Reale Júnior (2009), pp. 24–25.

principle of protection to a legal good with criminal dignity, or even of criminal subsidiarity, which already indicates the need for rejection of Criminal Law in such situations. However, beyond the harmful premise, it is often observed that Economic Criminal Law is inadequate, which also compromises its rationality.

This means that the means used in the construction of the most diverse types of crimes are too insecure and porous, compromising the criminal path through its technique. That is, beyond the inherent difficulties of regulating the economic environment, complex and dynamic by its very nature, dubious means are used, with a high degree of legal uncertainty, in the legislative technique of typification.

The abuse in the use of techniques of abstract danger crimes,[60] of open types,[61] of omission crimes,[62] of negligent crimes,[63] of blank criminal norms,[64] with abuse of administrative referrals, erects a system that supports state arbitrariness, vilifying legal security through the violation of the fundamental principles of legality and harmfulness in criminal law. The material reference of the incriminating types is seen as emptied.[65]

---

[60] As examples, we have Article 63 of Law 8.078/1990 (omission of statements or conspicuous signs about the harmfulness or danger of products, on packaging, wrappers, containers, or advertising) or Article 70 of the same law (use, in the repair of products, of used replacement parts or components, without consumer authorization).

[61] For example, the crimes of disseminating false or incomplete information about a financial institution and reckless management of a financial institution, provided for, respectively, in Articles 3 and 4, sole paragraph, of Law 7.492/1986, as well as the use of relevant information in the capital market (insider trading—Article 27-D of Law 10.303/2001).

[62] These are the hypotheses provided for in the sole paragraph of Article 10 of Complementary Law 105/2001 (unjustified omission or delay of information required under the legislation on financial operations) or in Article 73 of Law 8.078/1990 (failure to immediately correct information about the consumer contained in a register, database, files, or records that is known or should be known to be inaccurate).

[63] § 2 of the cited Article 63 of Law 8.078/1990 (culpable modality regarding omissions about product harms) and § 2 of Article 66 of the same statute (culpable modality of untrue statements about products or services).

[64] Case of Article 1 of Law 8.176/1991 (related to the exercise of fuel economic activities in disagreement with the norms established by law), Article 65 of Law 8.078/1990 (execution of a highly dangerous service, contrary to the determination of the competent authority) or Article 22 of Law 7.492/1986 (currency evasion). Regarding the latter, a paradigmatic example, as we understand it, note that, in addition to numerous normative elements of the type ("exchange operation," "currency," "currency evasion," "money," and "public office") and blank criminal clauses ("unauthorized," "without legal authorization," and "not declared to the competent federal office"), the number of administrative norms that have been issued around the type (such as Brazilian Central Bank Circulars 3.071/01, 3.181/03, 3.225/04, 3.278/04, 3.313/05, 3.345/06, 3.384/08, 3.442/09 and 3.496/10, and finally, National Monetary Council Resolution 3.854/10) denotes a violation of criminal taxativity, indicating, moreover, that the subject is much more related to the administrative sphere. On the subject, see Schmidt and Feldens (2006), passim; Schmidt and Feldens (2010), pp. 2–3; Prado (2004), pp. 329–339.

[65] Sgubbi (1998), p. 72.

Furthermore, analyzing the difficulties of establishing or proving causal relationships between conduct and results in environmental crimes, similar to crimes against economic order, Costa appropriately states:

> Attribution becomes even more problematic when it has to be carried out in business contexts. Starting from the inescapable assumption in criminal law that the illicit act is the product of the agent and not of other people, it is observed that in business activities there is a complex separation of tasks, information and functions that ends up making personal attribution as required by criminal law very difficult.[66]

To overcome such difficulties, part of the doctrine supports the use of corporate liability, which is, as seen, controversial in legal-criminal terms, fundamentally because of the principle of culpability, but would not present any problem in the administrative field.

Moreover, criminal and administrative protection, concurrently, can often represent a *bis in idem*.[67] As Reale Júnior notes when, e.g., comparing the criminal types and administrative infractions in Laws 8.137/90 and 8.884/94,[68] both have in common the protection of the same legal good, by prohibiting largely similar conducts.[69] In this sense, punishment in both spheres for the same conduct represents the consecration of a double punishment in a context of state power to punish that is unique. This is recognized in countries like Germany, Italy, Spain, and Portugal.[70]

Furthermore, Ferrari confidently asserts that the exclusive adoption of administrative protection in the economic field has the power to eliminate the slowness and bureaucracy of the penal system, which certainly enhances efficiency and prevents impunity in unwanted economic infractions:

> The reason for adopting this administrative view, strong in the field of economic issues, aims to increasingly avoid penal interference in the economic sphere, resulting not only in eliminating as much as possible the slowness and bureaucracy of the penal system, revaluing state agents, and, consequently, all society and the economic order; there is no way to avoid the perception that we live in a sphere, where the protection of the economic order is articulated, in our system, in a systemic vision of constitutional root.[71]

There are, therefore, structural and conjunctural incompatibilities that point to Administrative Sanctioning Law, instead of Penal Law, as, in general, the best way to protect the economic order, leading to a broad decriminalization of conduct in these cases, except for the most serious cases curtailed by clear and precise types.

---

[66] da Costa (2010), p. 154.

[67] On the subject, cf. Rando Casermeiro (2010), pp. 506–509.

[68] Law 8.137/90 is the Brazilian statute that defines crimes against the tax, economic order, and consumer relations, while Law 8.884/94 provides for the prevention and repression of offenses against the economic order within the country.

[69] Reale Júnior (1988), pp. 117 et seq.

[70] da Costa (2010), p. 242.

[71] Ferrari (2004), p. 295.

6.4 Legal Options as *Lege Ferenda*

As seen, among the legal options offered by doctrine as an alternative to Penal Law in the protection of diffuse interests, such as the case of the economic order, we have Intervention Law, two-speed Penal Law, and Administrative Sanctioning Law.

Hassemer's proposal for an Intervention Law, as seen, lacks greater concreteness. Thus, although it shows signs of approaching the ideology of Administrative Sanctioning Law as a system of counter-order to be used for the regulation of new social problems, the fact is that there is no precise delimitation capable of inscribing a safe and effective systematization. For this reason, there is no greater possibility of justification for its defense.

Silva Sánchez's proposal, in turn, as stated more than once, represents a systemic break and maintains the problem of abuse in the symbolic use of Penal Law, with which we do not agree. The fact of defending the non-use of prison sanction for the second penal speed does not mitigate the other grievous and infamous characteristics of this drastic means of legal protection. In this sense, this position is also rejected.

Administrative Sanctioning Law, on the other hand, represents a coherent alternative with the defense of new and complex social interests, consistent with the characteristics of a Democratic State of Law. At first, it is noted that the regulation of state functions, the scope of various economic norms, is a typical assignment of Administrative Law, not the penal branch.

Also, the flexible means of protection that is sought to impose on economic infractions can only be admissible in this sphere, never in the penal field. Such a flexible means, moreover, is consistent with the dynamism and complexity of economic activity, and enormously distant from the legal-penal structure, with its characteristics of strict legality and taxativity.

Also, the economic sanction, as well as the criminal liability of the legal person, are much more related to the administrative branch than to the penal system.

However, although there is a broad indication that infractions to the economic order should preferably be protected by Administrative Law, it is understood that it must be restructured with a view to its greater efficiency, according to concrete proposals such as those brought, for example, in our doctrine by Reale Júnior, Ferrari and Costa. It is not denied that Penal Law can offer types of infractions legitimate economic. But this will only occur if consistent verification criteria are respected, in the assessment of the legal good of economic order, in its structural adequacy, and verification of the efficiency of this serious means of restraint, respecting the idea of *ultima ratio*. Otherwise, the only legitimate option is decriminalization, opening up the possibility of other means for social pacification.

References

Bechara AELS (2010) Da teoria do bem jurídico como critério de legitimidade do direito penal. Tese de Livre Docência, Faculdade de Direito da Universidade de São Paulo, São Paulo

Bitencourt CR, Busato PC (2014) *Comentários à lei de organização criminosa*: Lei n. 12.850/2013. Saraiva, São Paulo

Bottini PC (2007) Crimes de perigo abstrato e princípio da precaução na sociedade de risco. Revista dos Tribunais, São Paulo

Coelho MP (2006) Ensaio sobre a tipicidade penal objetiva em um sistema teleológico-racional. Tese (Doutorado em Direito). Faculdade de Direito da Universidade de São Paulo, São Paulo

Corcoy Bidasolo M (1999) Delitos de peligro y protección de bienes jurídico-penales supraindividuales. Tirant lo Blanch, Valencia

Costa JF (2003) Direito penal económico. Quarteto, Coimbra

da Costa HRL (2010) *Proteção penal ambiental*: viabilidade, efetividade, tutela por outros ramos do direito. Saraiva, São Paulo

de Sousa SA (2023) Questões fundamentais de direito penal da empresa. Almedina, Coimbra

Dias JF (2001) Temas básicos da doutrina penal. Coimbra Ed, Coimbra

Dias JdF (2007) *Direito Penal*: parte geral: tomo I: questões fundamentais: a doutrina geral do crime. Revista dos Tribunais/Coimbra Editora, São Paulo/Coimbra

Feldens L, Diettrich EDR (2016) A privatização da função investigatória nos delitos empresariais. In: Feldens L, Estellita H, Wunderlich A (orgs) Direito penal econômico e empresarial. Lumen Juris, Rio de Janeiro

Ferrari ER (2004) Legislação penal antitruste: direito penal econômico e sua concepção constitucional. In: Reale M, Reale Júnior M, Ferrari ER (eds) Experiências do direito. Millennium, Campinas, pp 253–315

García Cavero P (2007) *Derecho penal económico*: parte general. Tomo I. Grijley, Lima

Gómez-Jara Díez C (2005) La culpabilidade penal de la empresa. Marcial Pons, Madrid

Gracia Martín L (2003) Prolegómenos para la lucha por la modernización y expansión del derecho penal y para la crítica del discurso de resistencia. Tirant lo Blanch, Valencia

Jakobs G (2009) *Tratado de direito penal*: teoria do injusto penal e culpabilidade. Trad. Gercélia Batista de Oliveira Mendes e Geraldo de Carvalho. Del Rey, Belo Horizonte

Machado MRA (2005) *Sociedade do risco e direito penal*: uma avaliação de novas tendências político-criminais. IBCCRIM, São Paulo

Martínez-Buján Pérez C (2007) *Derecho penal económico y de la empresa*. Parte general. Tirant lo Blanch, Valencia

Ortiz De Urbina Gimeno I (2013) Sanciones penales contra empresas em España. In: Kuhlen L, Montiel JP, Ortiz De Urbina Gimeno I (eds) Compliance y teoría del derecho penal. Marcial Pons, Madrid

Prado LR (2004) Direito penal econômico. Revista dos Tribunais, São Paulo

Ragués I Vallès R (2013) *Whistleblowing*: una aproximación desde el derecho penal. Marcial Pons, Madrid

Rando Casermeiro P (2010) *La distinción entre el derecho penal y el derecho administrativo sancionador*: un análisis de política jurídica. Tirant lo Blanch, Valencia

Reale Júnior M (1988) Parte geral do código penal. Revista dos Tribunais, São Paulo

Reale Júnior M (2009) *Instituições de direito penal* – parte geral. Forense, Rio de Janeiro

Salvador Netto AV (2018) Responsabilidade penal da pessoa jurídica. Thomson Reuters Brasil, São Paulo

Schmidt AZ, Feldens L (2006) O crime de evasão de divisas. Lúmen Júris, Rio de Janeiro

Schmidt AZ, Feldens L (2010) Os ativos declaráveis perante o Banco Central e os limites normativos do art. 22, parágrafo único, da Lei n° 7.492/86. Boletim IBCCRIM 217(18):2–3

Schünemann B (1991) La política criminal y el sistema de derecho penal. Anuario de derecho penal y ciencias penales, Madrid, tomo XLIV, fasc. III, pp 693–713

Schünemann B (2005) El derecho en el proceso de la globalización económica. In: Laveaga G et al (Dir) Orientaciones de la política criminal legislativa. INACIPE, México, D.F., pp 3–16

Schünemann B (2007) *¡El derecho penal es la ultima ratio para la protección de bienes jurídicos!* Sobre los limites inviolables del derecho penal en um estado liberal de derecho. Trad. Ángela de la Torre Benítez. Universidad Externado de Colômbia, Bogotá

Sgubbi F (1998) *El delito como riesgo social*: investigación sobre las opciones em la asignación de la ilegalidad penal. Trad. Julio E. S. Virgolini. Editorial Ábaco de Rodolfo Depalma, Buenos Aires

Silva Sánchez J-M (2002a) Aproximación al derecho penal contemporáneo. Bosch Editor, Barcelona

Silva Sánchez J-M (2002b) *A expansão do direito penal* – aspectos da política criminal nas sociedades pós-industriais. Trad. Luiz Otávio de Oliveira Rocha. Revista dos Tribunais, São Paulo

Silva Sánchez J-M (2016) Fundamentos del derecho penal de la empresa. BdeF, Montevideo-Buenos Aires

Silva Sánchez J-M (2022) El riesgo permitido en derecho penal económico. Atelier, Barcelona

Silveira RMJ (2003) A construção do bem jurídico espiritualizado e suas críticas fundamentais. Boletim IBCCRIM 122:14–15

Silveira RMJ (2006) Direito penal econômico como direito penal de perigo. Revista dos Tribunais, São Paulo

Silveira RMJ, Saad-Diniz E (2015) Compliance, direito penal e lei anticorrupção. Saraiva, São Paulo

Silveira RdMJ, Salvador Netto AV (2010) A tutela penal do mercado de capitais e o Sarbanes-Oxley-Act: novas considerações. In: Ruiz Filho A, Sica L (Coordenação) *Responsabilidade penal na atividade econômico-empresarial*: doutrina e jurisprudência comentada. Quartier Latin, São Paulo, pp 371–396

Tangerino DdPC (2017) Pessoa jurídica e culpabilidade no direito penal econômico. In: Lobato JDT, Martinelli JPO, Santos HS (org) Comentários ao direito penal econômico brasileiro. D'Plácido, Belo Horizonte

von Hirsch A (2007) El concepto de bien jurídico y el "principio del daño". In: Hefendehl R (ed) *La teoría del bien jurídico*: ¿ fundamento de legitimación del derecho penal o juego de abalorios dogmático? Marcial Pons, Madrid, pp 37–52

Chapter 7
Conclusions

1. In general history, the relationship between Criminal Law and economy presented the phases of mere casuistry of treatment, which lasted from Antiquity to the Modern Age; of protection to the liberal economic model, which had in the *Sherman Act* its consecration; of assurance of the policy of the Welfare State; and of reduction of the role of the State in the economy, to the function of regulatory agent, having in the *Sarbanes-Oxley Act* its peak.
2. From the period of search for protection to the liberal model until the present day, the criminal repression of actions of interest to the economy has been expanding, although for different reasons.
3. In Brazil, there is no correspondence with international phases until recently. However, from the second half of the twentieth century, economic criminalization begins to emerge in the country, with a radicalization in the 90s, without any systematization.
4. In the face of the exacerbation of this form of criminalization, it is fundamental to delimit the meaning, scope, and functionality of the connection between Criminal Law and economics, to reflect on its legitimacy in a Democratic State of Law.
5. The interpreter must then, preliminarily, focus on the conceptualization of Economic Criminal Law, which is controversial in doctrine.
6. From the studies of Sutherland, with a criminological slant, the theme was identified with its author, seen as a businessman (of "white collar"), in contrast to the traditional criminal.
7. There is also an understanding that recognizes Economic Criminal Law as a Corporate Criminal Law, that is, perpetrated through companies.
8. From the previous position, there is still doctrine that conceives Economic Criminal Law as that which encompasses criminal offenses perpetrated professionally within an economic activity (*occupational crime*).
9. For Tiedemann, according to a strict understanding, the purpose of Economic Criminal Law would be to protect the objectives of state planning of the

L. A. d. Souza, *Economic Criminal Law*,
https://doi.org/10.1007/978-3-031-87236-5_7

economy. In a broad sense, which gains the adherence of the German author, Economic Criminal Law would comprise violations of the state's intervening and regulatory activity in the economy, offenses against other supra-individual legal goods of economic life, which, by conceptual necessity, transcend individual legal goods, and, finally, classic property crimes, when these are directed against supra-individual assets or when they constitute abuse of measures and instruments of economic life.

10. The only safe and legitimate criterion in a Democratic State of Law, however, is the one that identifies in the legal-criminal intervention the protection of essential interests for peaceful social coexistence that cannot be protected in any less burdensome way. In other words, the principles of minimal criminal intervention and the exclusive protection of legal goods must be respected.
11. The criminal-legal good protected by a legitimate economic criminal law is the economic order, a supra-individual interest consisting of the structure of production, circulation, and distribution of wealth, representative of a value resulting from individual and collective life, indispensable for its maintenance and free development.
12. In identifying the legal good of economic order, trust proves to be an important value marker, of a critical nature, capable of delimiting valid typification, since a monetized free market system requires minimum social expectations for its regular operation.
13. Despite the possibility of verifying the legitimate criminal protection of the economic order, economic criminalization commonly resulting from the global risk society reveals serious structural problems, with complex behaviors being prohibited through anticipatory typifying formulations, inconsistent and with the character of a means of shaping behaviors of administrative scope, consecrating the administrativization of Criminal Law.
14. Thus, the formulations most often used are of abstract danger, open types, negligent crimes, omissive types, and blank criminal norms, fostering a merely symbolic Criminal Law.
15. In a context of minimal criminal intervention, after identifying the criminally protected legal good, the subsequent analytical vector to guide the interpreter is the principle of harmfulness, or offensiveness, consistent, according to classical thought, in the relevant affectation of the protected interest.
16. The understanding of harmfulness as a transgression to the order, erected as an alternative to the traditional conception of harmfulness, is illegitimate, as it understands the criminal offense as a mere violation of duty, aimed at protecting the validity of the legal system, which does not appear as a safe parameter for limiting the state's power to punish.
17. The difficulties in identifying the protected legal good and the principle of harmfulness in economic delinquency lead to the defense of relaxing rigor for the verification of abusive practices, which already shows better adequacy of protection by another branch of Law.
18. An example of the use of flexible criteria aimed at effectiveness of protection, in the Brazilian case, is found in the performance of the Administrative Council for

Economic Defense—CADE. Such parameters, however, are inadmissible in the criminal sphere.

19. The theory of cumulative offenses is linked to the idea of criminal punishment for behaviors that are *per se* incapable of affecting criminal-legal interests, but which, by political-criminal criteria, are prohibited, since their widespread practice would exponentially denote shock (by damage or by danger) to a certain legal good. In this sense, this theory could justify the current anticipatory economic criminal protection.
20. However, the idea of cumulative offenses does not reveal compatible with the paradigm of a liberal Criminal Law, based on the protection of a legal good essential for social coexistence, as well as the foundation in the principles of offensiveness, of proportionality and culpability, limiting criteria of repressive incidence. This is the normative framework that constitutes the validity foundation of Criminal Law in democracies and that does not find resonance in the theory in focus, thus affecting its legitimacy. The construction in focus is, however, consistent with the administrative sphere.
21. In the face of the penal expansionism of recent decades, where the expansion of Economic Criminal Law is inserted, erecting a merely symbolic criminal intervention, with structural, conjunctural difficulties and lack of legitimacy, proposals for equationing emerge in the doctrine. In this context, the thoughts of the Frankfurt School, the Intervention Law, the Two-Speed Criminal Law, and the Sanctioning Administrative Law stand out.
22. The proposal of the Frankfurt School, namely, to maintain the Criminal Law to a minimum core with direct reference to the individual, is unfeasible since it ignores social evolution.
23. Still within the context of the Frankfurt School is Hassemer's Intervention Law proposal, which, on the one hand, has the merits of seeking to safeguard Criminal Law in legitimate contours and not turning a blind eye to new social problems, on the other hand, lacks greater concreteness, there is no delimitation.
24. Silva Sánchez's proposal for a Two-Speed Criminal Law represents a systemic break and starts from the wrong premise of considering as of penal relevance only norms that impose prison sanction, ignoring all other consequences of the serious means of legal-criminal intervention. Furthermore, it paves the way for penal expansionism.
25. A reformed Administrative Law, of a sanctioning nature, with material and procedural guarantees, reveals itself as a legitimate and more effective way to protect the economic order. Thus, on the one hand, a broad decriminalization of economic infractions must come accompanied, on the other hand, by a restructuring of the administrative sphere, without losing sight, in both aspects, of the liberal contours inherent to a Democratic Rule of Law.

The manufacturer's authorised representative in the EU is Springer Nature Customer Service Centre GmbH, Europaplatz 3, 69115 Heidelberg, Germany. If you have any concerns regarding our products, please contact ProductSafety@springernature.com

Printed and bound by CPI Group (UK) Ltd, Croydon, CR0 4YY
01/10/2026
02225982-0007